LOVE THE WORK, HATE THE JOB

LOVE THE WORK, HATE THE JOB

WHY AMERICA'S BEST WORKERS ARE MORE UNHAPPY THAN EVER

David Kusnet

WILEY

John Wiley & Sons, Inc.

Published by John Wiley & Sons, Inc., Hoboken, New Jersey
Published simultaneously in Canada

Library of Congress Cataloging-in-Publication Data:

Kusnet, David, date.
    Love the work, hate the job : why America's best workers are more unhappy
than ever / David Kusnet.
      p. cm.
    Includes bibliographical references and index.
    ISBN 978-0-471-74205-0 (cloth)
  1. Job satisfaction—Washington (State) 2. Work environment—Washington
(State) 3. Profit—Washington (State) I. Title.
  HF5549.5.J63K78 2008
  331.01'209797—dc22
                                                2008000220

Printed in the United States of America

10 9 8 7 6 5 4 3 2 1

*For Ruth,
Michael, and Lylah*

CONTENTS

Introduction

THE BATTLE OF SEATTLE

When all hell broke loose in downtown Seattle, Verlene Jones's first thought was, "I've got to save those children."

It was shortly after two in the afternoon on November 30, 1999, the first day of the World Trade Organization (WTO) meeting. Representatives from 135 countries were gathered to write the rules for the global economy. Tens of thousands of labor union members and environmental activists were holding teach-ins and marches to protest the global economy's excesses, from child labor to ruined rainforests. Meanwhile, thousands of thrill seekers and advocates of exotic causes of all kinds, from anarchy to abolishing modern technology, were getting ready to run wild in the streets.

Just a few minutes earlier, Jones had heard the windows shattering on the Bank of America building. Then, the alarms blared. Soon, a group of rock-throwing rioters pushed a Dumpster into the middle of the street and set it on fire with matches. As if in response, the police sirens started to wail.[1]

STOPPING THE DISASTER MOVIE

Standing at the corner of Fourth Avenue and Pike Street in the heart of Seattle's downtown business district, Jones saw two menacing-looking armies—the police and the rioters—advancing on each other.

1

Running through the downtown area were groups of young people wearing all-black outfits with handkerchiefs or hoods covering their faces. They smashed windows and trashed businesses that were blamed for the excesses of globalization: multinational corporations such as the Bank of America and retail outlets like Nike and the Gap that sold products made by children overseas. They called themselves the "Black Bloc Anarchists," but Jones knew that underneath their costumes, most were white kids from middle-class families.

Marching west on Pike Street and north on Fourth Avenue, another army was advancing, also wearing black uniforms. Hundreds of Seattle police trooped toward the mayhem, wearing new equipment they'd gotten in anticipation of disturbances—black "hard gear," from ballistic helmets that covered their faces to shin guards like those worn by baseball catchers. Jones had been on enough protest marches to know that if the cops had all that riot gear, they would also be carrying pepper spray and tear gas canisters.

Across the street, and soon to be caught between the rioters and the riot police, were two women with three children who couldn't have been much older than seven or eight. The women were carrying signs that said, "Tell WTO, No Child Labor." But they didn't seem to realize that their own children were in danger. Instead, they watched with fascination as the anarchists ran wild and the police ran toward them. To get a better view, two of the children were standing on top of a small garbage can. "These women were looking around like it was a scene in a movie," Jones recalled years later. "They didn't realize it was a disaster movie, and they were about to become part of it."

The moment she saw the mothers and the children, Jones flashed on the worst thing that could happen. She had worried that "the police wouldn't stop and see young children there. They would just shoot tear gas at them." So she ran across the street and shouted at the women, "You've got to get those kids away from the corner now." As the mothers and the children ran away, Jones felt better than she would for the rest of the day.

Jones was wearing an orange cap that identified her as a marshal for the AFL-CIO (American Federation of Labor and Congress of Industrial Organizations), which coordinated protests against the WTO by labor union members, environmentalists, students, and other activists from the Seattle area and all across the country. She could already see the first group of union people who were marching to rally at the Seattle Center, a fairground and park within the city. Their route would take them through the intersection where she was stationed, and her assignment was to make sure they turned south on Fourth Avenue. No one had figured that the corner would be a battleground between kids who thought they were Che Guevera and cops who were dressed like Darth Vader.

Soon there was "a mass bedlam of people running and not knowing where they were running to," as she described the scene years later. Union members, environmentalists, and others who had planned to protest peacefully arrived at Jones's corner unsure of where they should go. "People told stories of how it feels to be tear-gassed," she said. "They had a burning sensation in the back of their throats and in their eyes."

She told them to go ahead if they still wanted to go to the rally, but they should understand that they might be tear-gassed or caught between the rioters and the riot police. As she later remembered, members of industrial unions who had lost jobs to low-wage competition overseas, including the Teamsters, the Steelworkers, and the United Auto Workers, "were very passionate and committed to go that route," no matter what. If they wanted to go back to somewhere safer, she suggested ways that they could avoid the mayhem, and she and other union activists walked with them for a city block or two to make sure they had safe passage through the police lines.

All the while, she was thinking about one person in particular, her eighteen-year-old daughter, Kristin, who was in her first year in college. Suspecting that there might be disturbances, Jones had advised her to "go to the labor march to be safe." But Kristin chose to go on the student march, and her mother was worried that while the police might hesitate to tear-gas burly blue-collar workers, they might have trouble distinguishing between grungy college kids and rowdy anarchists. (Fortunately, Kristin was not hurt that day.)

EXPERIENCED WITH EMERGENCIES

For Jones, responding to emergencies—whether on the city streets or in a hospital ward—had become second nature. Soft-spoken and youthful in appearance, she had moved from her home-town of San Francisco to Seattle in 1976. Soon after, she went to work at the Group Health Hospital in the acute care unit, where patients with urgent conditions such as heart attacks or bullet wounds were rushed after arriving at the emergency room. She became a telemetric technician, reading the heart monitors that revealed whether a patient was in need of immediate care.

She would work twenty-one years at the hospital, eventually becoming active in the union. At first, she looked askance at unions. A carpenter by trade, her father had grown up in Texas and moved to California. Usually, the local unions had refused to accept him, or any black man, as a journeyman or even an apprentice. But she saw that the hospital and the union were very different. Whites, blacks, Hispanics, and Asians all worked there and were welcome in the union. Her tendencies as a joiner and an activist took over. "When I had problems, I filed a grievance," she recalled. "The union rep came to the hospital to visit and talked to me about becoming a union steward."

She accepted. By the 1980s and 1990s, most unions bore lit-tle resemblance to what had always been the unfair stereotype that they were only for blue-collar workers, overwhelmingly male, resistant to change, and indifferent to organizing new members, especially workers who aren't native-born white men. Indeed, union membership had grown most rapidly among the very workers who were furthest from this typecasting: women, African Americans, Latinos, professionals and technicians, and workers in health care and the service sector. Moreover, a new generation of labor activists was emerging who understood that the well-being of workers and their unions depended upon the success of the enterprises in which they worked. Very often, these activists carefully studied the workings of industries such as health care, aerospace, and information technology and became at least as well informed about their companies' problems and prospects as were the executives whom they faced at the bargaining table or debated in the news media. So, after taking her first step toward becoming a committed unionist, Jones, like many other skilled workers, never looked back.

While continuing to work as a technician, she became a shop steward, the union's representative in the acute care unit, filing grievances on behalf of her coworkers. Then she became a full-time representative for her union, Local 6 of the Service Employees International Union (SEIU). By the time she joined the staff of the Central Labor Council, she was experienced at organizing picket lines, demonstrations, and other mass protests. But, unlike the anarchists, she learned how to keep the actions orderly, to make sure no one got hurt, and to portray the unions in ways that would appeal to, not antagonize, the news media and the general public. By the fall of 1999, Jones was one of Seattle's foremost liberal activists. A leader in the Central Labor Council and in what the AFL-CIO called its "constituency groups" representing women and African Americans, she was widely mentioned as a potential candidate for the City Council.

On November 30, while the police and the anarchists battled on the streets of Seattle, it was left to a small group of seasoned organizers like Jones to try to keep order when others were unwilling or unable to remain clearheaded. As she had done so often in the acute care room, Jones did her work well.

A MILESTONE MOMENT

With tear gas in the air, fighting in the streets, and President Bill Clinton, Secretary of State Madeleine Albright, and other world leaders trapped in their downtown hotels, the protests were broadcast internationally and became the subject of weeks of argument and analysis. In the words of the WTO's former director general, Renato Ruggiero, the meeting was supposed to create "the constitution of a single global economy."[2] Instead, it became a forum for groups with grievances against globalization, the governments that sponsored it, and the multinational corporations that benefited from it. Workers from the advanced countries who feared losing their jobs to low-paid workers in poor countries, environmentalists who dreaded large-scale deforestation and pollution, those from Third World countries who felt threatened by the domination of the wealthier nations, and Americans from the far Left and the far Right who worried about the erosion of national sovereignty—all took to the streets. "Teamsters and Turtles" (and, yes, there were environmentalists costumed as turtles) became the shorthand for the odd alliances that were being forged in the streets of Seattle. Unlike the turbulence of the 1960s, when construction workers and college students fought each other, the protests against globalization brought together the blue-collar workers who did the grunt work of the global economy and the angry youngsters who feared that the global economy was destroying the natural environment.

Faced with these protests, the WTO adjourned without reaching any new agreements about international trade. Understanding that many of the marchers were the same people who vote for parties of the mainstream Left, such as the Democratic Party in the United States and the Labour Party in Great Britain, President Clinton and his European counterparts revised their speeches to sympathize with demands that trade agreements include protections for the environment and workers' rights. By December 2, the world leaders, the trade negotiators, and the news media started to leave town, resolving never to hold another high-visibility meeting in a major city, especially one like Seattle, with its traditions of trade unionism and social protest.

Addressing Anxieties about the New Economy

Meanwhile, throughout the nation and especially in Seattle, something unusual happened. In the past, extremists rioting in the streets would have triggered a reaction against the peaceful protestors, just as, in the 1960s, the mainstream civil rights movement suffered from the backlash against black radicals. Even though the unionists and the environmentalists had marched peacefully, they could have been lumped together with the anarchists in the public mind and suffered a loss of support. Indeed, the nation's media, corporate, and political elites had all assumed Seattle would be unreceptive to protests against globalization. After all, the city had been selected for the WTO conference because so many of its major companies, such as Boeing and Microsoft, were successful exporters, and the city's skilled and well-educated workforce was prospering in the global economy.

But there was no backlash, nationally or locally. As the 2000 presidential campaign got under way, none of the Republican candidates attacked the WTO protestors, while the Democrats wooed the unionists and the environmentalists who had protested against globalization. In Seattle, in a survey conducted several weeks after the WTO meeting, more than 50 percent of the residents of the metropolitan area said they approved of the peaceful protestors.[3] Indeed, in every statewide election since the protests, including two presidential campaigns, two gubernatorial races, and two for the U.S. Senate, liberal Democrats have carried Washington State. Years later, in interviews with Boeing engineers, Microsoft employees, hospital staff, and aluminum workers, I found that most of them agreed with the protests against the WTO and few expressed anger even at the rioters.

Nor was the disillusionment with globalization and the sympathy for the protestors limited to liberals and labor union members. A self-described "conservative Democrat," Geoffrey Stamper, who was Boeing's chief negotiator with its white-collar union (and whose father had been Boeing's president), told me that when he watched the rioting on TV, his first reaction had been: "Why had we let those kids get so angry? Why hadn't we listened to them?"[4]

Why weren't the adults angrier? The kids were protesting globalization, and, as the United States approached the twenty-first century, globalization triggered all sorts of anxieties about a new economy where the old rules didn't apply and the new rules hadn't yet been written. These anxieties were about international competition and much more. Yes, blue-collar workers had seen their jobs shipped overseas. Moreover, professionals and technicians were beginning to realize that they, too, were vulnerable. The controversial H1-B visa program allowed companies like Microsoft and Boeing to bring immigrants from countries like India who would work as aircraft engineers or software writers at lower pay than Americans would. And there were already signs that instead of letting tens of thousands of foreign professionals immigrate to the United States, these companies would soon be sending hundreds of thousands of professional jobs overseas.

In addition to exposing U.S. businesses and workers to competition from other countries with lower wages and living standards, globalization symbolizes profound and bewildering economic changes in this country. New technologies are eliminating middle managers and manual workers. New management theories are encouraging companies to abandon established product lines, require workers to prove their worth every day, and value adaptability over expertise. The deregulation of major sectors of the economy is plunging entire industries, from trucking to telecommunications, into unforgiving competition. And the increasing influence of investors over corporate management, with the resulting emphasis on short-term gains that boost stock prices, is making these changes occur at warp speed. These trends are transforming U.S. corporations from stable institutions that provided permanent jobs with rising wages into loose networks of superstars, subcontractors, and short-term employees. Professionals and technicians who had been encouraged to pursue excellence at all costs now are being overruled by bean counters who care mostly about their companies' quarterly financial statements. The very employees who are committed to their companies and their callings are infuriated by the unwelcome changes all around them.

Although they don't put this insight into words, these skilled and dedicated workers are experiencing a fundamental contradiction of the new global economy: Companies that still make products in this country can compete in the international marketplace only by offering higher quality, not by paying lower wages. The only way to improve quality is to engage employees' emotions, energies, experience, and intelligence in their work. But many companies are responding to the challenges of the new economy by doing exactly the opposite, denying employees the resources, the respect, and the discretion that they need to do their best work. Indeed, many loyal workers who would be proud to devote their careers to their companies are being treated as transients.

A YEAR OF CONFLICTS

In the year that followed the WTO protests, the Seattle area became the scene of a series of conflicts that resulted from the new economy's wrenching changes and their disorienting effect on many of the most skilled and dedicated employees at some of the most respected companies. At Boeing, more than seventeen thousand engineers and technicians conducted the largest strike by professionals in private industry in U.S. history. At Microsoft, where more than six thousand of the employees were classified as temporary workers, a maverick union group maintained a muck-raking Web site that exposed the mistreatment of the workforce. At the Kaiser Aluminum Company, which was once a model employer, thousands of workers refused to accept reductions in their wages and benefits and eventually forced a change in the company's ownership. At Northwest Hospital, several hundred workers organized with the SEIU, bringing the union closer to its goal of representing a majority of the health-care employees in the metropolitan area. By the end of the year, the reporters at Seattle's two jointly operated newspapers, the *Times* and the *Post-Intelligencer*, conducted a brief strike themselves, using the nonpolluting outdoor heaters that the Boeing engineers had invented to warm their picket lines. "The year 2000 was a synergy, in which the energy from each succeeding struggle, starting with the WTO protests, fed into what came next," explained Jonathan Rosenblum, who worked with Jones at the Labor Council.[5]

Seattle hadn't seen so much labor strife since 1919, when shipyard workers protested pay cuts in the aftermath of the armistice that ended World War I, and workers from every industry joined them, staging one of the few general strikes that this country has ever seen. What caused these modern-day battles of Seattle?

Interviewing the Boeing and Microsoft employees in 2000 and again years later, as well as the Northwest Hospital Workers in 2005 and 2006, I found that their grievances were very different from the mostly economic concerns that had motivated generations of workers since the general strikers in 1919. Most of the aerospace engineers, the software testers, and the hospital workers told me that they enjoyed their work but worried that their employers weren't giving them the leeway to do their jobs as well as they could. The Boeing engineers feared that the company was getting out of the business of building civilian aircraft. The software testers complained that they had to rush to meet their deadlines. The hospital workers spoke of understaffing in their units that compromised patient care. To be sure, the Kaiser

Aluminum workers found their jobs physically exhausting. Still, they admired the company's founder, the legendary industrialist Henry J. Kaiser, who believed in motivating his employees by treating them well. And they regretted their company's loss of leadership in its industry.

Talking to these workers who want to believe in their bosses but ended up battling them, I couldn't help but reach this conclusion: They love their work—the careers they have chosen, the skills they have learned, the products they make, and the services they provide. But they are beginning to hate their jobs and the conditions under which they do their work. Their thwarted desires to do their best work contributed to problems in their workplaces. As I argue in this book, these events set the tone for a new kind of workplace conflict that will become increasingly common during the twenty-first century. Disputes will set workers who are concerned with quality against employers who are mainly motivated by their quarterly profit statements. Organizations, whether in the form of traditional unions, professional associations, cyberspace societies, or some new model still struggling to be born, will take up the cause of improving the products that workers make and the services they provide. At the turn of the last century, the pioneering labor leader Samuel Gompers summed up his demands with one word: "More." At the turn of the twenty-first century, an increasingly skilled but frustrated workforce would add one more word: "Better."

Ironically, the emphasis on making money quicker instead of making products better is driven by the demands of the global economy, whose excesses produced the WTO protests. But if the United States loses the very traditions of quality work that the engineers, the information technology workers, the health-care employees, and the metal workers fought to defend in Seattle in 2000, we will eventually lose out in the global marketplace.

In short, these skilled but dissatisfied workers and their concerns about the quality of their work matter very much. Seattle benefited from Verlene Jones's expertise and dedication in responding to an emergency on the city's streets during the WTO protests—strengths she'd developed as a hospital technician and a union activist. The nation needs more such skilled workers, along with the contributions they make to their companies and their communities.

As the saying goes, "The whole world was watching" the WTO protests. Those who care about the United States' future should also look back on the conflicts that took place in the region's workplaces during the year that followed the battle of Seattle.

After all, Seattle has always been on the cutting edge of change. Just as a leading industrial age corporation, Boeing, was built in the Seattle area early in the twentieth century, the leading information age corporation, Microsoft, was founded there late in the century. As the social conservatism of Boeing's blue-collar workers and engineers gave way to the postmodern cynicism of information technology workers—an attitude partly rooted in their ambivalence about their work—Seattle became the trailblazer and the talisman for new cultural trends: grunge rock, gourmet coffees, and gloomy celebrities such as Kurt Cobain and Courtney Love.

In addition to being on the cutting edge of social change, Seattle has been on the razor's edge of social protest. Just as the general strike of 1919 focused attention on the forthright militancy of manufacturing workers, the battles of Seattle in 2000 showcased the anxious ambivalence of U.S. professionals and technicians who love their work but not their jobs.

At the beginning of the last century, angry workers could cripple the industrial economy by not showing up for work. At the beginning of this century, ambivalent workers can put a crimp on U.S. competitiveness in the global economy by being unable to do their best work.

For better or for worse, the battles of Seattle foreshadow America's future. This book is the story of what happened, why it happened, and where it's going.

1

HENRY KAISER'S
ORPHANS

After thirty-two years at the Kaiser Aluminum plant in Trentwood, rolling molten metal into usable forms, Dave Carlson envied his father. Making aluminum is one of the hottest, hardest, and dirtiest jobs in modern America, but Dave's dad had worked at the same mill before modern technology had made the job just a little easier. So why did Dave think that things had been better for his father?

Sitting in his union's storefront office, Carlson explained, "All my father saw were the good days."[1] As with many families in Spokane, a gritty factory town in eastern Washington, there had been little question that he'd follow his father into the rolling mill located ten miles beyond the city line. The elder Carlson had gone to work at Trentwood in 1946, shortly after the legendary Henry J. Kaiser had founded the company, and he retired in 1976, when Kaiser's heirs were still in control. Dave was hired in 1973, so he worked for a succession of new owners, culminating with the financier Charles Hurwitz, who ended up locking out his own employees and bankrupting the company. Increasingly discontented with the new management, Dave became active in the union, eventually becoming president of Local 338 of the United Steelworkers.

From 1998 through 2000, negotiations for a new union contract deadlocked, the workers went on strike, and the company refused their offer to return to work. So Carlson took on new roles—bargaining with management, leading picket lines, and making sure that workers got their strike benefits. His life became more varied and challenging than his father's, but still he envied the settled world his old man had known, when a benevolent company and a strong union together guaranteed a stable livelihood. "Everyone enjoyed working for Henry J. Kaiser because he treated you right," he said. "It was a good place to work, great benefits, health care, and vacations."

Kaiser Aluminum's history was a parable of how workers could be encouraged to take pride in their work—and how that pride could turn to rage when their company morphed from model employer to corporate cutthroat. Ambitious, hardworking, and attuned to the temper of his times, Henry J. Kaiser began his business career during the conservative 1920s as an unusually demanding boss who drove his employees mercilessly. But when he found that workers were more responsive to respectful treatment, he became the prototypical progressive capitalist, practicing and preaching the New Deal doctrine gospel that businesses benefit from stable and satisfied workforces and cooperative relationships with unions. During Kaiser Aluminum's heyday, its policies proved that workers could take satisfaction in doing some of the most difficult and dangerous blue-collar jobs and could develop a remarkable degree of loyalty to a company that cared about them. When new owners treated their employees as costs to be cut, their loyalty turned into fury. The workers resolved to hold out "one day longer" than their employer, even though the strike and the lockout lasted for two years. Burdened with debt, fines for labor law violations, and underfunded health and pension plans, Hurwitz lost control of the company, and its new management returned to the founder's vision. By 2005, a slimmed-down Kaiser Aluminum sold specialty products to Boeing and Airbus. Once again, Kaiser Aluminum developed a partnership with the

Steelworkers Union, which now selected four of ten members of the company's board of directors.

"THE FABULOUS MR. KAISER"

In a society that turns successful CEOs into celebrities, Henry J. Kaiser was as famous during the 1930s and 1940s as Bill Gates, Jack Welch, and Donald Trump are now. But just as today's tycoons personify the practices of the unstable new economy, Kaiser advanced the values of the New Deal. By the time he became a national figure, it is impossible to imagine Kaiser having a third of his workforce consist of temporary workers (as Gates did during the 1990s), boasting that he closed down entire divisions of his company (as Welch did in his best-selling books), or making his most famous phrase "You're fired" (as Trump does on his television series). Instead, Kaiser was known as Franklin D. Roosevelt's favorite businessman, the inventor of prepaid health care for workers and their families and child care for their kids, and the advocate for a postwar prosperity built on a secure and growing middle class.

Because of Kaiser's high-profile progressivism, the conservative columnist Westbrook Pegler attacked him as being overly dependent on government contracts and a "soft touch" for the unions. But Kaiser was far from being a softheaded humanitarian. His background and earlier career cast him as a hard-driving Horatio Alger, a self-made businessman whose can-do spirit helped him to found successful companies in industries ranging from photography to construction, shipbuilding, steel, and aluminum. His enlightened employee-relations policies were all the more noteworthy because he began his career as a demanding boss who later learned that satisfied workers were more productive than insecure ones.

Born in 1882 in the small town of Sprout Brook in upstate New York, Kaiser dropped out of school at the age of twelve to help support his family. Kaiser's father, a German immigrant shoemaker, made leather boots by hand, but he was losing business to nearby factories that mass-produced footwear. While Henry J. Kaiser rarely talked about his father, several of his biographers suggested that his determination to be first in his industries was forged by his father's failure to keep up with the times. After leaving school, Kaiser took a job at a dry goods store in Utica, but he soon bought a photography business in Lake Placid and expanded it with branches in vacation spots in Florida, Nassau, and the Bahamas.

Then, perhaps following the proverbial advice "Go west, young man," Kaiser moved all the way across the continent to a community with which he would be connected for the rest of his career, Spokane. There, he founded a construction company that did business in the Pacific Northwest, California, and Canada. Beginning with state road and bridge projects, he eventually coordinated the construction of major federally funded projects, including the Hoover Dam in Colorado and the Bonneville and Grand Coulee Dams in Washington, both of which, decades later, would provide hydroelectric power for the Kaiser Aluminum Company. During the late 1920s and early 1930s, Kaiser's competitive advantage was his determination to complete his projects quickly and inexpensively.

Just a few years later, Kaiser would coin quotable sayings about improving working Americans' lives, but at first, all of his maxims were about the importance of outworking his competitors. To people who doubted that a job could be done, he said, "I'm a builder, and if you call yourself a builder, you ought to be able to build anything," To anyone who doubted that the job could be done quickly, he added, "There's no money in a slow job." And to those who still doubted that Kaiser's company could do whatever he set his mind to, he added, "Problems are simply opportunities in work clothes."[2]

In order to meet his deadlines and keep within his budgets, Kaiser drove his workers to the edge of exhaustion—and beyond—at a terrible toll in their health and even their lives. During the construction of the Hoover Dam, fourteen men died from the heat in a single day in 1931. Soon afterward, fourteen hundred workers went on strike over unsafe conditions and the simple lack of water. Kaiser fired them.

Although he never apologized for the terrible working conditions on this project, Kaiser did have what he later called "a transformation" of his attitudes toward workers and their unions.

In addition to whatever humane impulses he had, Kaiser had at least three practical reasons to treat workers better. First, his reputation was damaged by the deaths at the Hoover Dam, and the project was delayed by the strike. Second, Kaiser's companies were moving beyond construction to other industries that required stable workforces. And third, as he continued to seek government contracts and other opportunities that depended on the goodwill of public officials, pro-labor politicians were taking office, from President Franklin D. Roosevelt to other liberals in state and local governments.

Completing projects in remote areas of the Pacific Northwest, California, and the Rocky Mountain states, Kaiser and other contractors whom he coordinated found that they could not count on regular supplies of the construction materials that they needed. Always the can-do businessman, Kaiser built several sand and gravel plants of his own and a huge cement plant at Permanente, California. These plants helped him to get contracts to complete more mammoth projects, such as building the piers for the San Francisco Bay Bridge.

While construction projects employed itinerant workforces that often moved from job to job and contractor to contractor, these factories needed loyal, stable, and motivated workforces, as would later Kaiser ventures, such as aluminum mills. By the mid-1930s, Kaiser had raised the pay for his workers, improved health and safety conditions, and looked for new benefits to provide for employees and their families. He also invested in the most modern equipment, explaining that he would rather wear out his machines than his workers.

In 1935, Congress passed and President Roosevelt signed the National Labor Relations Act, which guaranteed workers' rights to organize unions and bargain with their employers. Although major auto and steel companies and some construction companies still opposed unions, Kaiser quickly got in step with the trend toward collective bargaining. That same year, Kaiser made sure that the Northern California association of rock, sand, and gravel producers, which he headed, signed an agreement with the American Federation of Labor (AFL). Two years later, as part of his proposal to supply cement for the federal government, Kaiser declared that he "faithfully followed the policies of this administration with reference to collective bargaining, both in letter or spirit." In 1943, the AFL recommended that Kaiser and another pro-union businessman get all the federal contracts for shipbuilding.

By the 1940s, Kaiser's businesses had branched out well beyond construction, and he was building relationships with and soliciting contracts from Roosevelt administration officials, starting with the president himself. As the historian Stephen B. Adams wrote in his perceptive biography *Mr. Kaiser Goes to Washington,* Kaiser was becoming the first "government entrepreneur" actively seeking business opportunities that filled public needs and advanced public policies. Adopting a new watchword, "Find a need and fill it," Kaiser took it upon himself to advance three goals of Roosevelt's New Deal: helping working people and their families; equipping the military for World War II, and introducing competition into industries dominated by only a handful of companies.

As the nation prepared for and entered World War II, Roosevelt and his advisers appreciated Kaiser's can-do attitude. Beginning in 1940, Kaiser started up seven shipyards in California, Washington, and Oregon, employing two hundred thousand workers and building a third of all the nation's new ships for the navy and the merchant marine, more than any other industrialist provided. Meanwhile, Kaiser also served one of the administration's domestic goals, entering industries where the New Dealers believed that powerful corporate combines were restricting supplies and raising prices. During the 1940s, Kaiser founded companies in the magnesium, steel, aircraft, and aluminum industries. As *Business Week* observed, "His approach is to find a field in which the Administration considers [there is] a monopoly. Kaiser then goes into the field as an independent operator, and, in so doing, assures himself of government support."[3]

Confident that leading New Dealers, including Franklin and Eleanor Roosevelt, would approve of his endeavors, Kaiser developed new ways to advance social goals with the same energy and imagination that he improved production processes in construction, shipbuilding, and other industries. Seeking to reduce absenteeism, promote productivity, and perhaps atone for the tragedy at Hoover Dam, Kaiser provided health care for workers at his dam projects and shipyards. First, Kaiser hired doctors and nurses to work at the facilities, treating workers who became ill or injured. Then he created a new program where, for a minimal annual fee, his employees and their families could get medical checkups and other types of health care. Soon, he called this service the Kaiser Permanente plan—the forerunner of what became the nation's largest health maintenance organization.

With what was, for him, a minimal amount of fanfare, Kaiser had invented prepaid health care and paved the way for today's HMOs.

Similarly, Kaiser invented the child-care center and created the forerunner for the Head Start program. With able-bodied men being drafted into the armed forces, millions of women flocked into factories on the home front—"Rosie the Riveters," they came to be called. At the suggestion of Eleanor Roosevelt, who believed that child neglect was a national scandal, Kaiser created child-care centers at his shipyards that served as models for other industries. At his Portland, Oregon, shipyards, Kaiser built playrooms for workers' kids, with the newest playground equipment, cafeterias staffed by nutritionists, and infirmaries staffed by nurses. As the historian Doris Kearns Goodwin wrote, these facilities were more advanced than daycare centers decades later—indeed, Kaiser had created "a Head Start a quarter of a century ahead of its time."[4]

To be sure, all of these government contracts didn't just fall into Kaiser's lap. Leading the way for other companies such as Boeing and Microsoft, Kaiser hired a staff of representatives in what Bill Gates would call "the other Washington, D.C." These included the leading lawyer-lobbyist Tommy Corcoran and a young attorney, Lloyd Cutler, who would later serve as White House counsel for presidents Jimmy Carter and Bill Clinton. While Kaiser remained a registered Republican, he led several campaigns that furthered the Roosevelt administration's political purposes, including a "nonpartisan" voter registration and mobilization effort during the 1944 presidential election. A frequent guest at the White House, he replaced Joseph Kennedy as the president's favorite business leader.

Meanwhile, Kaiser cast himself for the part later played by Lee Iacocca, Bill Gates, and Jack Welch—the business executive as national hero. With a staff of publicists and speechwriters, Kaiser received worshipful coverage from newspapers and magazines, particularly Henry Luce's *Time, Life,* and *Fortune,* which breathlessly branded him "the fabulous Mr. Kaiser." In the spring of 1945, a Roper poll found that the public believed that Kaiser had done more than any other civilian to help the president with the war.

Apparently, President Roosevelt agreed. Aware that he was ailing, Roosevelt dumped his left-leaning vice president, Henry Wallace, in 1944 and searched for a running mate who could replace him, if necessary. As his cousin and confidante Margaret Suckley revealed decades later, Roosevelt told her that the best-qualified candidate was Henry J. Kaiser. "I have a candidate, but don't breathe it to a soul—there is a man, not a politician, who, I think I could persuade the country to elect," he told her. "There would be such a gasp when his name was suggested that I believe I would have a good chance if he were sold to the country in the right way."[5] Asking his political advisers to explore the possibility of a Kaiser candidacy, Roosevelt was dissuaded when they discovered that many Americans mistakenly believed that the industrialist was Jewish.

Although the White House wasn't in Kaiser's future, yet another new industry was. In a meeting on February 18, 1942, Interior Secretary Harold Ickes (whose son and namesake would be Bill Clinton's liaison to the labor movement) asked Kaiser to enter the aluminum industry in the Pacific Northwest. There were shortages of aluminum for aircraft production, Ickes explained, and the administration believed that the leading producer, Alcoa, was creating production bottlenecks. The idea languished, and instead the government decided to operate its own aluminum plants—an extreme measure even for the New Deal. But Ickes had planted an idea in Kaiser's mind, and immediately after the war, Kaiser bought two government-operated aluminum plants, the Trentwood and Mead mills outside Spokane, while building or buying other plants in Tacoma, Washington, not far from Seattle, and in Newark, Ohio; and Gramercy, Louisiana. He called his new company Permanente Aluminum but soon changed the name to Kaiser Aluminum.

"It was called 'Kaiser's Folly' when it was opened," recalled Alan Link, a former local union president at the Trentwood plant, whose father had also worked there (and led the local union). "Everyone knew, after the war was over, there was no need for aluminum."[6] But, once again, Kaiser could see around corners. With the growth in civilian aircraft and the Cold War's continuing demand for missiles and military aircraft, companies like Boeing demanded more aluminum than ever. Kaiser Aluminum would be the nation's third-largest producer, after Alcoa and Reynolds, benefiting from its location in the Northwest.

GOOD TIMES AT "THE LAZY K"

Lightweight, rust-free, and capable of conducting electricity, aluminum is a valuable and versatile metal. It's used in automobiles, airplanes, trucks, ships, railroad cars, bicycles, cans, foil, and electrical transmission lines. In many working-class communities across the country, the houses (usually built after World War II) have aluminum siding. In the movie *Tin Men,* Richard Dreyfuss and Danny DeVito portray salesmen peddling aluminum siding in Baltimore during the 1950s. As a high school kid in New York City in 1968, I had a summer job going door-to-door in the east Bronx selling a product that was supposed to protect aluminum doors against the rain and the snow. It was unnecessary, and I remember one angry homeowner, clad only in his shorts and T-shirt, chasing me away, screaming, "This stuff is crap." He was right. Aluminum doesn't rust and only corrodes slightly.

Making aluminum is much harder than selling it. In its natural form, powdery white alumina is found in bauxite ore. To turn alumina into a useful metal, aluminum, the alumina is placed in huge high-temperature vats—"pots," as they're called in the smelting mills—in a "bath" of sodium aluminum fluoride and other materials. As the electric current is passed through a series of the pots in a "pot line," temperatures in the "pot room" become almost unbearably hot. Eventually, the alumina separates into two constituent elements, aluminum and oxygen. At rolling mills like the Trentwood plant, workers take the molten metal and turn it into usable forms, such as rods, sheets, and coils.

No way around it, working in these mills is as agonizing as any job in modern America. As Jim Woodward, who worked at the Tacoma smelter, recalled, "The pots burned at 1,300 degrees centigrade. There were a hundred or so pots in a room. Each pot was the size of a small room. The room was a building the length of a football field." Workers wore heat-resistant suits, like astronauts, that covered their entire bodies, from their heads to their electrically insulated boots. With the work-suits and the excruciating temperatures, everything was more difficult. "A wrench weighed about five to six pounds," Woodward remembered. "In the heat it feels like two hundred pounds."[7]

Workers were covered with sweat and soot. "You were wet from top to bottom," Woodward recalled. "Your clothes were soaked. Caked ore is from the plant. Cake stuck to your skin and your clothes. You would shower when you left." Once his wife went to the plant to bring him something. "She didn't recognize me." Most people, even young men who'd worked in factories or on construction sites, couldn't last at jobs in the smelters and the rolling mills. Looking back on their years at Kaiser Aluminum, workers keep telling the story of hiring in right after high school, often following their fathers into the mills, and watching while other newcomers quit or were fired. "I hired in during the summer time," Woodward recalled. "You might have twenty workers starting and seventeen would quit the same day. . . . A newly hired worker would walk in the lunchroom. The older guys would say, 'Hey, kid, when you quit tomorrow, what size are your boots?' . . . If you could make it thirty days, you had a job for life." Woodward's father was a guard at Boeing, and Woodward remembers that even as a twenty-year-old, he made more than his father made.

Kaiser did his best to make these arduous jobs bearable. In its union contracts with the Steelworkers, the company usually paid a little more and offered better benefits than Alcoa and Reynolds did. Sometimes, Kaiser broke with the other two companies in contract negotiations, earning the enmity of its competitors and the gratitude of its workforce. In addition to the state-of-the-art work-suits and boots, the company provided water bottles and later Gatorade and doctors and nurses in the plants to treat injuries and heat exhaustion and provide annual checkups. In an innovation unheard of anywhere except in colleges and universities, Kaiser Aluminum offered its employees ten weeks off at thirteen weeks' pay every five years. The workers could do whatever they wanted—go back to school, go on a vacation, fix up their homes, stay home with the kids, or, as most did, take temporary jobs and collect two paychecks. Professionals would have called this time off a "sabbatical." Kaiser workers called it "my long vacation," and, decades later, they still thank "Henry J."—no one calls him anything else—for it.

Looking back on the years when Henry J. and his heirs ran the company, workers remembered that the supervision was no stricter than absolutely necessary. "They left you alone," Carlson recalled. "You did your job, and you went home." In fact, if workers could do their jobs in less time than their eight-hour shifts, supervisors let them "take a nap somewhere without being interrupted," especially on the graveyard shift (midnight to eight A.M.). Because of the naps and the sabbaticals, the Kaiser workers' neighbors in Spokane called the company "the Lazy K." They smiled when they said it, though, because everyone knew that even working for Henry J., making aluminum was the toughest job in town.

Even now, with the Kaiser family long gone and the smelters in Mead and Tacoma closed, workers speak proudly of their work, their products, and the company as it used to be. Because their jobs were so difficult, people were proud that they could do the work, and they relished the respect of their coworkers and supervisors. That was especially true for the handful of women who worked at Kaiser. The first woman to become a welder at Tacoma, Rosanna Miller—"Yes, they called me Rosie the Riveter"—still speaks with pride of every promotion she received. Starting out in the most difficult place of all, the pot room, she was threatened with firing by a supervisor who said that she, literally, couldn't take the heat because she was a woman. She was rehired to work in the "paste room," which mixes the carbon in the aluminum reduction process. Three years later, she heard that as part of an affirmative action program that Kaiser Aluminum and the Steelworkers had introduced, she could apply for an apprenticeship as a welder. She applied, was accepted, completed the program successfully, and, as she proudly remembers, instead of being pushed out, she moved up.[8] That program was historic: it was unsuccessfully challenged by a white man, Brian Weber, in a case that reached the U.S. Supreme Court in 1979, and, for the first time, the AFL-CIO under an aging George Meany, filed a friend-of-the-court brief in support of an affirmative action plan.

"It was fun to go in—I looked forward to work every day," said Kevin Dupus, a machine operator at the Trentwood plant. "You got along with everybody. Management treated you decently." There was a camaraderie that extended from the factory floor to the union hall. "Each crew became a family, working these weird hours," Woodward said. "You did things with the other guys and their kids—hiking together, picnics together. The union was a big deal, guys were involved. I worked two union jobs before Kaiser, and I don't remember monthly union meetings." There was also a fierce pride in the product. Years after leaving Kaiser, Link boasted that the plants used the best processes for smelting and rolling aluminum: "We made 99.99999 percent pure metal, as good as you can make."

Moreover, workers took pride in knowing Henry J., a national hero who never lost touch with his workforce and with the city of Spokane, even after he moved his base of operations to Oakland, California, and later to Hawaii. Together with hiring in and watching other newcomers quit, the stories that Kaiser workers tell most often are about the times that they, their fathers, or their grandfathers first met Henry J. when he toured their plants. Decades later, they remember and agree with his philosophy. "I always heard stories of how his workers came first," Dupus remembered. "He believed it is important to provide a good reliable job for the family man."

When the topic is working at Kaiser, the talk soon turns to families and fathers. It was the kind of company where sons followed their fathers into the factories, and young men (and the occasional young woman) were proud that they could do the jobs their dads did. Soon someone mentions the day their dad met Henry J., and the impression is inescapable that in a company that was at once egalitarian and paternalistic, the founder was the greatest father figure of all. Long after Kaiser and his heirs were gone and the new owners made the company crueler, the workers sounded like Henry J.'s orphans.

"They're Not Going to Settle"

Henry J. Kaiser died in 1967, at the age of eighty-five. His heirs held onto the company until the late 1970s, when it was sold to British investors who maintained its management team and traditional policies. Without the innovative Henry J. Kaiser at the helm, with aluminum prices declining, and with stiff competition from Alcoa, Reynolds, and foreign companies, Kaiser Aluminum's fortunes declined. Shortly after the stock market fell in October 1987, Kaiser was sold to a Texas financier, Charles Hurwitz, and his company, Maxxam.

Hurwitz bought Kaiser Aluminum with junk bonds, saddling the company with a huge debt that eventually contributed to his downfall. To hear Hurwitz's numerous critics tell it, Hurwitz combined the least attractive features of the corporate raiders of the 1980s and 1990s, such as Frank Lorenzo, Michael Milken, and the fictional Gordon Gekko, whom Michael Douglas portrayed in the movie *Wall Street*, famously proclaiming, "Greed is good." Hurwitz had owned a failed savings-and-loan, the United Savings Association of Texas, and the bailout cost taxpayers $1.6 billion and was the third-largest in the nation's history. He had also acquired Pacific Lumber, a family-owned California timber company. He soon doubled its cutting of old-growth redwoods, infuriating environmentalists—a situation the Steelworkers would use to their advantage when they searched for allies.

At first, Hurwitz was content to keep Kaiser's veteran managers, but as the company lost its market share and profit margins, he took a tougher line against the workers, their union, and the company's generous wages and benefits. The sabbaticals and supervisor-sanctioned naps were the first to go. Then came a drumbeat of demands for freezes or cuts in pay scales and other costs.

In 1983, the company and the union negotiated a wage freeze. Then, as Woodward, who served on the union's negotiating committee, recalled, there were two years of "concessionary bargaining" that resulted in $4.80 an hour in cuts in wages and benefits. In return, the workers received company stock, but in 1988, in a decision that Kaiser workers and retirees still debate, they cashed in their holdings, losing their stake in the company's future. Meanwhile, in a costly move that eventually went sour, the company diversified into real estate and chemical divisions. During this period, workers grew discontented with the company and the union, and many local union officers were defeated for reelection.

Once again, in 1994, the workers agreed to new concessions, totaling $50 million. Many jobs were combined so that workers assumed new responsibilities. Hundreds of workers were laid off in Spokane, Tacoma, and elsewhere. The workers thought they would be rewarded in good times, but the company kept coming back for more.

In 1995, the workers staged a nine-day protest strike that resulted in restoring some of their lost wages. "There was a terrible frustration among people who made sacrifices, got stock, and now had no way to get money back from the stock," Woodward recalled. "A lot of people thought you could shut them down for a ten-day strike, everything would be fine. We juggled things around, passed the agreement, and back to work." It looked like a victory, but, as Woodward explained, the ultimate result was, "Kaiser said, 'We might have been caught with our pants down once, but we ain't gonna get caught with our pants down again.'"

By then, the older generation of executives and supervisors whom Henry J. Kaiser had trained was retiring, and tougher bosses were taking their places. A former manager at Trentwood, Ray Milchovich, became the CEO. He may have had blue-collar roots, but he had blue-chip aspirations, which aroused the union members' anger. "Ray was a short little guy with a big ego and expensive tastes," Woodward remembered. "I can still see him with starched French shirts. . . . After all these years at Trentwood, if he got a chance to get rid of the union, he would." Soon, the company was taking every union grievance victory to arbitration, denying workers the satisfaction of ever winning and costing the union thousands of dollars in arbitration expenses.

As the negotiations for the 1998 contract got under way, it was clear that this time, Kaiser was playing for keeps. "When we went into the 1998 negotiations, this was a normal pattern bargaining that we had been used to," Woodward recalled. "They [Kaiser] wanted to take a contract that took fifty years to build and basically throw it in the shit can and turn it into a few pieces of paper." Among other changes that the company proposed, all the workers would go on annual salaries without overtime and shift differentials. Each facility would have its own agreement, eliminating the union's collective clout as the representative of all of the company's blue-collar workers. "They would have made us a company union," Woodward said, using the labor movement's traditional phrase for an employee organization that exists at only one facility and is subservient to the employer.

Kaiser's negotiators didn't dispel the view that they were out to break the union. In the opening bargaining session, Kaiser's vice president of administrative operations, Wayne Hale, referred to the union disparagingly, as if it were a social group: "Listen, I think everyone should belong to a club at some time. But we have to make changes in order to compete."

Meanwhile, Kaiser was already advertising in the Spokane newspapers for "replacement workers" (union members call them "scabs") in the event of a strike. During the summer of 1998, managers interviewed and conditionally hired these workers at the Redpath Hotel in town. "Management had a book with job descriptions with pictures, a private scrapbook for scabs," recalled John Wheeler, who worked at the Mead smelter. In preparation for a strike, "they brought in trailers, washers and driers, and portable kitchens."[9]

Workers also remembered unlikely candidates being hired and promoted for regular jobs at the company, with the implicit understanding that they would work during a strike. Wheeler served on the joint labor-management apprenticeship committee, and he said that the company was placing people with unusual backgrounds in training programs. "They were hiring ex-navy people—military people follow orders—not people who were union members elsewhere. They were hired in the bargaining units and then promoted." Prim, precise, and well-groomed, the new hires stood out from their coworkers. "They looked like Republicans," said Roseanne Miller, who herself had graduated from the apprenticeship program but as a trailblazer, not a strikebreaker.

As the negotiations crept along, Alan Link, who had become an official of the state AFL-CIO, told the labor group's president, Rick Bender, to expect a long and grueling strike. "They [Kaiser] don't want to settle," Link predicted.[10]

A LADDER TO LUNA

On October 1, 1998, as the old contract expired, the union's bargaining committee rejected the company's latest offer. Characteristically, the company and the union couldn't even agree on what Kaiser was offering. The company claimed that it would raise base wages by $2.75 an hour over five years—a meager offer, by most standards. But the union maintained that even this increase would be eaten up by eliminating overtime and shift differentials.[11]

The workers walked off their jobs. The usually soft-spoken Roseanna Miller remembered, "We were escorted out of the plant by jackbooted guards and goons." For the next two years, the company and the union fought on three fronts: the bargaining tables, the plants and the picket lines, and the public stages on which the union conducted a campaign of guerrilla theater.

The actual bargaining was a textbook case of the conflict between a company that was intent on drastically cutting costs in order to become competitive in the global marketplace and a union that wanted to limit the concessions it would make after workers had already made substantial sacrifices to keep Kaiser Aluminum in business. Indeed, the Bureau of Labor Statistics later commissioned a dispassionate study of the negotiations, authored by a staff economist, Edward J. Wasilewski Jr.

After the walkout began, the company and the union continued to conduct negotiations, off and on and usually with the assistance of the Federal Mediation and Conciliation Service. But on October 30, the bargaining was temporarily derailed when the union objected to a talk that Kaiser's CEO, Ray Milchovich had delivered at a conference of New York industry analysts. Upping the ante on the company's earlier proposal, Milchovich said that he wanted to reduce the number of jobs at the five plants by between six hundred and nine hundred.

Returning to the bargaining table on November 21, the union made a counteroffer that recognized that Kaiser had to streamline itself but that limited the sacrifices that workers would make. The union suggested an early retirement incentive to reduce the workforce, coupled with protections against plant closings, contracting out work, or layoffs of workers with two years or more of service. Rejecting the union's position, Kaiser said that the proposal still failed to increase productivity.

On December 11, Kaiser presented the union with an unwanted Christmas present—a 1,200-page proposal to eliminate "antiquated" work rules, cut seven hundred jobs, postpone capping the company's contributions to health premiums, and increase wages by $3.13 an hour. "It was so huge, it was delivered with a fucking forklift, as someone said," recalled Steelworkers lawyer Paul Whitehead. "They photocopied it for every negotiator." The union rejected the proposal.[12]

After resuming negotiations in Chicago on January 7, 1999, and talking again from January 11 through 13, it became clear that the two sides were far apart. After the bargaining, "We had a real come-to-Jesus meeting among the union people assessing the situation," Whitehead said. "We decided to offer to return to work and continue negotiating." The company rejected the offer and declared that it was locking out—in effect, firing—the striking workers, a hardball tactic that was never used at Kaiser and had only rarely been used in U.S. industry. For the next year, the real action would be on the picket lines and in the guerrilla theater that the union staged.

When the workers walked off their jobs on October 1, the company ran the plants in Spokane, Tacoma, and elsewhere with more than a thousand strikebreakers and supervisory employees. A security firm—IMAC—provided guards for the plant. Wheeler, Miller, and other workers described them as "black-booted guys in black uniforms"—fearsome garb that anticipated how the police and the anarchists would dress at the WTO protests less than a year later. Meanwhile, the mills became self-contained cities, with the replacement workers putting in two twelve-hour shifts every day and eating, sleeping, and washing their clothes inside.

Receiving unemployment compensation because they had been locked out and striker benefits from the union, most of the workers maintained picket lines around the mills. At the Tacoma smelter, which was on the waterfront, Miller recalled, "We picketed at the back gate, the front gate, the port, and the railroad gate." Occasionally, there were encounters between the striking workers and the guards. Miller remembered: "I was picketing at the port on Sunday. I saw a 'goon guard' cross a line and use a men's restroom. I told the longshoremen and the police. The police told him to use the restroom in the plant."

In addition to strike benefits, the union maintained a food bank at the union hall, with a cargo trailer. Compared to the company's absentee owners and replacement workers, most residents of Spokane and Tacoma saw the striking workers as the home team. Longshoremen and local businesses brought over hotdogs, hamburgers, pizza, and other food to the picket lines and the union hall.

But the Steelworkers had learned from bitter battles with other companies, including the financier Mark Rich, who had acquired an old Kaiser plant in Ravenswood, West Virginia, that unpopular employers were most vulnerable far away from their factories. Foreshadowing the WTO protests that united blue-collars and greens, the union forged an alliance with environmentalists, who hated Hurwitz because he was clear-cutting California forests.

On May 19, 2000, nearly three hundred workers and environmentalists traveled to Texas for Maxxam's annual stockholders meeting at a remote country club in a Houston suburb. Clearing security guards and metal detectors, the protestors— each of whom had bought a share of the company's stock— heckled Hurwitz and nominated former Ohio senator Howard Metzenbaum and former Illinois congressman Abner Mikva to serve as members of the board of directors. Although the insurgency was supported by public employee pension funds from California and New York, it was defeated, but not before Hurwitz got more unfavorable news coverage.

Calling themselves the "road warriors," Kaiser workers visited the company's customers in the United States and Canada, claiming that the replacement workers didn't know their new jobs and were making unsafe products. For instance, Richard Prete, a maintenance mechanic at Trentwood, traveled to Calgary, Alberta, where Crown Cork and Seal bought rolled coil that was produced to make aluminum cans. "I tried to persuade them not to use the metal made by replacement workers because of quality concerns," Prete remembered. "The workers agreed there were problems, and the managers said they'd take a closer look."[13]

In their most unusual action, the Steelworkers traveled to Eureka, California, where Hurwitz's company was cutting down forests and, the union believed, recruiting strikebreakers for Kaiser. Together with environmentalists, the union members rallied against the financier. Then a delegation of Kaiser workers paid a visit to Julia Butterfly Hill, a young woman who lived on a two-hundred-foot-high platform in an ancient tree that she named "Luna." Other young people rigged up ropes and ladders and brought her food. The Steelworkers' group was muscular and mechanically savvy, but with larger body builds than the vegetarians who usually visited Hill. Still, the Steelworkers rigged up their own ropes and ladders and huffed and puffed their way up to visit the environmental heroine, who endorsed the strike. Soon, they were hanging out with rock stars and other celebrities who were participating in the environmental protests.

The experience brought the workers into a world that their fathers wouldn't have recognized but their kids appreciated. "Julia Butterfly Hill is a lovely young woman," Woodward said years later. "Bonnie Raitt is one of the nicest people you'll ever meet. Joan Baez is remarkably unpretentious." Years later, when these performers were playing in Seattle, Tacoma, or Spokane, the workers went to their concerts.

When Jackson Brown came to Eastern Washington, Woodward went to a backstage party with the star, his sidemen, and the road crew.

Ultimately, three body blows forced Hurwitz to settle with the union. The debts he ran up when he bought the company had continued to grow. With the 2000 elections coming up, the Clinton administration threatened to prevent Kaiser from reselling the hydroelectric power it purchased at low rates from Bonneville. And on May 1, the National Labor Relations Board announced plans to charge Kaiser with unfair labor practices that could have cost the company more than $200 million in back pay.

Kaiser agreed to binding arbitration, and on September 18, 2000, the arbitration panel split the difference between the company and the union. Workers received modest wage increases totaling $3.42 an hour over five years, without cuts in their health benefits. Massive layoffs were ruled out, but the company was allowed to combine many job titles and loosen many work rules. With some grumbling, workers ratified the agreement.

Returning to work at Trentwood on October 24, the workers were greeted by a mile-long chain of cars as they drove up Euclid

Avenue to the mill for their first morning shift in more than two years. Friends, family, and other supporters cheered and waved. When some workers rolled down their windows, supporters reached inside and shook their hands.

Over the months ahead, it became clear that while the workers hadn't won, Hurwitz had lost. He hadn't broken the union, but the company was broke. Rising debts, increasing electrical bills, unpaid health and pension costs, lost business during the lockout, and the prospect of back pay awards all plunged Kaiser into bankruptcy court. As we'll see in the afterword, the company emerged slimmer than even Hurwitz had wanted, with the smelters at Tacoma and Mead closed but jointly managed with the union and focused on high-quality specialty products for customers such as Boeing and Airbus. Once again, workers would say that the company was treating them right.

Somewhere Henry J. was smiling.

2

FROM BLUE-COLLAR BLUES
TO WHITE-COLLAR WOES

In today's United States, work is getting better, but jobs are getting worse. During the first three decades after World War II, most Americans disliked the content of their work but liked the wages, the benefits, and the overall economic security provided by their jobs. Now, for growing numbers of Americans, it's the other way around: they like what they do every day, but they're dissatisfied with the economic insecurity and frustrated with the obstacles to doing their best work.

What happened? More people than ever before are doing work that challenges them intellectually, rather than exhausting them physically. But there are also fewer jobs like those that Kaiser Aluminum used to offer—secure jobs with regular raises, stable health coverage, and guaranteed pension benefits. For most workers, downsizings can come suddenly, raises depend on their supervisor's discretion, their health insurance keeps costing more and covering less, and defined pension plans are a thing of the past. For growing numbers of workers in professional and technical jobs, there are no more corporate dress codes, but there is also less discretion in how they do their jobs.

These new realities have produced new kinds of worker discontent. As recently as the early 1970s, the typical angry worker was a production worker trying to slow down his assembly line at an auto factory. Now she's a nurse trying to increase staffing levels at her hospital. How did we get from the blue-collar blues to the white-collar woes?

PAID NOT TO THINK

Back in the days when millions of Americans worked on assembly lines, they performed the same tasks over and over again. The problem was not that workers weren't able to think for themselves. The problem was that most companies wouldn't pay workers to think—in fact, they paid them not to think. Corporate managers were afraid that their employees knew their crafts too well and wouldn't surrender the control of the pace and the processes of their work to their supervisors. Knowledge, after all, is power, and as long as workers knew things that their bosses didn't, they might not work as hard and as quickly as the companies wanted. And if the workers went on strike, they'd be able to shut things down, without their supervisors knowing how to start things up again.

That was why, early in the twentieth century, the industrial engineer Frederick Taylor was so sought after as a management consultant. Taylor figured out how to take the skill and the autonomy out of blue-collar jobs, turning skilled machinists, electricians, and carpenters into indistinguishable factory "hands" who performed the same tasks repeatedly. Taylor and his colleagues conducted "time-motion studies" of factory workers to determine exactly what they did, how they did it, and how they could do it faster. Eventually, workers' jobs were broken down into simple and separate tasks, and they were given only one or two tasks to do, over and over again. Factory life became a manager's paradise and a worker's purgatory, with the managers doing the planning and the workers doing the drudgery.

Supposedly, this was the most efficient way of doing things, but discouraging and defeating strikes was—and sometimes still is—part of the reason for conducting "time-motion studies" of workers' jobs. As recently as 1998, when the Kaiser Aluminum Company was preparing to provoke a strike, management consultants studied workers' jobs to determine how strikebreakers could replace the regular employees.

By the middle of the twentieth century, this "scientific management" had spread from factories to offices. Bookkeepers, claims representatives, secretaries, receptionists, file clerks, and other white-collar workers found themselves subject to micromanagement. In his classic study *White-Collar*, the sociologist C. Wright Mills described how most office and sales work resembled factory work, with employees churning out paperwork as methodically as their blue-collar brethren bent metal. Typing pools, keypunch rooms, and bookkeeping units were managed with a discipline that Taylor would have envied.

The old ways—narrow job descriptions, strict supervision, and workers doing the same things to churn out the same products, over and over again—worked well for the first three decades after World War II. Manufacturers were equipped only to make their standard models, consumers were satisfied with fewer choices, and only a few companies and countries were competing in most industries. In those days, mass production allowed for enormous economies of scale, and companies made money by making and selling large numbers of the same models of trucks, tape recorders, or TV sets.

WHEN NIXON SANG THE BLUE-COLLAR BLUES

By the 1970s, computerization (in those days, they called it *automation*) and foreign competition (then the word was *imports*) began to change how Americans worked and did business. Corporate America's first response was to micromanage their employees to make them work even harder and faster. In the most infamous example of turbo-charged Taylorism, General Motors built a new fully automated Chevrolet assembly plant in rural Lordstown, Ohio, to churn out its new subcompact passenger car, the Vega, which was supposed to compete with small-size German and Japanese models. Soon, the plant was producing a hundred cars or more an hour with the fastest assembly line in history. But the youthful workforce rebelled against the unbearable pace of the line. First, they sabotaged the cars, cutting the ignition wires, slitting the upholstery, denting the bodies, scratching the paint, and loosening the bolts. In the spring of 1972, their United Auto Workers (UAW) local conducted a three-day strike that convinced the company to slow down the line. By then, the Vega had become a symbol of poor-quality U.S. cars, Lordstown was a warning that young workers would rebel against regimentation, and, for a brief moment, the nation's business and political leaders paid attention to the problems of workers who were stuck in intolerable jobs.[1]

Long before the Lordstown strike, President Richard M. Nixon had been paying attention to working-class discontent. Since Franklin D. Roosevelt's presidency, blue-collar workers had been the mainstay of the New Deal coalition—they figured that Democrats fought for working people, while Republicans favored the idle rich. But now, circumstances were setting them against other groups of people who were easily stereotyped as not working as hard as blue-collar Americans. Many of their sons were fighting in Vietnam in a war that was being demonstrated against and dodged by the children of the upper middle class—hippies who sat around, slept around, or marched around, apparently without studying or working. The civil rights revolution and the antipoverty program seemed to be benefiting others, while burdening the hard-pressed lower middle class. In an era when everyone else—women, students, and minorities—was protesting, white working-class discontent could be expected to reach a boiling point, too. Indeed, popular culture was already producing blue-collar characters who always seemed one tax bill, layoff notice, or unwanted social encounter away from going on a rampage. In the movie *Joe*, a factory worker played by Peter Boyle announces that he wants to kill a hippie—"just one." In the sitcom *All in the Family*, a warehouse worker named Archie Bunker rages against blacks, Jews, hippies, and his own layabout son-in-law. In a rare acknowledgment of the fact that African Americans also worked hard for a living, the film *Blue-Collar* presents three auto workers—two black and one white—who are increasingly infuriated by the company, the union, and every aspect of life in a decaying Detroit. Life seemed to be imitating art when construction workers (then called "hardhats") attacked antiwar demonstrators in lower Manhattan in the spring of 1970.

In real life, most working-class Americans—white, black, or Latino—hadn't become violent, but they were becoming volatile voters. In the 1968 presidential election, Alabama's segregationist governor, George C. Wallace, became a tribune of white working-class discontent before the unions successfully challenged him with populist appeals in behalf of a pro-labor Democrat, Hubert H. Humphrey, who lost narrowly to Nixon. In 1970, Democrats and Republicans fought to a standstill for the support of working-class voters—Republicans and Democrats wore American flag pins in their lapels, and Democrats also marched with union members who struck at GM, GE, and other companies. With the 1972 election looming, Nixon prepared to do what his Republican successors, including Ronald Reagan and two George Bushes, wouldn't do: appeal to lower-middle-class voters not only as patriots and traditionalists but as workers.

Nixon appointed two task forces (one coordinated by the Department of Labor, the second by the Department of Health, Education, and Welfare) to study what his advisers called the "blue-collar problem." Reporting first, the Labor Department task force recommended a set of initiatives that included job training and retraining, adult education, mass transit, and child care for kids with two parents working outside the home. While Nixon was willing to work with congressional Democrats to pass progressive programs on most initiatives except child care, this report did not inspire any initiative that Nixon himself promoted.

Entitled *Work in America*, the second study was more ambitious and made sweeping pronouncements about the quality of work life that liberals would have hailed and conservatives would have ridiculed if the report had been released during a Democratic administration. Sounding more like a university sociology department than a corporate personnel department, the task force concluded that "classically alienating jobs (such as on the assembly line) . . . allow the worker no control over the conditions of work and . . . seriously affect his mental and physical functioning off the job."[2] Prophetically, the report continued, "a growing number of white-collar jobs have much in common with the jobs of autoworkers and steelworkers."[3] Indeed, discontent with the intrinsic factors of work had spread even to those with managerial status. The report warned that this widespread worker discontent was a major cause of economic problems, including "low productivity, increasing absenteeism, high worker turnover rates, wildcat strikes, industrial sabotage, poor-quality products, and a reluctance by workers to give themselves to their tasks." Moreover, worker alienation also caused social problems, such as alcoholism, drug abuse, and racial conflict. These notes had been sounded for years by labor leaders such as the visionary UAW president Walter Reuther (who had originated the slogan "Humanize Work"), but no one expected them to be echoed by a Republican administration.

So, what was to be done? In addition to the kinds of government programs that the Labor Department report had recommended, *Work in America* called for a redesign of jobs throughout private industry that would make work more interesting and challenging by offering workers more discretion and responsibility. Always a complex figure, Nixon responded to the report with rhetoric that melded a New Dealer's sympathy for the working class, a conservative's contempt for the indolent, and a centrist's support for pragmatic programs that would encourage Americans to work more cheerfully and productively. Honoring and rewarding work became a theme of his speeches, and Nixon began his talks sounding like the labor leader George Meany and concluded by echoing the white backlasher George Wallace. Thus, in his Labor Day speech on September 6, 1971, Nixon declared, "In our quest for a better environment, we must always remember that the most important part of the quality of life is the quality of work, and the new need for job satisfaction is the key to the quality of work." In the same speech, he also warned of "a new welfare ethic that could cause the American character to weaken."[4]

To be sure, by praising "the work ethic," Nixon appealed to workers who resented welfare recipients, student protestors, and lazy hippies. But he also persuaded people who were working hard, barely breaking even, and receiving little respect from their employers or the nation's news media that the president understood and respected them. Ironically, this was the same message that Roosevelt had sent working Americans during the Great Depression (a textile worker once told a reporter that Roosevelt "knows that my boss is a son of a bitch"), and it is a message that few presidents, from either party, have sent since then.

(Nixon's Labor Day speech was drafted by one of his star speechwriters, William Safire, who later became a columnist for the *New York Times*. Nixon and Safire considered this a major speech, and, with Nixon's approval, Safire spent several weeks during the summer of 1971 traveling around the country, talking to workers, and identifying himself only as "a writer."[5] More than twenty years later, I was a speechwriter for President Bill Clinton. If there was any issue I cared about, it was restoring workers' rights to organize unions, so I made sure to be the writer who drafted Clinton's Labor Day speeches. When self-styled "New Democrats" on his staff questioned my speech drafts' emphasis on workers and unions, I showed them excerpts from speeches that an earlier president had delivered. They assumed that the words were Roosevelt's, Harry Truman's, or Lyndon Johnson's and were amazed to learn that these tributes to the working class had been uttered by Nixon. If an old-style Republican had recognized that unions were an essential American institution, then why couldn't a New Democrat like Clinton? In fact, Nixon himself was obsessed with winning over, or at least neutralizing, the labor movement, and his staff included several shrewd students of the working class, including his labor secretary George Schultz; the speechwriters William Safire, Patrick Buchanan, and William Gavin; the scholarly Daniel Patrick Moynihan and Kevin Phillips; and the civil rights activist and former union organizer James Farmer.)

Nixon's embrace of the *Work in America* report was a little-known factor in reforming U.S. workplaces. In the U.S. Department of Labor, a division was set up to encourage labor-management cooperation, employee involvement in management decisions, and the redesign and enrichment of jobs. The assistant labor secretary, Jerome Rosow, who had first suggested the administration's "blue-collar initiative," later created his own research and education center, the Work in America Institute, which has spread the gospel of job redesign and employee involvement to several generations of leaders in business, labor, and government. Employee involvement ("EI," for short) has become a catchphrase for the business community, often falsely raising workers' hopes and producing the very discontent that these programs are supposed to preempt.

WHY TAYLOR'S WALL CAME TUMBLING DOWN

Technological change made it possible to restructure the workplace, and globalization made it necessary. During the 1980s, more sophisticated software, personal computers, and the intraoffice networks that preceded the Internet all allowed individual workers to store, retrieve, and exchange information in miraculous new ways. Meanwhile, international competition reached gale force, sweeping away established companies and old ways of doing business. By 1989, when the Berlin Wall between communism and capitalism was being torn down in Germany, "Taylor's Wall" between doing and thinking (the phrase was coined by the social critic Ralph Whitehead) was being demolished in U.S. workplaces. Fewer jobs were being cut apart, carefully choreographed, and closely supervised. Instead of being stripped of every area of competence except the capacity to keep doing the same things faster and faster, workers were encouraged to become skilled generalists again, performing many tasks, exercising more discretion, and taking responsibility for the quality of their work. Instead of being bossed around by supervisors, workers were often assigned to autonomous work teams, either without any supervisors at all or with the management representative functioning as a "coach." Many factories also created other problem-solving groups, often known as "quality circles," where workers and managers discussed and decided issues such as hiring policies and health and safety. By 1997, a survey of major manufacturing companies showed that more than 38 percent were using self-managing work teams, problem-solving groups, job rotations, or all of these methods of humanizing their workplaces. These innovations were most common in companies that used advanced technologies, made high-end products, offered sophisticated services, and competed in international markets—companies very much like Boeing and Microsoft.

I saw these changes as early as 1988, when I wrote about two unionized factories in the industrial Midwest that had reorganized their workplaces to make quality products (and whose managers and unions had been influenced by the Work in America Institute). At the LS Electrogalvanizing plant in Cleveland, a joint venture of the American LTV Corporation and the Japanese Sumitomo conglomerate, workers made high-quality, rustproof, lightweight "specialty steel" for U.S. auto companies. Unlike the traditional steel mill where foremen shouted orders at workers in more than forty job classifications, LS Electrogalvanizing's workers could learn every skill. They worked in teams, and at the end of every "turn" (steel industry lingo for "shift"), they met to learn what had happened on the last turn and to plan what they would do on their turn. Instead of foremen, there were "process coordinators" who helped their work groups to reach consensus. Similarly, at its plant in Sharonville, near Cincinnati, Ford produced a new trans- mission, the E40D, with four speeds, a lock-up torque converter, and overdrive control, which was fitted into trucks and vans. Blue- collar employees worked in self-managing "business teams," and, in a remarkable change from traditional factory rules, they could stop the assembly line whenever they spotted defective parts. As Ron Eads, who worked on the "final line," told me, "It used to be they hired us just for our shoulders and below. Now they finally understand we have something valuable above the neck."

LS Electrogalvanizing, the Ford Sharonville plant, and General Motor's experimental Saturn plant in Spring Hill, Tennessee, fre- quently hosted visitors from school districts, government agencies, high-tech companies, and other white-collar organizations that wanted to learn more about how to make workplaces more partic- ipatory and less bureaucratic. If blue-collar workers weren't being treated like cogs in machines, how could companies continue to treat professional and technical workers that way? Moreover, one new technological application in particular—e-mail—allowed top management to communicate directly with employees and employees to communicate with one another without the need for middle managers to mediate between the higher-ups and the lower-downs or between workers in different departments. Along with new theories about management, this new means of communication broke down rigid hierarchical and departmental structures, allowed workers to collaborate in teams, and resulted in eliminating layers of middle managers or encouraging them to become "team leaders," rather than direct supervisors.

During the 1990s, white-collar workplaces transformed themselves from the rigid hierarchies and enforced conformity of the 1950s sociological tract *The Organization Man* to the freewheeling informality of the contemporary sitcom *The Office*. Just as assembly lines symbolized the humiliation of workers handling products that careened down a conveyor belt, networked computers signified the hope that workers could exchange ideas up, down, or sideways in an organization. As with other outbreaks of discontent throughout history, white-collar workers' frustrations would be fueled by their eventual disappointment that even with "flattened" corporate hierarchies, most professionals and technicians ultimately have little say in how their companies are run.

Now Thinking Is Part of the Job Description

While companies have been restructuring themselves and redesigning their jobs, the new economy has generated many jobs that encourage employees to think for themselves and relatively fewer that merely require routine and repetitive work. Of course, there aren't any official tabulations of how many jobs are "challenging" and how many are "boring" (and in work, as in other activities, different people are stimulated by different things). But several statistics do suggest how much work in the United States is changing.

Between 1900 and 2005, the percentage of the workforce that is "white-collar"—a category that usually includes professionals, technicians, clerical workers, and salespeople—grew from less than 18 percent to more than 62 percent. More than thirty million workers—24 percent of the entire workforce—are considered "professional and related," and six million more professional jobs are expected to be created by 2014. Almost three-quarters of the growth will be in three sectors: education, training, and libraries; health-care practitioners and technicians; and information technology.[6]

Many of these large and growing occupations consist of traditional professions such as medicine, law, nursing, teaching, engineering, architecture, and library science, which require specific academic degrees and professional certifications. Newer fields are populated by professionals such as computer programmers, hospital technicians, and software testers, whose jobs require training and skill but have not yet developed clearly defined requirements for entry and advancement. All of these occupations, however, fit the broader definition of professional and technical jobs: they require extensive training, specialized skills, and the exercise of independent judgment.

Meanwhile, the new economy is creating a new kind of skilled worker, with expertise in emerging technologies and vast opportunities for advancement but usually without a degree from a four-year college. Trained at two-year colleges, trade schools, or on their jobs, these technicians do highly skilled and increasingly important work. Their jobs range from reading heart monitors, as the WTO protest organizer Verlene Jones did in a Seattle hospital, to interpreting the specifications for aircraft, as the union negotiator Doug Smith did at Boeing. Similarly, growing numbers of blue-collar and service workers, from drivers at FedEx to security guards at large buildings, need to work with computers. Among the first observers to note the melding of blue-collar and white-collar jobs, Ralph Whitehead (who's also the brother of Paul Whitehead, the Steelworkers' union lawyer who was involved in the negotiations with Kaiser Aluminum) coined the phrase "new-collar workers" in 1985. As early as 1990, *Fortune* magazine featured technicians on its cover as the "Stars of the New Economy." But these skilled workers with roots in the working class harkened back to earlier figures in U.S. history. Thomas Jefferson and Andrew Jackson considered skilled artisans indispensable to democracy because their knowledge of their crafts gave them a stake in society and a sense of independence.

Not all technicians' jobs are newly created; many are evolving from blue-collar jobs. For instance, two of the leading blue-collar jobs in telephone companies used to be "lineman" and "cable splicer." When building phone networks, workers used to splice cables containing 3,600 pairs of wires, and a team worked all day to connect two 500-foot sections of cable. Now, instead of heavy copper cable, a single strand of fiber optic cable, about the size of a human hair, can transmit thousands of phone calls at the same time, together with Internet connections and television signals. Workers can splice 500-foot lengths of fiber in about two hours, and fewer repair workers are needed to maintain the system.[7] Monitoring the network at computer consoles miles away, workers can detect many problems, and linemen and splicers make fewer repairs on the scene than they used to. These workers are fewer in number now but better paid than in the past. Under agreements negotiated by the Communications Workers of America—the same national union with which WashTech (Washington Alliance of Technology Workers; see chapter 5) is affiliated—many long-term employees were retrained for these jobs.

Meanwhile, traditional factory jobs are decreasing. Blue-collar workers declined from 41 percent of the workforce in 1950 to only 23 percent in 2005. Manufacturing workers accounted for only 14 percent of the workforce, and experts estimated that only 1 or 2 percent of the workforce earned its pay on fast-paced assembly lines. That last statistic is the most stunning of all since many Americans who haven't been around factories in a long time still assume that the typical worker is on an assembly line.

So the good news is that jobs generally require more skills and allow more discretion than in the past. For most policy makers and opinion leaders, that's the whole story. To hear them tell it, the new economy is a meritocratic marketplace, talent and training are always rewarded, and those who suffer from layoffs or low wages lack the skills they need to compete. But the story about skills and schooling—and the part they play in determining what workers do and how much they're paid—isn't quite that simple.

First, the United States still has a working-class majority. As of 2000, the median—or typical—income for U.S. households was about $39,000, scarcely enough to afford a modest middle-class lifestyle. More than three-quarters of all adults do not have a four-year college degree or a professional or managerial job.[8] Americans no longer work on assembly lines, but they still live on an economic treadmill.

Second, the new economy is creating lots of jobs at both ends of the spectrum of skills and wages: more professional and technical jobs and also more low-wage service jobs. Although traditional factory jobs are declining, less rewarding jobs are increasing. Without union representation, jobs on cleaning crews, in hospitals and nursing homes, and at discount retailers like Wal-Mart tend to offer poverty wages, few benefits, and unpleasant working conditions. While good-paying factory jobs were mostly held by white men, these low-wage service jobs usually are held by women, African Americans, Hispanics, and recent immigrants, whether documented or undocumented.

Third, these and other jobs may be "unskilled," but that doesn't mean the workers are "unskilled." Anyone who has watched a window cleaner or a nurse's aide—not to mention a carpenter or an electrician—knows that these workers have strong skills that enable them to do their jobs. To be sure, jobs may be structured so as to be routine and repetitive and to follow a rulebook. But that says something about the job and not about the intrinsic nature of the work or the inherent abilities of the worker.

In the past, workers were discontented when they found themselves trapped in large organizations that didn't recognize their individuality. Now, major companies are casting off their former responsibilities to their employees, and workers like the veteran employees at Kaiser Aluminum are less likely to consider themselves imprisoned than to feel abandoned.

THE ORGANIZATION MAN DOESN'T WORK HERE ANYMORE

For all their faults, the large corporations that thrived during the decades after World War II made a bargain with their workers that built the middle class. Under the terms of this unspoken agreement, employees would work a full day, make an honest effort, and follow the corporate rulebook. They wouldn't bad-mouth their employers, slip secrets to competing companies, or keep jumping from job to job. In return, workers would get a steady job with regular raises, health coverage for themselves and their families, and a guaranteed level of pension benefits when they retired at age sixty-five. Companies cast themselves as com-munities or even families (for instance, Boeing called itself a "family" well into the 1990s), with softball, basketball, and touch football teams; holiday parties; and summer picnics for workers, their spouses, and their kids. Working at such companies was not the most exciting experience imaginable, but the generation that grew up during the Great Depression and served in World War II had already had enough excitement and sought its satisfaction in fam-ily life, community service, religious observance, hobbies, sports, and cultural pursuits.

Enjoying huge and seemingly stable shares of the national and international markets and remembering the labor strife of the 1930s, corporations considered predictability the key to profit-ability. Major companies like GM, GE, and IBM became large, lethargic bureaucracies built along standardized organizational lines and management principles. At the bottom of the pyramid were the blue-collar workers, who were paid by the hour and took orders from foremen. Then came the white-collar employ-ees, arranged in corporate hierarchies with ascending layers of clericals, technicians, low-level professionals such as bookkeep-ers, middle managers, top executives, and, at the top of the pyr-amid like an ancient sun king, the CEO. While every company was hierarchical, the largest companies also consisted of separate divisions that produced different kinds of products, as well as other units that handled sales, service, research and development, and other functions.

Industrial feudalism this may have been, but just as in the Middle Ages, the lords of the manor followed a code of honor, took care of their people, and followed a faith that had clear concepts of right and wrong. Top executives, middle managers, professional and technical staff, clericals, foremen, and factory workers all followed a personnel code—or, with unionized workers, the union contract. In addition to their remarkably similar rulebooks, companies organized themselves on the basis of narrowly defined jobs. In fact, there were dozens of different jobs in every steel mill or auto plant, not to mention the companies' offices. Often, these positions were arranged as if on a ladder, so that workers would climb "step" by "step" as they performed satisfactorily in one position and moved up to the next-highest position. Pay scales were set by analyzing the content of each job—a process similar to a time-motion study—and a comparison with what workers in similar jobs in other companies in the same industry were paid. Following these studies, workers were assigned job titles and pay grades. Their performance on their jobs was reviewed regularly by their supervisors and evaluated according to the personnel code or the union contract. How much money workers made from the day they were hired to the day they retired depended on what position they were in, how long they had worked in it, and whether they had earned step increases and promotions; their income was not based on abstract assessments of their abilities and accomplishments.

Because major corporations were so strong and stable, they assumed the responsibility for providing the services and the supports that workers needed to make their way throughout their working lives, from training and tuition assistance to health insurance and pension plans. With hundreds of jobs that were clearly defined and connected to one another step by step on a ladder pointed straight upward, ambitious and capable workers could spend their entire careers at one company, which rewarded their exchange of loyalty for security. Although companies such as Boeing would "lay off" workers when hard times hit, they would "call them back" when good times returned, without workers losing credit for their years of service before the layoff. Other companies prided themselves on not letting workers go even during recessions. For instance, well into the 1990s, IBM—the company that Bill Gates made sure that Microsoft did not model itself after—declared in its personnel manual: "In nearly 40 years, no person employed on a regular basis by IBM has lost as much as one hour of working time because of a layoff. When recessions come or there is a major product shift, some companies handle the workforce imbalances that result by letting people go. IBM hasn't done that, hopes never to have to. . . . It's hardly a surprise that one of the main reasons people like to work for IBM is the company's all-out effort to maintain full employment."[9]

It all seemed so fair; it all was standardized; and, for major corporations at the middle of the last century, "standardized" was synonymous with "fair."

Most middle-class Americans may have craved security, but intellectuals lust after excitement. Not surprisingly, this boring bargain spawned a specialized literature of social protest, from popular sociology to socially conscious novels. In his 1956 best-seller *The Organization Man*, the business journalist William Whyte described the technicians, the professionals, and the middle managers who worked for large organizations, sacrificing their individuality and often their integrity to become team players. Anything that made people stand out, even excessive competence and creativity, was discouraged. Whyte claimed to have found an unnamed engineering company whose watchword was "no geniuses here; just a bunch of average Americans working together." In novels such as *The Man in the Gray Flannel Suit* by Sloan Wilson and *Revolutionary Road* by Richard Yates, a new antihero emerged, the intellectual with creative aspirations, often an aspiring novelist-turned-copywriter, who sold his soul for the security of working at a large company. By the 1960s, young people were less willing to "sell out," as the saying went—the hero of the novel *The Graduate*, which became a movie starring Dustin Hoffman, rejects an older man's advice to take a job with a company that makes "plastics."

Thirty years later, few companies were offering recent college graduates the opportunity to sell their souls in return for lucrative lifetime careers. Instead of protesting the benevolent bureaucracies that the baby boomers rebelled against, members of Generations X and Y were writing protest novels like Douglas Coupland's *Microserfs*, which told the stories of young people working sixty hours or more a week in "veal pen" cubicles at short-term junk-jobs for employers who might fire off encouraging e-mails to them on a Friday and fire them on Monday.

THE END OF THE JOB?

Unlike the GMs and the IBMs of earlier decades that offered well-plotted careers in return for white-collar conformity, today's start-up companies and their reengineered rivals provide little more than this week's paycheck. Following the new rules preached by Jack Welch and practiced by Bill Gates, these companies offer good-paying jobs with promising futures to a shrinking number of workers with high skills in what these firms consider their "core competencies." As for less-skilled workers or workers whose specialties are outside the company's "core competency," they're given short-term jobs or their jobs are shipped out to subcontractors. One by one, the risks of the relationship between employer and employee are being handed off to the worker. Employer-paid health insurance, guaranteed levels of pension benefits, and even the basic guarantee of a regular job—that you'll be paid during the slow times, as well as the busy periods—all are becoming things of the past. Just as careerism was the norm several decades ago, contingency is typical today. As AT&T vice president James Meadows said, "We all have to recognize that we are contingent employees in one form or another."[10]

During the 1990s, a famous article and a flashy book celebrated the trend toward free-form companies and short-term jobs. In a cover story in *Fortune* on September 19, 1994, William Bridges proclaimed "The End of the Job" and pronounced it a good thing. Using the high unemployment rates of what was still a "jobless recovery" as his starting point, Bridges declared, "What is disappearing is not just a certain number of jobs—or jobs in certain industries or some parts of the country or even jobs as a whole. What is disappearing is the very thing itself."

Treating high unemployment, corporate downsizings, and the growing numbers of freelancers and temporary workers as if these developments were one phenomenon—and a favorable one—Bridges announced that companies and individuals alike were being "dejobbed." Because "Most societies since the beginning of time have done just fine without jobs," Bridges saw no reason why modern Americans also couldn't do well without regular sources of income. While his business executive readers may have breathed sighs of relief that their laid-off employees and their layabout kids wouldn't suffer for being dejobbed, Bridges didn't explain how most people could find the security to raise their kids, support their families, get medical checkups, and provide for their retirements without steady work and regular paychecks.

In 2001, just as the new economy's euphoric era was coming to an end, Dan Pink published a provocative potboiler, *Free Agent Nation*, which lumped together temp workers, freelancers, independent professionals, and self-employed entrepreneurs as "free agents" who were pioneering a new ethos of self-reliance and self-fulfillment.[11] Although Pink did cite the use of long-term temporary workers at companies like Microsoft as examples of a problem, not a promising new trend, he exaggerated the extent to which short-term employment and self-employment were voluntary. After all, how many downsized executives, professionals, and technicians describe themselves as "consultants," rather than as job hunters, because admitting that they were laid off sounds perilously close to labeling themselves "losers"? And how many employers are only too happy to classify temp workers as "independent contractors," Microsoft's original stratagem with the perma-temps? (As it happens, Pink was a speechwriter for Vice President Al Gore and, before that, for Labor Secretary Robert

Reich. Neither Gore nor Reich accepted Pink's view that dejob-bing was a positive development. Indeed, Reich attacked corpo-rate downsizings, and Gore bragged about the eventual growth in employment under the Clinton-Gore administration. I know Pink a little and find him intelligent and engaging but apparently unaware that well-connected freelancers like him and me enjoy advantages that most temp workers don't have.)

In fact, the growing numbers of part-time and temporary jobs are not good news for most working Americans. By the year 2000, about 30 percent of all workers—some thirty-seven million people—earned their living without full-time, permanent jobs. Part-time workers accounted for about 13 percent of the work-force. Temporary workers, the self-employed, independent con-tractors, and on-call workers made up the remaining 15.9 percent.

According to surveys by the Bureau of Labor Statistics, more than 50 percent of both groups—the part-timers and the temps—would rather have full-time, long-term jobs. And no wonder. These workers earn about 15 percent less per hour than regular employees do. Only 17 percent receive health insurance benefits from their employers. And only 21 percent are included in their employers' pension plans.

The growing number of part-time and temporary workers and their precarious economic condition triggered several high-profile conflicts during the late 1990s. At Microsoft, the plight of the "perma-temps" prompted an IRS decision, a class action lawsuit and a huge backpay award, a union organizing campaign, and an enormous amount of unfavorable publicity for the software giant. Similar struggles also took place among blue-collar workers in older industries. Founded in Seattle, United Parcel Service (UPS) became the nation's leading package-delivery company and one of the ten largest private employers in the world. Its workers were represented by the Teamsters Union; many of its profits had been plowed into the Annie Casey Foundation, which advocates for children; and UPS enjoyed a reputation as a generous employer and a responsible corporation. But by the middle of the 1990s, its workforce was sharply divided, with 40 percent consisting of well-paid, full-time drivers and 60 percent who were lower-wage, part-time loaders and sorters. In contract negotiations in 1997, UPS demanded that more positions become part time, prompting a strike by the 185,000 Teamsters. Using the slogan "Part-Time America Won't Work," the union struck a responsive chord among opinion leaders and the general public—a rarity for the controversial union. After a well-organized and well-publicized two-week strike, UPS agreed to create ten thousand new full-time jobs by combining existing part-time positions.[12]

Similarly, in Seattle and nearby Tacoma, more than seven hundred "port truck drivers" haul containers of cargo from the piers to railroad yards and warehouses. These workers used to be regular employees of the truck companies, working under a contract negotiated by the Teamsters union. By the middle of the 1990s, the trucking companies had reclassified them as "independent contractors" and paid them by the trip, eliminating their health benefits, job security, and payment for waiting in line to pick up their loads. During 1999, the drivers struck in an effort to become regular unionized employees again. They lost the strike, but they disrupted the port, encouraging other protestors to try to shut down Seattle's downtown business center during the WTO meeting later that year. At a remarkable public hearing in Seattle on June 24, 1999, the two star witnesses were Harry Lucia, a port truck driver, and Barbara Judd, a temporary worker at Microsoft. The blue-collar man and the white-collar woman agreed that their situations were surprisingly similar.

During the 1990s and the first years of the twenty-first century, worker discontent would increasingly be represented by workers like Judd. These professional, technical, or health-care employees are doing work that they like, but their situations are increasingly insecure, and they worry about whether their employers are cutting corners on quality.

3

GRAVEYARD SHIFT

It all started in the cemetery.

An attractive five-story building in North Seattle, Northwest Hospital and Medical Center was built adjoining a cemetery. Understandably, its founders figured that hospital patients don't want to look out on a graveyard while they're recovering from their illnesses and injuries. So the side of the hospital that's nearest to the cemetery has unsurprisingly few windows, and trees block the views from many of the rooms that do have windows. Although the architects didn't intend to protect the privacy of the hospital workers, if an employee wants to do something secretly—have a late-night party, arrange an assignation, or attend a union meeting—all she has to do is go to the cemetery and almost no one inside the hospital can see her.

By August and September of 2000, union organizers were meeting with workers from Northwest Hospital, and the cemetery was the location of choice. Deanna Swenson, who works in housekeeping at the hospital, remembered a session with the union organizer Mia Barcelongo near the entrance of the cemetery. She and several other workers were sitting in the organizer's car, but just to make sure no passersby understood what was going on, Swenson sat in the front seat, and Barcelongo was in the back.

Swenson had expected a high-powered pitch, most likely from a tough-talking man, so Barcelongo, a soft-spoken young woman, was a pleasant surprise. "Mia, she's harmless; she's okay," Swenson recalled years later. "She's very personable; didn't force anything on me. She got me to talking about everything."

"It was just like talking to someone I work with. She was down-to-earth, friendly, she drew me out," Swenson continued. "She was not like the stereotype of a union rep. I was very surprised."[1]

Years later, after she'd become active in the union, Swenson would not have been surprised that its organizers were so skillful at reaching out to hospital workers like herself. Barcelongo's union, Local 1199NW of the Service Employees International Union (SEIU), had been organizing hospital workers in the Seattle area since 1983. Beginning as a group of idealistic nurses, the founders of Local 1199NW built a base among their colleagues who wanted a stronger organization than a traditional professional association. Years later, the union successfully organized service and technical workers in the hospitals by appealing to aspirations that these lower-paid workers share with higher-paid professionals. As it turned out, in addition to wanting wage increases, the workers who prepare the patients' meals, empty their bedpans, and launder their bedsheets are concerned about the quality of care that the patients receive, and they worry about how hospitals are becoming less friendly and more cost-conscious.

But raising wages and improving care costs hospitals money. As the union's strategists were painfully aware, they had to organize the great majority of health-care facilities, community by community, so that hospitals that did well by workers and patients wouldn't be islands of high costs in an ocean of penny-pinching. At a time when most unions were unable to respond to wrenching changes in their industries, Local 1199NW carefully developed a plan to organize one hospital after another, starting with the likeliest targets and concluding with the holdouts.

By 2000, Northwest Hospital was one of the last major nonunion health-care institutions in the Seattle area. The organizing campaign there was remarkable for being unremarkable—almost everything worked according to plan, especially the union's appeals to dedicated workers who were distressed by the changes in the hospital and who desperately wanted to love their jobs again.

The campaign had actually begun several months before the meetings in the cemetery. Back in the spring, Local 1199NW's organizing director, Curt Williams, got a phone call from a nursing assistant at Northwest Hospital who said that people wanted to organize. Williams drove out to North Seattle to meet the woman for lunch and took her to the nearby Hardee's fast-food restaurant, a high-cholesterol choice for a health-care worker. The woman worked in the day surgery unit, a small group within the hospital. "I asked her what the number one issue was," Williams remembered. "She said parking. . . . The hospital was starting to charge people for parking to build a new parking lot. And they figured they would build the lot with the workers' money. The workers would have to pay for a new parking lot for a hospital that was making money."[2]

Sure, the fees sounded like a legitimate gripe. But when it came to making parking the leading issue in an organizing campaign among health-care workers, Williams's reaction was "Give me a fucking break." So sophisticated had Local 1199NW become in its analysis of the attitudes of health-care workers that even one of its most hardboiled organizers understood that the union had to emphasize patient care, not parking fees. As Williams later explained, "It is not uncommon for us to get a call from a hospital where a worker has a pet grievance. My concern was, if someone raises economic issues as number one—and it isn't 'I can't take care of the patients or the hospital doesn't respect the workers'—I'm a little suspicious."

Williams's strategic insights are especially persuasive because, in a union whose leadership and staff are evenly divided between former nurses and veteran organizers, Williams is an organizer's organizer. An intense, solidly built man in his late thirties, Williams organized for the Steelworkers' union in Michigan and a health-care workers' union in Baltimore. Although his father is a surgeon (upper-middle-class backgrounds aren't unusual among today's organizers), Williams never worked in a hospital himself. But having spent more than a decade organizing health-care workers, he is familiar with their concerns, which he filters through what he learned growing up as a doctor's son. If hospital workers cared most about their paychecks, that's what Williams would gladly talk about. When this seasoned organizer stresses patient care, it's a sign that hospitals are changing in ways that trouble their most dedicated employees.

SELLING MOTHER JOSEPH'S LEGACY

When Emily Van Bronkhorst went with her family to Washington, D.C., in the summer of 2000, she took them to the Capitol Building. Touring Statuary Hall, where each state has contributed two sculptures of distinguished residents, she saw the statue of Mother Joseph. Born Esther Pariseau in Quebec in 1823, Mother Joseph had been a pioneer in more ways than one. At age twenty, she entered a convent of the Sisters of Providence. Later, she led five other nuns on horseback and in full habits on a journey to the Pacific Northwest, where they founded the first hospitals in the state of Washington. Van Bronkhorst had been born in the Sisters of Providence Hospital in Seattle, which had been part of the charitable order, so she should have been proud to see the statue in the nation's Capitol Building. Yet she couldn't help but think about how Mother Joseph's legacy was being sold to various health-care empires. The huge nonprofit Swedish Medical Center had acquired the Seattle hospital. Health Management Associates, a profit-making corporation based in Naples, Florida, had bought the Providence Health System properties in Central Washington, which included a hospital in Yakima that had been owned and managed by the Sisters of Providence for more than a hundred years.

Van Bronkhorst had professional as well as personal reasons for her mixed feelings about visiting the statue of Mother Joseph. As vice president of Local 1199NW, she'd seen what she called "an enormous change in hospitals from very professional, community-oriented institutions to a corporate model of business."[3]

By the early 1990s, four mutually reinforcing trends were making hospitals and other health-care facilities more cost-conscious and less community-oriented. Health-care costs were increasing by about 10 percent a year, provoking a backlash by everyone who ended up paying the bills. Insurance companies refused to pay for many medical expenses and insisted that hospitals, physicians, and other providers start to cut costs. The large companies that provided health insurance for their employees resisted increases in their insurance premiums and also shifted some of the costs to the workers. Even government programs like Medicare and Medicaid became more cost-conscious. All of a sudden, individuals and their families found themselves paying higher premiums and deductibles for less health-care coverage, and that was only the beginning of the wrenching changes in the health-care system.

To be sure, while these changes left health-care workers and patients anxious and angry, the system really was in need of a shakeup. During World War II, when the government discouraged wage increases but allowed boosts in benefits, large unionized companies such as GM and Boeing began to fund health coverage for their workers, and companies like IBM that wanted to duplicate union benefits followed their lead. Insurance companies picked up the tab for most procedures, exacerbating a fee-for-service system that encouraged expensive treatments, technologies, and medications. Eventually, the most pinch-penny nonunion companies like Wal-Mart gained an enormous advantage against unionized or paternalistic competitors, and U.S. companies were disadvantaged against competitors from countries where health care was provided by the government, not by employers. Something had to be done, and presidents from Richard Nixon through Bill Clinton proposed plans that gave government, private companies, and the insurance industry their own roles in providing coverage and controlling costs. But none of these initiatives was enacted.

So, while the Clinton initiative stalled and failed in 1993 and 1994, companies herded their employees into health maintenance organizations, HMOs for short. As with so many other innovations, Henry Kaiser had originated employer-financed, prepaid, preventive health care. Indeed, the nation's oldest and largest network of HMOs, Kaiser Permanente, had been created for employees of Kaiser's construction projects and shipyards (but not of the Kaiser Aluminum Company, which offered traditional health coverage because its factories were far from Kaiser Permanente's hospitals). While Kaiser Permanente and a few other like-minded plans offered a wide range of services at low costs, most HMOs followed the insurance industry's priorities: higher subscription fees for less care. By the mid-1990s, when a mom played by Helen Hunt complained about her HMO in the movie *As Good as It Gets,* it was enough to prompt cheers for her character and boos for the HMO from audiences across the country.

Some of the new breed of HMOs were at least nominally non-profit, many others were for-profit, and almost all followed the priorities of the insurance industry. Meanwhile, sensing that health care was a lucrative growth industry, many for-profit companies entered the field of owning and operating hospitals, expanded their existing operations, and bought up nonprofit institutions, just as Health Management Associates had acquired the Sisters of Providence hospitals in central Washington. These for-profit hospital chains, such as Health Management Associates and Columbia/HCA, introduced contemporary business practices into health care, from sensibly trying to cut costs on supplies by buying items in bulk to seeking to reduce the less lucrative kinds of care, such as lengthy hospital stays for moderate-income patients, and offered more services that generated higher revenues, such as costly operations for the wealthiest patients.

Soon, these for-profit chains set the tone for most nonprofit facilities as well, and health-care administrators at institutions of all kinds were sounding more like MBAs than MDs, talking about "cost consciousness," "market share," and other concepts that seemed more appropriate for corporate boardrooms than hospital emergency rooms. These executives tended to come from business backgrounds, commanded high salaries, and managed networks of facilities with hierarchies of managers, supervisors, superstar professionals, less prestigious professionals, and low-paid service workers. For instance, in Seattle, the nonprofit Swedish Medical Center acquired Ballard Community Hospital, Doctors Hospital, Seattle General Hospital, and, finally, the Sisters of Providence Hospital, where Emily Van Bronkhorst was born. With 1,245 beds and 7,000 employees, Swedish Medical Center marketed itself with newspaper advertisements and direct-mail pieces targeted to the most affluent neighborhoods in the Seattle area. Swedish was a respected health-care network and a responsible employer, but it had come a long way from being a small facility founded for Scandinavian immigrants and their families.

As Diane Sosne, the president of Local 1199NW, observed early in the 1990s, the new corporate culture in health care was reflected in the growing use of management consultants in facilities in Washington State. "Hospitals have even gone so far as contracting with management 'cost-efficiency' consultants like West Hudson, which is based in Los Angeles, and Ernst and Young, based in Seattle, to conduct time, motion, and productivity studies to cut back on staff," she reported. "These consultants, who are not patient care providers, have created a profitable new growth industry as the supposed cure to hospitals' budget woes."[4] Swedish Medical Center had already paid West Hudson $1 million for consulting on cutting costs, and Valley Medical Center was paying $500,000. At a time when many industries were allowing employees to exercise more discretion on the job, hospitals were imitating factories from the turn of the twentieth century. Early in the 1990s, the WTO protest organizer Verlene Jones was still working as a medical technician at the Group Health Hospital in Seattle. She was closely observed on her job by time-study consultants. "Taylorism comes to the hospital," she called it in an interview a decade later.[5]

Hospitals had become very different places, and the consequences were being felt by patients, physicians, nurses, and service workers. Hospitals hardly had to pay millions of dollars in consulting fees to get their marching orders from the marketplace: Hire more superstar specialists and encourage them to provide the most advanced services for the most affluent patients. Limit expensive procedures and medications for less affluent patients and shorten their hospital stays. Have fewer nurses at the bedsides of the great majority of patients. Replace registered nurses with lower paid and often poorly trained assistants. And work everyone harder.

While superstar specialists were being wooed and richly rewarded, most doctors found that their decisions were being micromanaged by insurance companies and HMOs. For nurses, whose professional lives had always required them to work in a medical model with physicians in strict control, the changes in their hospitals were even more traumatic. Although registered nurses are credentialed, college-educated professionals, their occupation has always been defined by the fact that it overwhelmingly consists of women, often women from working-class backgrounds who were the first in their families to be formally educated beyond high school. As with people in other professions, nurses often felt a sense of mission about their work, but with nurses, their sense of calling was often perceived by others to be quasi-religious in nature. Decades ago, nurses wore special uniforms, almost like habits; the best-known nurse, Florence Nightingale, was portrayed in popular culture as a secular saint; and nurses were seen as assisting the physicians (who are still stereotyped as overwhelmingly male) and serving the patients.

As with classroom teachers, another traditionally female profession, nurses were considered too self-sacrificing to demand better pay, benefits, and working conditions; too indispensable to be allowed to unionize and strike; but not so essential that their professional judgments would be fully respected or their professional contributions fully rewarded.

In fact, nursing is an indispensable profession with its own body of knowledge, standards of practice, and responsibilities in the hospital. Nurses provide bedside care for the patients, while doctors usually spend only a few minutes every day with each patient. The nurses are the advocates for the patients and the early warning system for the medical team. Usually, the nurses are the professionals who conduct the tests, administer the treatments, and determine how the patient is responding. To be sure, nurses also play the role that the public knows best, comforting patients and their families. But nurses are not merely guardian angels—they are skilled professionals. Especially compared to inexperienced young doctors, nurses are likely to understand how the human body will react to an illness, an injury, an operation, or medication and whether a course of treatment is succeeding or failing.

Nurses know how important their skills and experience are, and they are very loyal to their profession and to one another. Just as members of the U.S. Marine Corps always describe themselves as marines, nurses always identify themselves as nurses, no matter how they earn their living. When I interviewed nurses in New Jersey in 2000 and nurses in Seattle in 2005, several told me that the character played by Juliana Margulies on the TV series *ER* had become a folk hero to nurses. The reason? She was a registered nurse, and even after she became a doctor, she still identified herself as a nurse.

Especially because of their dedication to their profession, nurses are offended by the commercialization of health care. As the journalist Suzanne Gordon has written, the newly business-oriented hospitals "have viewed physicians as revenue generators and nurses as revenue drains" and therefore have reduced the number of nurses on their staffs.[6] With the number of patients increasing, the number of nurses decreasing, and the length of hospital stays shortening, fewer nurses have found themselves caring for more patients for shorter periods of time. Thus, many nurses think they can no longer provide the quality of care that they are committed to, and some even worry that they are being forced to violate their professional standards and that they could lose their licenses. As Local 1199NW president Diane Sosne, herself a registered nurse, wrote during the early 1990s,

> One nurse who works nights taking care of patients told me that she sometimes takes care of nine patients. She is frustrated because she barely has enough time to speak to a patient before she has to [go to] the next bed. One morning, while she was rushing to do chemotherapy, the father of one of her patients came to ask her what it would be like when his son died. She said, "It broke my heart because I didn't even have time to sit down and talk with him. I feel that a large part of my responsibility as a nurse is to care for the emotional needs of my patients and their families, as well as the physical ones."[7]

In the Seattle area, the discontent among nurses bubbled up during the late 1980s and early 1990s, when Local 1199NW was founded, grew rapidly, and staged a successful eighteen-day strike. The union emerged at Group Health, an HMO that had been founded for union families in the area. Over the years, Group Health grew into a network of two hospitals and thirty clinics. By the early 1980s, it was being managed more like a business than a community service. Group Health's fourteen hundred nurses were represented by the Washington Nurses Association, but a group of disaffected nurses thought that the association wasn't assertive enough. In an election supervised by the National Labor Relations Board, the Group Health nurses voted out the association and chose the insurgent group as their new representative.

The campaign at Group Health produced two leaders who would play a part in organizing Northwest Hospital. A psychiatric nurse, Diane Sosne was a transplanted New Yorker from a family with a tradition of what she called "fighting injustice." (Indeed, she later learned that her grandmother had survived the historic Triangle Shirtwaist Factory fire at a Manhattan garment factory.) Sosne became the president of the new nurses' organization, and another nurse at Group Health, Chris Barton, became the secretary-treasurer. They shared a vision of building their new group into a union that would represent most nurses and, eventually, most health-care workers in every occupation in the entire state.

Soon after winning the election at Group Health, the new nurses' organization, merged with District 1199, a health-care workers' union based in New York City with a heritage of leftist politics and aggressive organizing. During the 1980s and 1990s, the newly named Local 1199NW won elections to represent nurses at most hospitals in the Seattle area. When its parent union broke up into several units early in the 1990s, Local 1199NW joined a larger and stronger national union, SEIU, which encouraged it to organize service and technical workers, as well as nurses. Northwest Hospital was one of the first facilities where Local 1199NW wooed these lower-paid workers without first representing the nurses.

MR. HART AND "HIS HIGHNESS"

It had taken a long time for the workers at Northwest Hospital to reach out to the union—and for the union to reach out to the workers. Compared to Group Health and Swedish Medical Center, Northwest Hospital is relatively small, with a little more than four hundred beds and a thousand employees. Instead of being alongside many of the major hospitals in the downtown area that health-care industry leaders irreverently call "Pill Hill," Northwest is located in a residential area about thirty blocks from the Seattle city line. In fact, Northwest really is what many health-care facilities call themselves: a "community hospital." Its located in North Seattle, which is mostly middle class, with many residents now middle-aged or retired. North Seattle has few dot-com millionaires, fashionable young professionals, grungy young people, or desperately poor people and seems like a relic of the old Seattle, before the city became the country's cultural trend setter. As it turned out, the neighborhood was a throwback in another way—there were lots of union members and retirees who would support an organizing campaign at their community hospital.

Also, the neighborhood is predominantly white, mostly of Scandinavian, German, or Irish heritage, as is the workforce at Northwest Hospital. Having met with hospital workers in New York, Chicago, Los Angeles, and other large cities when I worked for AFSCME (American Federation of State, County and Municipal Employees) and throughout New Jersey when I interviewed nurses for the Albert Shanker Institute, I was surprised at first to see so few African Americans or Hispanics among the workforce. Traditionally, members of groups that suffer discrimination have worked in the housekeeping, dietary, and laundry departments in hospitals. At Northwest, the main ethnic minority group in these departments is Filipino Americans.

As Local 1199NW leaders acknowledged several years after the organizing campaign, Northwest Hospital wasn't an especially stingy or inhumane employer. Wages and benefits for the service workers were a bit lower than at unionized hospitals. The nurses were organized, belonging to the state nurses' association. This would be one of the first campaigns in which Local 1199NW tried to organize the service workers at a hospital without first representing the nurses. As it happened, the management at Northwest Hospital made little effort to oppose the organizing campaign—there were no high-priced attorneys and consultants, no leaflets and mailing pieces, no mandatory meetings for the employees, or any of the other tactics that hospitals and nursing homes often use to frighten workers out of organizing. Indeed, several of the hospital's features seemed to reflect an effort to make the facility friendlier for patients, their families, and the employees. For instance, most hospital cafeterias serve greasy food in gloomy settings. The cafeteria at Northwest serves healthy food and great coffee (this is, after all, Seattle), and it is the first hospital cafeteria that I have ever visited that is on the first floor, with long and wide windows, so that the sunlight comes in and the fresh air can circulate. As workers did at Microsoft, the hospital staff spoke to me in the cafeteria, explaining their grievances against their employer but without looking nervously over their shoulders to see whether someone from management was listening.

One summer afternoon in 2005, I sat at a table in Northwest Hospital's cafeteria talking to two experienced employees who had led the organizing campaign. Dona Aring, from the medical records unit, and Deanna Swenson, from the housekeeping department, had been so active that their colleagues started to call them "Dona and Deanna," as if they, together, were the union at Northwest Hospital. As workers often do now that the healthcare industry is changing so rapidly, they spoke of the hospital's history as if it were a morality play in three acts: the good old days when the facility was run as a community service, the fall from grace when corporate-style management took over, and the hopeful new dawn now that the workers have a union.

Looking back more than a decade, Aring and Swenson recalled the hospital as a happier place for patients and workers. "In the beginning," Aring explained, as if remembering the expulsion from Eden, "we had a good rapport with management. We felt we were treated fairly. Maybe the pay wasn't so great, but more people were happy. They felt they had a voice."[8]

The current CEO's predecessor was Jim Hart, and Aring and Swenson emphasized his last name, as if it symbolizes what

Northwest Hospital has lost. "He could walk through the hospital—everyone knew who he was," Aring said. "We called him Mr. Hart out of respect—it wasn't out of fear." In the old days, she continued, the hospital was "all-around friendlier" for the employees and the patients. When asked what they had appreciated about the hospital's former management, Aring and Swenson stressed seemingly small gestures that must have cost the hospital relatively little but reinforced the sense that it was a caring community. Hart often walked through the hospital, greeting the employees by name and asking them about their families. At Christmas, the hospital gave its employees bonuses, usually about $300 per person. There also were parties during the Christmas season and picnics in the summer. At the picnics, one of the most popular activities was the "bed race." As Swenson described it, "You get the smaller, skinnier person to sit on the mattress. The stronger person pushes the mattress. We would match the littlest, tiniest person with the biggest guy in the department. That way, we would win."

While all this may sound trivial for low-wage workers in high-stress jobs, Swenson offered two serious explanations for why workers were grateful for the parties and the picnics. "When you deal with what we deal with every day"—helpless patients, frantic family members, and paychecks that don't cover the cost of living—"you need an outlet," she said. Also, workers want a sense that their work is appreciated, and these seemingly small favors "were Jim Hart's way of saying, 'Thank you, you've done a good job.'"

For the workers, the differences between Hart and the man who replaced him came to symbolize the transformations that were taking place at Northwest Hospital and in the entire health-care industry. While workers remember Hart as a friendly father figure, the descriptions of Bill Schneider also attained mythic proportions, as if a jet-setting corporate chief executive had somehow alighted in North Seattle and set up shop in the local hospital. Playing Scrooge to Hart's Marley, Schneider abolished the Christmas bonuses, ended the summer picnics, and turned the Christmas party into a sit-down dinner. Just as important for several employees, Schneider never took the trouble to learn most of their names, and, as Swenson put it, "His highness doesn't do walk-arounds."

Having dealt with many more management officials, Local 1199NW's officers took a bemused view of Schneider's mannerisms and consider him a relatively innocuous example of the new breed of health-care executives. Almost affectionately, Sosne described him as "a real character" but added, philosophically, that management people "all have a uniqueness to them."[9] Calling him "a slick Armani-suited guy," Van Bronkhorst gave him credit for being "a talented businessman who has done a lot to turn the hospital around." Although Schneider is less approachable than Hart, Van Bronkhorst credited him with keeping Northwest friendlier than many other hospitals, at least for the supervisors. "The place still has family values," she said. "A lot of the senior managers have been there a long time. It's different from other institutions that have a lot of turnover with the managers."

Sosne and Van Bronkhorst recognized that as do other community-oriented, nonprofit hospitals throughout the nation, Northwest faces a financial squeeze. It is the only hospital on the north side of town and is frequently flooded with emergency-room patients. Since Northwest is in a working-class neighborhood where most people aren't poor enough for Medicaid or wealthy enough for gold-plated health coverage, it serves patients whose insurance plans tend to question many treatments and try to shorten many hospital stays. Up against the economic realities of a changing industry, Northwest Hospital does have to find new ways to increase its revenues and cut its costs—or, in other words, to act more like a business. Unlike other hospitals that emphasized high-priced services for high-income patients, Northwest Hospital invested $6 million in its emergency room in 2001, renovating the unit and promoting it in the community. Unusual as such an investment is in the new world of commercialized health care, Northwest Hospital still is a community hospital, and about half of its admissions come in through the emergency room (and 80 percent of those decide for themselves to go to Northwest), compared to a national average of about 16 percent of hospital patients arriving through the ER.

Still, many workers at Northwest felt that the quality of care was deteriorating as the institution became less congenial and more cost-conscious. Describing her work as a housekeeper, Swenson expressed her concern for the patients with much the same passion that a nurse would display. "It should take ten minutes to clean a room," she explained. "You clean it while the patient is in there. You put on gloves, rinse a rag in disinfected water, clean the sink, the table and chair, the window sill and telephone. You take care not to dust over the head of a patient who is in bed. Then you do the dirtier jobs—the bathroom, the shower, disinfecting the toilet, and mopping the floor. You also try to cheer the patients up and make a human connection. The patients are not here for a luxury vacation, they are here because something is wrong. You understand that and try never to get in an argument. Remember that when patients start to complain about the food and the hard bed, it's a sign that they're getting better." By 2000, Swenson and other employees believed, with the patient population increasing and the number of staff members decreasing, it was becoming more difficult for service workers to perform their assigned tasks, much less to befriend the patients and try to brighten their days.

By 2000, workers were concerned about their paychecks as well as patient care. Throughout the hospital, across-the-board pay raises had been replaced by a "merit system" where the supervisors determined whether employees would receive wage increases and how large these increases would be, usually between 1 and 3 percent a year. But, as Swenson recalled, "One year, I got a 2 percent raise. I had gotten 3 percent the year before. But my performance was the same as the year before.

I was told, 'We can't give the same raise to everybody, all the time.'" During their annual "personal development review meetings," supervisors told individual employees whether they would be getting raises the next year. But workers weren't supposed to know how much money their coworkers were making—indeed, as Swenson remembered, "When you hired on, you signed a confidentiality agreement not to discuss how much you were paid."

Meanwhile, following the lead of most major companies, the hospital was considering plans to subcontract many of its services. In the housekeeping department, during the late 1990s, much of the work was farmed out to the company Service Master, although the hospital eventually terminated the contract and had the work done by regular employees once again. Similarly, in the medical records department, much of the work was to be outsourced to a company called Transcend, based in Atlanta. As Aring explained, she and other medical records workers would have been assigned to Transcend, paid and supervised by the company. "After working here for fifteen years, I would have had to start out as a 'new employee' of Transcend," she said. Angry and anxious about the proposed changeover, five coders in medical records gave notice that they intended to resign in 1999.

Now that Northwest Hospital's employees were caring for more patients, weren't getting regular raises, and were anxious that their jobs would be contracted out, they were ready to consider something that had never occurred to most of them—voting for union representation.

WE WORE SMILEY-FACE BUTTONS

During the late summer and early fall of 2000, as more Northwest Hospital employees expressed an interest in Local 1199NW, the union's supporters communicated with one another in a kind of code. Rather than wear union buttons, "We wore smiley faces as a way to spot each other," as Aring recalled. "It was our little badge of courage," Swenson added. If they wanted to know whether someone was going to a union meeting in the cemetery or at Hardee's, they would ask one another, "Are you going to Arby's?"—another nearby fast-food restaurant but not one where union meetings were being held.

At first, even the strongest union supporters were afraid that if their sentiments became known to management, they would not receive pay increases, they would be disciplined on trumped-up charges, or they might even be fired. Such fears are almost always present in organizing campaigns, if only because employers control employees' livelihoods, and they often use their positions of power in order to discourage workers from organizing.

In 1999, Dr. Kate Bronfenbrenner of the School of Industrial and Labor Relations at Cornell University studied four hundred organizing campaigns that resulted in elections conducted by the National Labor Relations Board, in which workers voted on whether to be represented by unions. In 20 percent of these elections, employers illegally fired workers simply for having supported the unions. In 92 percent, employers required employees to attend meetings in which managers made the case against the unions—"captive audience meetings," as union organizers call them. In 70 percent, the employers also conducted one-on-one meetings between employees and their supervisors, where the workers' immediate bosses told them not to support the union. This personal pressure by the people who supervise workers and provide their paychecks makes it difficult for workers to exercise free choice in the elections in which they decide whether to be represented by unions.

That is why, in the Northwest hospital election, Local 1199NW organized community residents to put pressure on management not to conduct an active campaign against the union. As the headquarters for the community campaign and the organizing campaign, Local 1199NW rented an unheated upstairs room in a local church, Broadview Community United Church of Christ, on 125th Street, just a few blocks from the hospital. Eventually, sixteen elected officials, including Democratic congressman

Jim McDermott, sent letters to Schneider urging Northwest Hospital to remain "neutral" while the workers decided whether to unionize. While Schneider and his team were hardly friendly to the union and its supporters during the organizing campaign, they conducted a low-key campaign whose purpose appeared to be less to dissuade workers from voting for the union than to dampen their expectations about what the union would do for them. Thus, hospital officials (but not Schneider himself) held a briefing in the auditorium about the hospital's budget and also sent out low-key information mailing pieces to the employees. In some units, the supervisors actually hinted that they were pro-union, some of them because of their personal views and others because they, too, were anxious about rumors that the hospital planned to contract out many services. "The supervisors knew that if we were outsourced, they would be gone also," said Swenson. "In our housekeeping unit, we were lucky that we had a manager who was very active in the sixties and seventies pro-test movements and who wasn't going to be antiunion."

Meanwhile, the union methodically proceeded to build support among the workers. As the campaign began, the earliest union supporters, including Swenson, Arig, and the woman who had complained about parking fees, met with yet another organizer from Local 1199NW, Vanessa Veselka.

The interaction between the middle-aged and somewhat sub-dued hospital workers and the flamboyant young union orga-nizer was tenuous at first. In her twenties at the time, Veselka is the daughter of television newscaster Linda Ellerbee. Tall, freck-led, dark-haired, and extremely intense—she describes herself as looking like a "sturdy Czech peasant"—Veselka had worked in a warehouse for the online bookseller Amazon.com, played guitar in a punk-rock band, and aspired to be a novelist. As the work-ers and Veselka agreed on the issues they needed to confront, her confidence rubbed off on them.

Veselka used a tactic that organizers have favored for many years: "inoculating" the workers against the likeliest attacks by management against the union, such as warnings about strikes, violence, and union dues. "Because I'm a writer, I anticipated what management might say," she recalled. "She took us step by step through the campaign, explaining that we would never take the next step until we were ready," said Swenson.

Meanwhile, Aring and Swenson became bolder union advocates, although each, in her own way, had first been inclined to be more bashful. "Dona [Aring] was very well spoken," Veselka recalled. "She was white-collar, almost Miss Perfect." For her part, Swenson became more assertive. "The thing that blew me away about Deanna was watching this woman, who had never driven a car, who had been a single mother, a housekeeper who had been around a while. She was not a confrontational personality and had been underestimated by everyone in her life. But she turned into a union leader."

Soon, Veselka was giving the workers organizing missions of their own. First, she asked the union supporters to give her the names of other potential union backers. Then she asked them to talk to other coworkers to see whether they'd support the union. "My names were other housekeepers," Swenson remembered. "I made home visits and phone calls. I got to know a lot of people I didn't know before." Within weeks, the union's staff organizers and the workers themselves had collected signed cards from a majority of the workers authorizing Local 1199NW to represent them.

After holding a hearing, the National Labor Relations Board divided the employees into three separate "bargaining units," each of which would vote separately on whether to be represented by Local 1199NW. Northwest Hospital already had one bargaining unit, the registered nurses, who were represented by the State Nurses Association. As with politicians drawing the lines for legislative districts, the hospital and the union each argued for definitions of the new bargaining units that would be advantageous for them. Since the union was certain to carry the lowest-wage workers in the housekeeping, dietary, laundry, and maintenance units, the union would have benefited either by having one big bargaining unit or by dispersing enough of its supporters into several units so that it could carry them all. But for the hospital to weaken the union, it would have had to carve out at least one unit of higher-paid workers who would be likely to vote against union representation.

The eventual unit determination offered something for both sides, although the hospital may have gotten a little more of what it wanted. Most of the low-wage workers went into the "service and maintenance" unit. Separate "technical" and "professional" units were created, and often the distinctions between the two groups were difficult to anticipate or understand. For instance, radiologists were placed in the technical unit, while laboratory technicians went into the professional unit.

As it turned out, the "professionals" were more pro-union than the "technicians" were. The radiologists and other technicians were mostly young white men who, as Local 1199NW organizer Curt Williams explained, tended to be suspicious of collective action in general and unions in particular.

Meanwhile, about 80 percent of the laboratory technicians, who found themselves in the professional unit, were women. Although they did not seem to be rugged individualists like the radiologists, some of the lab techs did express the kind of doubts that professionals often voice about whether unions are only for blue-collar workers and not for more highly skilled employees. In order to ease the lab techs' doubts about whether unions understand professionals, the union brought in two expert witnesses. Christopher Malloy was a lab tech at Stevens Hospital, where the workers had voted for Local 1199NW earlier that year. He was also a member of the union's executive board. Malloy met with the lab techs at Northwest, making the case for the union in the dispassionate, factual terms that these workers, like the engineers at Boeing, tend to appreciate. As Williams later explained, "Lab techs evaluate the union in a very different way from a lot of other health-care workers. They are like scientists doing a cost-benefit analysis. With lab techs, an organizer who works off of passion and agitation is less effective than a fellow lab worker."

Toward the end of the campaign, Sosne herself met with the lab techs and other professionals. "The issue was whether they were comfortable being with the blue-collars," she recalled. "I talked from my experience. I have a master's of science degree in nursing. I thought I was able to connect with some of the workers. I talked about the fact that we negotiate about professional practice issues, that we negotiate leaves for professionals to attend professional association meetings, and that professionals are paid for continuing education, which they need to keep current in their fields."

While the outcome in the service and maintenance unit seemed to be a foregone conclusion, the union, as methodically as ever, made sure to consolidate its support among the main ethnic group in the hospital's workforce. In most big-city hospitals, the service workers are overwhelmingly African American and Hispanic, but in Northwest, most workers are non-Hispanic whites, and the largest ethnic minority is Filipino Americans, who are concentrated in the housekeeping unit. In addition to assigning a Filipino American organizer, Mia Barcelongo, to the campaign, Local 1199NW invited a friendly Filipino American state legislator, Velma Veloria, to meet with the workers at a Catholic church where many of the workers worshipped regularly. By the end of the organizing campaign, almost all of the Filipino American workers had agreed to be photographed and listed as union supporters in leaflets that Local 1119NW distributed.

After an unusually tense Christmas season at Northwest Hospital, the workers voted on January 5, 2001, in an improvised polling place in the Transitional Care Unit Auditorium. By margins of about two-to-one in each group, the workers in the service and maintenance unit and in the professional unit voted to be represented by Local 1199NW. By a smaller margin, the workers in the technical unit voted against union representation.

WE JUST CELEBRATED THE DOWNPOUR

Now, the union's next challenge was bargaining a contract with Northwest Hospital. First contracts are often the most difficult for a union to negotiate. Having just won an organizing campaign, the workers often expect to win every improvement that they want, all at once. But employers have just lost a measure of control of the workplace, thus are often determined not to give another inch, and, besides, if they didn't believe their existing policies and pay structures were fair and reasonable, they wouldn't have instituted them in the first place. As for the union, it has just gone through a campaign in which it most likely assured the workers that they wouldn't have to strike. Therefore, the union is usually reluctant to ask the workers to take more risks. This understandable caution limits its capacity to put pressure on management. For these reasons and more, the first negotiations often drag on for months and months.

As with the organizing campaign, Local 1199NW began by reactivating its community campaign. Now, the union support committee had a name, "Northwest Neighbors for a Fair Contract." The slogan on the yard signs was still usable, "Northwest Needs to Be Fair to the Employees." Once again, the union asked local elected officials, Democratic precinct captains, and other allies to contact Northwest Hospital management. But this time, they asked the hospital to agree to bargain in good faith for the contract. An experienced union organizer, Gretchen Donart, went door-to-door in North Seattle. She remembered speaking with many retired union members who were dismayed that their local hospital might be using delaying tactics at the bargaining table and who were only too eager to send postcards to Northwest urging management to take a more conciliatory stance.[10]

Meanwhile, Local 1199NW conducted a survey of the workers, asking what they wanted to propose at the bargaining table. Not surprisingly, they wanted across-the-board pay increases, no cuts in health coverage and other benefits, and some sort of ratio of patients to employees that would allow workers to provide personalized care. With Van Bronkhorst leading the union's bargaining committee, the negotiations began in April 2001. Once again, Schneider did not participate in the negotiations, leaving them to the human resources director.

When the negotiations appeared to stall, the union called one more action—an "informational picket line." Such actions are intended to attract the attention of workers, the general public, and the news media, but no one is asked not to go to work or not to use the hospital. On this afternoon, as happens so often in Seattle, there was a rainstorm. "But this one wasn't just a drizzle—it became a downpour," Chris Barton remembered. Then, almost all at once, the picketing workers seemed to get the same idea. Instead of calling off the picket line or huddling under the canopy, why not just keep picketing? "We're used to the wet," Barton explained. "It's like that all the time. So we just celebrated it."

"It was like going to a party—people were dancing in the rain," Veselka later recalled. A worker named Mark from the housekeeping department took one of the union bullhorns and started reciting hip-hop rhymes about working at the hospital and picketing in the rain. Several of the certified nursing assistants started kick-dancing like chorus girls.

By December, 2001, the union and management negotiating teams reached an agreement that was accepted by the workers in yet another vote. The contract provided for three 3 percent increases over three years, no changes in the benefit plans, and assurances that staffing levels would not be reduced.

In the years ahead, things never seemed to get easier. In the second contract negotiations, in 2004 and 2005, Northwest Hospital tried unsuccessfully to cut back its employees' health insurance—an irony that was not lost on the workers. Shortly after the second contract was finalized, a group of workers, backed by a conservative think tank, tried to vote out the union. Once again, the union prevailed. While the union struggled to survive at Northwest Hospital, it continued to grow throughout the Seattle area and statewide. When I interviewed Sosne, Barton, and Van Bronkhorst in December 2005, they had trouble remembering some details of the organizing campaign at Northwest Hospital. "That was ten campaigns ago," Van Bronkhorst said.

As for the union's earliest supporters, they appreciated the fact that when they wanted to get together to complain about their problems and plan what to do about them, they no longer had to sneak off to the cemetery or say they were going to Hardee's. As for the decertification, the downpour, or the difficulties at the bargaining table, they took most problems in stride.

"We were schooled by Vanessa," Swenson said. "Your work is never done."

4

CARING ENOUGH
TO GET MAD

Just before Boeing's contract negotiations with its engineers and technicians deadlocked, C. Richard Barnes, the federal mediator assigned to the talks, offered a shrewd analysis of what was going on. He said, "The social contract at this company is breaking down."

That statement described what was happening at Boeing. It also applied to workplaces all across the United States as the twentieth century drew to a close. For most of the second half of the century, a set of unwritten rules governed most U.S. workplaces. If you showed up every day and did your job well, and if your company made money, you could count on a lifetime job, rising wages, secure health coverage, a fair shot at a promotion or two, and guaranteed pension benefits when you retired. This social contract served employers and employees well enough as long as the nation's economy grew and prospered.

But by the end of the twentieth century, as U.S. corporations faced cutthroat competition in global markets, even the best companies like Boeing were telling their employees that the deal was off. From here on out, everything that workers used to be able to count on now would be up for grabs. Experienced employees would have to prove their worth every day. They could no longer depend on keeping their jobs or holding onto their current levels of health and pension benefits. Every corporate subdivision would be expected to make a profit and pay its own way. Just because a company had made a product for years—even if the company was closely identified with that product, as IBM was identified with making computers, first the mainframes and then the laptops—the employees couldn't rely on the company continuing to make and modernize it. Meanwhile, the newer companies, such as the software start-ups in Seattle that emerged in Microsoft's shadow, already followed the corporate model that Microsoft was moving toward—temporary jobs with low wages and few benefits for those working at routine jobs and skyrocketing salaries with stock options for the superstars.

Well-educated, highly skilled workers like the engineers at Boeing also felt that another implicit agreement was being violated. Since the days when they first arrived at Boeing, with their dreams of designing jumbo jets or space shuttles, the engineers had done much more than simply show up for work, do as they were told, and mark the months on their calendars until they retired. Every day, they did more than was asked of them—they'd created one more design for the cabin of an aircraft, conducted one more test of the airplane's wings, or headed home worrying that there was some problem with their project that they hadn't imagined yet. They made an extra effort, and they thought that they were entitled to receive something extra in return; they needed some assurance that Boeing respected their work and trusted their professional judgment. After the company kept making decisions that seemed to jeopardize the quality of its airplanes and even its future in the commercial aircraft industry, the engineers began to believe that they, not management, had the company's best interests at heart. When the engineers went on strike, their picket signs didn't declare, as most unions would, that they were "On strike against Boeing"; they proudly proclaimed they were "On strike *for* Boeing."

During the strike, the engineers' union received millions of hits on its Web site. At first, the engineers suspected that someone, maybe management at Boeing, was trying to sabotage their Web site. As the unusually high Web traffic continued, the engineers concluded, almost in spite of themselves, that they were staging a struggle that inspired skilled and committed workers well beyond Boeing. The engineers liked this—as their leader, Charles Bofferding, said, "We're not comfortable with conflict in our own behalf, but we love to lead crusades"—and they ratcheted up their rhetoric in an effort to speak for disgruntled professionals everywhere.[1] When the engineers said that they were fighting for their professional integrity, that the bean counters wouldn't let them do their jobs properly, and that they cared more about Boeing than their bosses did, they struck a responsive chord with hundreds of thousands of people who also worried that something was wrong with work in the United States.

All across the economy, other workers were voicing similar concerns. Doctors and nurses worried that their decisions about patient care were being questioned by number crunchers at the insurance companies. Software designers wondered why they were rushing their programs out the door before these were adequately tested. And teachers and social workers watched their class and caseload sizes increase, while their ability to provide personalized attention to their students and clients decreased.

TWO BROKEN BARGAINS

By the year 2000, two social contracts were breaking down in U.S. workplaces. The first broken bargain involved things that can easily be measured and grasped: a job that lasts a lifetime, regular raises every year, health insurance for your family, and a pension waiting for you when you retire. This deal could be summed up as "security in return for loyalty," and when the nation's companies called it off, the nation's workers felt betrayed. The second understanding was less universal or understandable. If you poured your energy and intelligence into your work, then your employer had better show you some gratitude and allow you some discretion to do your job the best way you knew how. That deal might be described as "trading commitment for respect," and when companies such as Boeing defaulted on this implicit agreement, some of the nation's most valuable workers reacted like jilted lovers.

The workplace conflicts of the twenty-first century will be about breaches of faith and, increasingly, about the second kind of betrayal. The first broken bargain hits workers in their paychecks and bank accounts, which is bad enough. The second shattered promise hits workers in their hearts and souls, which may be even worse.

Moreover, much has been written about how working Americans are being shortchanged by corporate America, and it is all well worth repeating: Job security is becoming a thing of the past. When inflation is taken into account, wages are flat-lining. Employer-paid health insurance and guaranteed pension benefits are becoming endangered species, preserved mostly in government jobs. In the first decade of the twenty-first century, the poor have been getting poorer again, the middle class is more anxious than ever, and a fortunate few are becoming wealthy beyond the dreams of avarice.

But much less has been said about how much satisfaction Americans take in our jobs, perhaps because this story is more complex. Although only the top 20 percent of Americans have seen their incomes increase dramatically over the last quarter century, it would be more difficult to maintain that only people in a similarly small share of the workforce are deriving a lot more satisfaction from their work. For most Americans, their work has become more pleasant. But people are also concerned about a cluster of problems that make their jobs more frustrating. Their companies care more about short-term profits than about long-term success in their fields. Skilled workers are losing control over the quality of their work. And employers are treating even their most skilled and committed employees as costs to be cut, rather than assets to be invested in.

These problems are about more than money, but they are also about money. Companies that care most about short-term profits end up shortchanging the investments that improve the quality of their products and services. When companies take a hard line on wages and benefits, as Boeing did with its engineers, or seek to save money by making some positions part time or temporary, as Microsoft did with its software testers, they also send the message that they are devaluing these employees' work. Even in the public and the nonprofit sectors, budgetary decisions have important impacts on quality; it costs money to cut social workers' caseload sizes or teachers' class sizes.

Just as job satisfaction problems have economic causes, they also have economic consequences. For individual companies and entire countries, their capacity to compete in the global economy depends upon having skilled workforces that are fully engaged in their work and actively committed to quality. When the most capable and committed workers lose faith that their judgment is respected and their contributions are appreciated, the quality of the nation's products and services will suffer. Eventually, the world's consumers will be more reluctant to buy what the United States is selling, and the economy will suffer as surely as if our own consumers' purchasing power had declined. So, when Americans love our work but hate our jobs, not only our emotional well-being but also our economic well-being is at risk.

A DEEP-ROOTED DISCONTENT

By the turn of the twenty-first century, many of the most discontented workers were also the most skilled and best educated and trained: aerospace engineers, information technology professionals, doctors, nurses, and social workers, all of whom felt that they were losing control over the conditions of their work and the quality of their products. This wasn't the first time that skilled workers became alienated from their work and angry at their employers because the standards of their crafts, their standard of living, and their standing in society were being threatened by far-reaching economic changes. These changes put them at the mercy of big companies and other large institutions that cared more about making money than about doing things right. At such times of change, the very quality that the sociologist Richard Sennett identifies with professionals, craft workers, and other people of skill—the commitment to doing their jobs well for the sake of excellence and service—becomes a profoundly subversive impulse.[2]

Toward the end of the nineteenth century, workers in scores of skilled blue-collar occupations found that their jobs were being transformed by the transition to mass production and Taylorite management techniques. In the past, carpenters, plumbers, iron-workers, machinists, and other skilled workers had trained, hired, and managed their colleagues and set the standards for quality work. Respected in their communities, they considered themselves independent artisans, the self-reliant citizens whom radical democrats such as Thomas Jefferson and Andrew Jackson believed to be the backbone of a self-governing society. Because these workers refused to be bossed around, Taylorism was attractive to employers not only because it made factories run more efficiently but also because managers could be sure that they would have unchallenged control. With the advent of mass production in factories and foundries, skilled craft workers were required to become—or be replaced by—laborers whose special skills had been rendered obsolete by machines. In a revealing turn of phrase, these workers were often called "factory hands." Compared to craft workers, these deskilled factory workers were paid less, were managed more heavy-handedly, and enjoyed less respect in the larger society.

An untold aspect of U.S. labor history is the extent to which the union movement has always been founded, organized, and led by the most skilled workers. These workers are more self-confident, enjoy the respect of their peers, and are frequently frustrated that their employers won't let them do their best work. Thus, the American Federation of Labor was founded by craft workers in construction, transportation, and other early industries. When industrial workers organized in the 1930s and 1940s, largely through the Congress of Industrial Organizations (CIO), their leaders also included many skilled workers. The legendary president of the United Auto Workers (UAW), Walter Reuther, was a tool-and-die maker, as were many other early UAW organizers. The longtime presidents of the International Ladies Garment Workers Union (ILGWU) and the Amalgamated Clothing Workers, David Dubinsky and Sidney Hillman, were both cutters, the most skilled occupation in the garment workers. Although many of the current leaders of the public employee and service sector unions are career unionists who have never worked in their industries, those who come from the rank-and-file tend to be professionals. For instance, the president of the Service Employees International Union (SEIU), Andrew Stern, was a social worker; the secretary-treasurer of AFSCME, William Lucy, was a civil engineer; the longtime president of the American Federation of Teachers, Albert Shanker, was a high school mathematics teacher who was a dissertation away from a PhD in philosophy; and Leon Davis, the founder of the health-care workers' union, Local 1199, was a pharmacist.

There is also a long-standing tradition of unions seeking to improve the management of their industries and the quality of their products. Perhaps the most gifted union leader in history, Walter Reuther frequently sparred with auto industry executives about whether he could have become president of one of the big-three auto companies (he hinted that he'd have preferred the largest one, General Motors) and whether he'd do a better job than their CEOs. Over the years, Reuther offered plans for converting auto factories to aircraft production during World War II; converting defense plants to peacetime production in the aftermath of World War II and, decades later, during the Vietnam War; and producing smaller and more energy-efficient cars—an idea that Reuther offered when the Volkswagen first made inroads into the U.S. market.

By the middle of the last century, the ILGWU and the Amalgamated Clothing Workers had efficiency experts on their staffs who advised the hundreds of small garment manufacturers how to improve the efficiency of their operations. Similarly, the United Steelworkers had a department headed by a cost accountant turned mill worker named Joe Scanlon that helped steel mill managers, local unions, or both to improve productivity in their workplaces. Decades later, when public schools came under criticism from business leaders, parent activists, and national commissions, the teachers' union president Shanker became a leading advocate of education reform, originating ideas such as charter schools with flexible work rules and peer review where teachers would mentor or weed out underperforming colleagues.

Although workplace conflicts over policy issues, as well as pay, were infrequent until recently, they did occur. In 1946, with Reuther's leadership, UAW members struck at GM, demanding pay increases without the company raising prices for its cars. Using the slogan "Open the Books," the union maintained that GM could afford to raise wages without charging more for its cars and would benefit by selling more automobiles and building a loyal consumer base among recently returned veterans and their families, who were prepared to make purchases that had been deferred for decades during World War II and the Great Depression. Since the 1960s, striking nurses, social workers, and teachers have demanded improved staffing levels and reduced caseloads and class sizes, as well as better pay and benefits.

But Do Employers Really Want Skilled Workers?

During the transition to the Industrial Age, skilled workers clearly understood—and bitterly resented—the fact that the nation's largest and fastest-growing companies no longer wanted independent artisans. Instead, these employers wanted workers who could be managed more, paid less, and treated worse.

At the beginning of the Information Age, professionals, technicians, and other skilled workers are struggling to understand

and address a more complex and confusing reality. The most prestigious companies, such as Microsoft and Boeing, insist that they want well-educated, highly skilled, and intensely motivated employees. Indeed, these companies frequently complain that their current employees and job applicants are not educated enough or sufficiently skilled. But at the same time, these companies often seek to cut the salaries and the benefits of their skilled workers, scour the world for lower-paid workers, and micromanage the very employees whose active involvement they claim to crave. Trying to make sense of their situation, professionals, technicians, and other skilled workers are often maddened by mixed messages. Companies seem to want the finest talent, on the cheap, and employees who will contribute their energies and ideas, while being second-guessed and closely controlled.

To be sure, more jobs require academic credentials and professional and technical skills, and more Americans are meeting these requirements. Between 2000 and 2010, the number of jobs demanding at least an associate or bachelor's degree are expected to grow by 23 percent—nearly twice the rate at which other jobs are increasing. Of the twenty fastest-growing occupations, ten are associated with college degrees and ten demand strong skills in information technology. Meanwhile, 34 percent of adult workers now have bachelor's degrees or more advanced degrees, an increase from 29 percent at the beginning of the 1990s.[3]

But there are real reasons to question whether many employers want well-educated, highly skilled, and strongly dedicated employees enough to pay them well, keep training and retraining them, and allow them autonomy on their jobs and a voice in decision making. Supposed shortages of skilled workers may really represent difficulties in hiring and holding onto skilled workers who are willing to work long hours for low salaries. As Stan Sorscher, a leader of the engineers at Boeing, has explained, there is little statistical support for the view that employers just can't find capable and qualified employees. From 2001 to 2006, the U.S. economy grew by about a million jobs a year, or 0.7 percent annually. Meanwhile, the population grew by 1 percent a year. So, throughout the economy, the story wasn't employers desperately searching for workers—the story was people searching for jobs.[4]

What about professionals and technicians in particular? Overall, the growth in computing and math occupations amounts to about 50,000 a year, while the increase in engineering jobs is about 15,000. Meanwhile, U.S. colleges and universities graduate about 125,000 engineering, computing, and science students a year, creating a surplus of about 65,000 potential professionals in these fields, not a shortage of educated people. Since 2000, the number of graduates in these fields has grown, but the number of jobs has not increased.[5]

And what has happened to wages in these fields? If there really were a skills shortage, qualified workers would command rising salaries. But, recently, salaries have stabilized. Yes, salaries (even when adjusted for inflation) rose slightly during the late 1990s, but this may have been due to companies being flush with money during the tech bubble of the dot-com boom more than to there being a scarcity of skilled workers. Since 2000, there has been little or no wage growth for entry-level computing jobs, while workers in other occupations had their inflation-adjusted wages increase through 2003 but decline afterward.

Contributing to stagnant wages and salaries, and indirectly influencing young people's reluctance to enter these occupations, employers have replaced U.S. engineers and information technology professionals with lower-paid workers from overseas, first by importing the workers and then by exporting the jobs. During the late 1990s, Microsoft and other high-tech companies relied heavily on the federal H1-B program, which provides temporary visas for skilled foreign workers. From granting sixty-five thousand visas in 1997, the program increased to two hundred thousand visas for foreign workers by the middle of the next decade.[6] These workers tend to be paid less than their American counterparts and cannot quit their jobs, demand pay increases, or threaten to organize unions because their visas are revoked if they leave or lose their jobs with their sponsoring companies.

Shortly after 2000, with the Internet allowing the transfer of information and images anywhere on earth, companies began to "offshore" jobs to professional and technical workers in other countries, especially India, which has millions of educated English-speaking people. By the middle of the decade, an estimated 300,000 to 600,000 jobs were being offshored every year, and economists estimated that more than 10 percent of the jobs in the United States could be sent overseas. While business, government, and opinion leaders had long suggested that education and skills would secure Americans' jobs, dozens of professional and technical positions, including programmers, accountants, and radiologists, to name a few, were vulnerable to offshoring.

The threat of offshoring affected millions more workers who kept their jobs. If their employers could move their jobs to India, then how could they afford to demand pay increases, challenge their supervisors' decisions, or refuse to work late nights or weekends? Meanwhile, large numbers of young people began to avoid occupations that were vulnerable to offshoring and prepared for positions that might be less challenging or rewarding but could not be moved to another country.

Only a few years into the new century, professional and technical workers felt as aggrieved, economically and in other ways as well, as blue-collar workers had been decades earlier. Between 2000 and 2004, the inflation-adjusted annual earnings of college graduates had actually declined. Meanwhile, these workers were falling behind the real winners of the new economy: corporate chief executives, top managers, hedge fund managers, and other financiers. A new kind of class conflict was emerging between professionals and technicians and the people who managed them, outearned them, and lorded it over them, politically and culturally. As the conservative columnist David Brooks wrote, it was a battle between "the aristocracy of the mind" and an "aristocracy of money."[7]

In the past, blue-collar discontent contributed to the growth of the Populist Party, the Socialist Party, the progressive movement, and eventually the New Deal, which recognized unions and transformed the economy. Now, the discontents of professional and technical workers are being felt in the popular culture, the political process, and the workplace.

WAITING FOR DILBERT

Angry professionals and technicians are joining alienated blue-collars as cultural icons. In the 1992 movie *Falling Down*, one of the first depictions of a worker who's hot under his white collar, Michael Douglas portrayed an aircraft engineer who had been laid off from his job as a result of the cutbacks in defense spending in the aftermath of the Cold War. Mirroring the blue-collar rage depicted two decades earlier in *Joe*, Douglas's character goes on a rampage throughout Los Angeles and its suburbs, threatening women, Asian Americans, and African Americans.

In succeeding films, sitcoms, and cartoons, white-collar rage was presented as more stereotypically white-collar—passive aggression rather than rampages. In the famous cartoon series *Dilbert*, an engineer by the same name is depicted as rumpled, caged in a cubicle, and mouthless (symbolizing his lack of a voice?). Meanwhile, his boss has two tufts of hair sticking up from his bald head like the Devil's horns. Although the cartoons avoid explicit mentions of economic, political, or labor issues, they satirize such management fads as reengineering, total quality management, and downsizing, rightsizing, outsourcing, and offshoring. Most workers are presented as competent but frustrated; however, as the cartoon's creator, Scott Adams, explained, "The most ineffective workers are systematically moved to the place where they can do the least damage: management." A former technician at Pacific Bell, Adams is intimately familiar and thoroughly disillusioned with corporate practices in information technology, telecommunications, and other cutting-edge industries.

Similarly, in the 1999 film *Office Space*, two consultants named Bob arrive at a software company called Initech. While they are interviewing the employees to determine who will be downsized or outsourced, one docile but disillusioned worker accidentally ingests a mind-altering drug. He leads a rebellion that infects the accounting system with a computer virus, and the film stumbles to an inconclusive but amusing end.

By 2007, such comedy found its way to prime-time network television, with the NBC show *The Office*. It depicts a money-losing paper-distribution company in Scranton, Pennsylvania, whose clueless boss, Michael Scott, mouths business-book clichés while scheming to "counsel out" some employees and ingratiate himself with others, particularly the attractive women.

WHITE COLLARS, BLUE STATES

Professional and technical workers' discontents are beginning to be felt in the political process, where these workers tend to support progressive Democrats in the general elections and insurgent candidates in the Democratic primaries.

Traditionally, most professionals and technicians tended to identify with managers and executives in the workplace and with Republicans in the political process. As recently as the 1960 presidential election, professionals supported Richard M. Nixon over John F. Kennedy by 61 percent to 38 percent, while managers supported Nixon by a slightly smaller margin. In 1968, professionals once again supported Nixon—an intellectually curious man who affected an anti-intellectual manner—against Hubert H. Humphrey.

Meanwhile, a minority of professionals were developing a new politics that offered a taste of the future. In 1952 and 1956, the Democratic presidential nominee, Adlai E. Stevenson, combined moderately progressive policies with a cultivated patrician manner that beguiled academics, social service professionals, and other educated liberals. Detached from blue-collar concerns and from the Democrats' populist traditions, Stevenson lost overwhelmingly to Dwight D. Eisenhower, but his followers remained active in the Democratic Party. His political heir, the liberal Catholic intellectual Eugene McCarthy, nominated him at the Democratic convention in 1960 and challenged President Lyndon B. Johnson in the party primaries in 1968, introducing a new generation of activists into the political process. While Stevenson and McCarthy were professorial in manner, their quixotic campaigns appealed to educated people who believed themselves to be beleaguered by mass culture and large institutions.

From then on, almost every presidential campaign included at least one candidate whose greatest appeal was to liberal professionals, from George McGovern in 1972 to Morris Udall in 1976, John Anderson (the lone Republican in this line) in 1980, Gary Hart in 1984, Michael Dukakis in 1988, Paul Tsongas in 1992, and Bill Bradley in 2000. Of these candidates, McGovern was something of a populist, Bradley campaigned as a risk-taking liberal, Hart and Dukakis stressed technological change, and only Anderson and Tsongas were self-consciously centrist. In personal style, Udall, Dukakis, Tsongas, and Bradley resembled Stevenson and McCarthy in their lack of aggression and disdain for populist appeals. (In September 1988, when I was working as a speech-writer in his campaign, Dukakis rebuked me in front of other staff members for drafting populist speeches that attacked "country-club Republicans.")

As the ranks of professional and technical workers grew during the 1990s, some Democratic strategists contended that these "wired workers" would resemble their more centrist and cerebral predecessors who preferred Stevensonian uplift to traditional Democratic populism. For instance, in a book that was circulated widely among centrist Democrats, the AT&T executive Morley Winograd commented, "Today there is an emerging class known as knowledge workers who earn their living by sharing information and solving problems, usually within an organizational setting. . . . These self-governing teams of knowledge workers serve as the organizational model of the Information Age, creating values and metaphors for Americans that are light-years removed from Henry Ford's assembly line and the pyramidal organization Alfred

Sloan created at General Motors."[8] Such workers, Winograd maintained, did not identify with lower-paid workers, neither did they resent their employers or identify with New Dealish economic liberalism.

But in the 2000 campaign, when Vice President Al Gore initially heeded such advice and muted his ancestral populism, he found himself vulnerable to a surprisingly strong challenge by Bradley and then losing ground by a wide margin to George W. Bush. At the Democratic Convention in August, he reemerged as a full-throated populist, championing "the people against the powerful," gained ground against Bush, and ended up winning the popular vote but losing in the Electoral College (and, before that, in the Supreme Court). In the final months of the campaign, Gore gained among professional and technical workers as well as among the blue-collar workers who were presumed to be predisposed to populism, while losing among executives and other managers. His theme that individuals were thwarted by large institutions, especially major corporations, resonated among well-educated professionals who worked for corporations and other institutions toward which they were ambivalent.

After 2000, Gore's populism-for-professionals took on an angrier tone. With the disputed 2000 election, the unpopular war in Iraq, the seeming passivity of establishment Democrats, and the growing grievances of professional and technical workers, these educated but aggrieved Americans became the core constituency for an angry progressive politics—McGovernism with an attitude. Using the Internet as an organizing tool, building new Web-based organizations such as Moveon.Org, and developing thousands of new Web sites that featured leftish commentary (first known as weblogs and then shortened to blogs), younger people in professional and technical jobs propelled the obscure former governor of Vermont, Howard Dean, into contention for the Democratic presidential nomination in 2004 before his pugnacity (a far cry from Stevenson and his heirs!) led to his defeat in the Iowa caucuses.

Meanwhile, professionals and technicians had become a progressive, even a populist, constituency. From 1988 through 2000, as the demographer Ruy Teixeira and the journalist John Judis have noted, professionals supported the Democratic presidential nominees by an average margin of 52 percent to 40 percent.[9] And John Kerry won by a similar margin among these voters in 2004.[10] Regions with large concentrations of high-tech workers, including the Seattle metropolitan area, had become solidly Democratic. In 2006, professionals and technicians in northern Virginia contributed to the victory of Senator Jim Webb, a warrior intellectual who melded economic populism with some socially conservative views. In the run-up to the 2008 elections, discontented professionals and technicians, including the progressive bloggers, were wooed by the major Democratic presidential contenders, from the frontrunner Hillary Rodham Clinton to the insurgents Barack Obama and John Edwards.

Growing numbers of professionals and technicians, especially younger workers in high-tech, were becoming the populists of the twenty-first century. One of the first skirmishes between minds and money was fought in the year 2000 in the most successful company of the era, Microsoft.

5

CYBER PROLES

David Larsen has the kind of face—and the sort of work history—that used to grace the jacket covers of first novels. Forty-four years old in 2000, with unkempt blond hair and a mustache to match, he usually wore the lumberjack's shirt, blue jeans, and running shoes that were the uniform for plumbers, poets, or programmers in Seattle.

Larsen's work history fit his laid-back looks. With a BA in communications from Evergreen State College, he'd studied acting, dancing, and creative writing, fields that, he later acknowledged, prepared you for waiting tables or standing in unemployment lines. Over the years, he had worked on a farm, at a lumber mill, and repairing roadways.

"The weirdest job of my life was driving a cab," he remembered years afterward. "I didn't actually meet drug dealers, but I found myself ferrying people from their homes to meet some shady characters on the streets of downtown Seattle, after which I ferried them back home. I can only imagine that they were acquiring drugs." Next, he went to the Divers Institute of Technology and became a deep-sea diver, but an injury ended that career.[1]

Then he went back to school again. This time, he attended a technical college to study something practical—HVAC engineering.

"That's HVAC, as in heating, ventilating, and air conditioning," he explained, pausing to see whether the person he was talking to had expected that HVAC would stand for something more exotic than installing central heating systems or fixing air conditioners. "That's what got me next to a computer," Larsen added, and it was a turning point on his life's journey. Fixing air conditioners didn't interest him, but he was fascinated by the computers that the technical college used in order to teach him how to troubleshoot heating and cooling systems.

Soon, he bought himself a computer to use at home, and, amazingly, "it turned out to be a lot of fun." That came as a surprise to him because, as he later recalled, "I'd bought into the popular portrayal of the computer scientist as a sexless, soulless entity who lives in his brain." But it turned out that learning how to work with computers was like playing video games every night—video games that you could earn a living playing with in a boomtown like Seattle in the late 1990s. "I had a good friend who'd worked with computers for years," Larsen remembered. "A software developer. And he helped to teach me how to use various software programs. Eventually, I figured, this was how I would make a living."

GUERRILLA WARFARE IN THE NERDS' NIRVANA

So instead of writing the Great American Novel, Larsen went to work for the Great American Software Company. Founded by Seattle native Bill Gates and headquartered in the nearby suburb of Redmond, Microsoft is the greatest success story of the Information Age. Starting out as a partnership between two college dropouts, it became the world's leading creator of the software that makes computers run and eventually grew into the largest company in the entire computer industry. Creating software is grueling intellectual labor, and Microsoft prides itself on hiring the smartest people to design its software, rewarding them generously with six-figure salaries and stock options that made many of them millionaires.

But Microsoft also needed workers to do relatively routine tasks, such as testing its software and writing guidebooks on how to use its products. Rather than fill these positions with permanent employees, Microsoft relied on temporary workers who eventually accounted for about six thousand of the approximately twenty thousand employees at its corporate headquarters. Hired as a software tester, Larsen became one of these temporary workers. As were many other temps, he became dissatisfied with the low pay, the skimpy health benefits, and the uncertain prospects of being hired for a permanent job. By 2000, Larsen emerged as a leader in a fledgling union formed by several hundred of the temps. Calling itself the Washington Alliance of Technology Workers, or WashTech, for short, it was a quirkily creative organization that maintained a maverick Web site that exposed the ways in which Microsoft mistreated its temporary workers. While WashTech's dues-paying membership was relatively low, its regular e-mail bulletins about abuses in the information technology industry were subscribed to by thousands more workers at Microsoft and other companies, generating buzz in the break rooms at offices throughout the Seattle area.

Why were so many of Microsoft's temporary workers so disgruntled? Headquartered on a suburban campus, providing free espresso and fruit juice in its cafeterias, and encouraging employees to dress informally, Microsoft is a pleasant place to work. For its superstars, young people doing work they loved for pay packages beyond their wildest dreams, Microsoft was a nerd's nirvana. But for the temps, this paradise must have seemed more like a purgatory, an ordeal that was bearable only because they held onto the hope of ascending into the heaven of gaining permanent positions. For most of Microsoft's temps during the 1990s, permanent status was an impossible dream, and the insecurities and indignities that they endured every day made many of them angry at the company they'd once admired.

If Microsoft had been a fraction as imaginative in employee relations as it was in software development, the temporary workers might have channeled their energies into perfecting the process by which the company tested its software and corrected the defects before putting its finished products on the market. Many of the software testers worried that they might be failing to find and fix all the defects in the software during Microsoft's panicky, last-minute, round-the-clock work-a-thons to meet the deadlines to get the products out the door. But the company never asked the temp workers for their thoughts about how they could do their jobs better, so the temp workers rarely offered their ideas. Meanwhile, the temps had so many problems with basic issues like overtime pay, health insurance, and impending terminations that the activists who joined WashTech became more interested in embarrassing Microsoft than improving it.

Most of the temp workers hadn't developed a strong commitment to Microsoft because Microsoft had made only a casual commitment to them. Even though the temps worked at Microsoft's offices and tested its software, Microsoft maintained that they weren't really Microsoft employees. Instead, the temps were officially employed by outside staffing agencies that wrote their paychecks, provided them with bare-bones health coverage, and sent them termination notices when their short-term stints were over. Microsoft constantly reminded them of their second-class status, requiring them to wear special badges and excluding them from the company's frequent picnics and parties. The temps were also overlooked by the nation's labor laws, which make it difficult for workers in such "triangular" situations—temporary employees who are nominally working for staffing agencies but are really working for the company where they spend their days— to organize unions, bargain with their employers, and, if necessary, conduct a strike. So, if the temps were to confront Microsoft, their uncertain legal status and insecure job situations required them to conduct guerrilla warfare, which was just what WashTech did during the late 1990s.

Companies get the workplace conflicts they deserve. At Seattle's other major employer, Boeing, the workforce consisted almost entirely of permanent employees, with health care, pension benefits, and long-established unions that represented the engineers and technicians, as well as the blue-collar workers. But Microsoft had purposely distanced itself from the temporary employees who comprised a third of its workforce and offered them no formal avenue for airing their complaints. Thus, the Boeing engineers staged a successful strike that demonstrated their passionate concern for their company's future, forcing the company to reaffirm its commitment to building commercial aircraft and, some would say, contributing to the company's recovery after 2000. For their part, Microsoft's workers fought a series of skirmishes on their Web site, in the news media, and in the state legislature, with little hope of improving the company's policies in the near future and costing Microsoft money, energy, and public esteem.

THE MILLIONAIRES' MATH CLUB

As Microsoft grew, it developed a distinctive corporate culture that reminded outsiders of a high-tech start-up, a Harvard reunion, a math club, or a frat house. Microsoft was successful because of the meritocracy that attracted so many brilliant and dedicated professionals, the insecurity that kept it nimble and flexible, and the informality that built team spirit among its most valued employees. But these same strong points put it on a collision course with its lower-level short-term employees.

As Gates's intellectual soul mate, Nathan Myhrvold, said, "The personality of Bill Gates determines the culture of Microsoft."[2] At the time of the events described in this book, Gates was Microsoft's chairman and "chief software architect"— a combination of the roles of CEO and superstar that calls to mind Anderson Cooper serving as president of CNN. In 2000, Microsoft was the House that Bill Built, reflecting his vision and also his blind spots.

More than three decades after Gates dropped out of Harvard, he still remembered his SAT scores—1590 out of a possible 1600, including a perfect score on the math part of the test. He and his inner circle were used to being the smartest kids in the class, and when it came to hiring new employees, Microsoft looked for what Gates called "super-smart" people with "incredible processing power." In 1993, the publisher of the business magazine *Forbes*, Rich Karlgaard, sat next to Gates on the Delta Shuttle from New York to Washington, D.C. "Halfway through the flight, Gates closed the book that he was reading and started talking. Out of nowhere, he told me that he had recently figured out who his competition was," Karlgaard recalled. "It was not Apple, Lotus, or IBM. He [Gates] waited a couple of beats. 'It's Goldman Sachs.'" "Is this a scoop?" the publisher asked. "Is Microsoft getting into investment banking?" "No," Gates replied. "I mean the competition for talent. It's all about IQ. You win with IQ. Our only competition for IQ is the top investment banks."[3]

When recruiting new employees, Microsoft's management team resembles the Guardians in Plato's *Republic*, an intellectual elite seeking new initiates. The company searches for brilliant young people—"Bill Clones," some call them, not always admiringly—who can be inculcated with the corporate culture. Being "super-smart" is more important than being experienced. During their job interviews, applicants are asked questions that they can't anticipate, such as "If you wanted to figure out how many times on average you would have to flip the pages of the Manhattan phone book to find a specific name, how would you approach the problem?" The process favors self-confident and articulate young people, often recent graduates from elite colleges and universities, rather than more experienced workers who have lost the knack of doing math in their heads or explaining how they would respond to hypothetical challenges. These whiz kids would get permanent positions developing the software, while job seekers like Larsen would get temporary slots testing the products.

To be sure, Microsoft's standards for potential talent resemble the late Supreme Court justice Potter Stewart's famous definition of pornography—the company can't explain exactly what talent is, but Microsoft knows it when it sees it. Throughout the information technology industry, however, there are no clear standards for the education, the training, and the credentials required for software developers and workers in related fields, such as software testers. By way of comparison, in order to design aircraft at Boeing, professionals need advanced degrees in engineering or physics, and many positions also require special certifications from the Federal Aviation Administration. But Microsoft was founded by brilliant college dropouts, and it wasn't about to insist that job applicants have credentials that Gates himself didn't possess. Many other software companies were also led by self-taught geniuses, so the entire industry evolved without a system of professional training and credentialing. Thus, in 1999, the Seattle-based industry analyst Steve McConnell reported that only about 40 percent of all software workers had four-year college degrees in software-related disciplines; while 20 percent had degrees in math, engineering, or completely unrelated subjects; and the remaining 40 percent had completed two-year colleges or had only graduated from high school. Several colleges and universities offered courses in software engineering—the preparation for designing software—but "practically none" of the nation's software developers hold degrees from these programs. (An advocate of professionalizing software design—and improving employees' salaries and working conditions—McConnell influenced the thinking of several disgruntled Microsoft workers, including WashTech activists. Ironically, his manifesto *After the Gold Rush: Creating a True Profession of Software Design* was published by Microsoft Press, a division of the giant software company.)[4]

In the absence of professional standards, Microsoft drifted into a caste system. After an interview where first impressions often trumped experience, the most promising applicants were offered permanent positions such as software developer, hard code programmer, or program manager. Less promising applicants often were shunted into temporary positions as software testers, and, since the software industry has no clearly defined career paths, they had few opportunities for promotions.

As Marcus Courtney, a software tester who led protests by the temp workers, explained, "The industry has a bias that there are true technical workers who belong in the industry—and then there's everyone else whom we have to let in because the industry is expanding."[5]

Gates and his inner circle would have disagreed with at least one of Courtney's points. No matter how successful Microsoft became, they were never confident that their industry, or at least Microsoft's share of it, would always be "expanding." If meritocracy was Microsoft's first article of faith, insecurity was its second dogma. While their clothes were casual, Microsoft's inner circle was always on the alert for new technologies, new products, new consumer preferences, and new competitors that could threaten the company's dominance in the marketplace. One of Gates's watchwords was, "Success today is no guarantee of success tomorrow." His sidekick Myhrvold often said, "No matter how good your product, you are only eighteen months away from failure."

Having helped to found the software industry, Gates understood that it was inherently unstable. At first, software was stored on plastic diskettes, just like the single 45 rpm records that people of Gates's age grew up with. But, as with the record industry, most software companies were only as successful as their latest offerings. Sure, MS-DOS, Windows, and Word had been successful. But what if Microsoft's new products didn't sell? Would the company be reduced to reissuing its golden oldies, just like a record label whose blockbusters were behind it? Moreover, in yet another scary similarity to the record industry, as Gates had known since his "Open Letter to Hobbyists," a manifesto he released in 1976, even the most successful products were vulnerable to piracy.

More alarming still was the prospect that entire product lines—perhaps entire technologies—would become outmoded, just as tapes replaced records and compact disks replaced tapes. Often, when the nature of an entire industry fundamentally changes, old companies fall by the wayside and new companies speed ahead. Gates and his inner circle were always looking nervously in their rearview mirrors because they knew that a scrappy newcomer like the Microsoft of 1980 could be gaining on them. Back then, they remembered, IBM was the seemingly unchallengeable leader of the information technology industry, making the mainframe computers that companies, universities, and government agencies kept buying, while Microsoft was a start-up company with a contract to create the operating system for the personal computers IBM planned to make. Not long afterward, Microsoft was dominating the software industry, while IBM was losing money and laying off employees. This much Gates and his colleagues knew: they didn't want to end up like IBM—fat, sluggish, and ready to be roadkill.

By the middle of the 1990s, Microsoft almost became a casualty of technological change, but the company responded just in time. During the early 1990s, Microsoft had become the leader in information technology by providing the user-friendly software that the new personal computers required. But just a little more than ten years later, Microsoft almost ignored the emergence of the Internet and the dramatic growth in e-mailing and Web browsing. An innovative newcomer, Netscape, developed an Internet browser that used Java, a programming language that allows applications to run on many operating systems, not just on Windows. Not only Windows but also Microsoft's other application programs, which benefited from their links with Windows, would have been in danger of losing their overwhelming share of the market. Microsoft responded just in time by offering a browser of its own, Internet Explorer, which was offered as part of a package with Windows. Microsoft's hard-ball tactics—building its application programs on the Windows platform—became an issue in the antitrust action, but the company retained its industry leadership and eventually dodged the antitrust bullet.

Being lean, nimble, and alert helped Microsoft to move quickly to seize opportunities. But as with his emphasis on recruiting the best and the brightest, Gates took a sensible concern to an extreme. From the first, Gates feared hiring full-time employees, insisting that the company never take on debt and keep enough cash in reserve to function for a year. After joining the company in 1980, Steve Ballmer recommended that with the business expanding rapidly, Microsoft hire seventeen new employees. Gates refused, telling Ballmer, "You're trying to bankrupt me." Soon, Microsoft's managers developed a new word, *headcount*, to describe the number of permanent employees in their divisions. The message was clear: "headcount" was to be held down at all costs.

Over the years, as Microsoft grew, it relied more and more on temporary workers who were hired to work on developing one software product and were let go when the project was completed. Why would a fast-growing, enormously profitable company on the cutting edge of technological change choose to have a two-tier workforce? Even Microsoft's harshest critics acknowledged that Microsoft originally had good reasons.

Growing from 128 employees in 1981 to more than 11,000 ten years later, Microsoft still had a start-up mentality when it began to hire large numbers of temps. Other companies had gone from boom to bust, and Gates feared Microsoft might, too. Why not maintain the mentality that Microsoft was a new company moving from project to project, rather than a bloated bureaucracy burdened with tens of thousands of timeservers? Also, Gates had grown up reading about how Boeing had laid off thousands of workers when it hit rough spots, generating sympathetic stories about the newly unemployed and bad publicity for the aerospace giant. Why not avoid the sob stories by hiring workers who knew they were only onboard for temporary assignments?

As its temporary workforce grew, Microsoft began to see the temporary workforce as a business necessity, even as a visionary business model. During the 1990s, celebrity CEOs such as GE's Jack Welch called for a new corporate model. Cut your permanent workforce down to the workers who are best at your basic functions. Outsource everything else to freelancers, staffing agencies, or outside contractors.

Gates didn't worship Welch or any other CEO; the software whiz was his own management guru. Moreover, he had the advantage of building a company from the ground up, not taking an already established company and cutting it down to size. So, as the business writer G. Paschal Zachary explained, Microsoft became "the model of the new postmodern corporate culture, perfectly suited to survive in an era of rapid technological change." Thus, Microsoft became the prototype for a new corporate paradigm, with a permanent "core" of essential employees and a "periphery" of temporary workers. Inevitably, this model resulted in large numbers of workers becoming estranged from the company that considered them peripheral.

For the temp workers, being outsiders at Microsoft was particularly painful because the insiders were obviously having so much fun. In an effort to create a relaxed workplace, Microsoft designed a corporate headquarters in Redmond that consists of thirty-five low-rise buildings sprawling across a campus that includes parks and athletic fields. Free shuttle buses take employees or visitors from building to building, and, to make Microsoft even more welcoming, the buses are stocked with baskets of free candy for the passengers. Similarly, the employee cafeterias feature a variety of meals at low prices, including gourmet cuisine, vegetarian dishes, and delicatessen-style sandwiches, with free beverages. Appropriately for a company where people work around the clock, the cafeterias offer free beverages at all hours, from fruit juices, soft drinks, and herbal teas to—this is Seattle—coffees of all kinds. Employees can buy Microsoft's software products at discounts of 70 percent or more at a shop called, with at least a touch of irony, "The Company Store." For the athletically inclined, there are basketball courts, tennis courts, and fields for playing softball, soccer, and touch football.

In its folkways, as well as its amenities, Microsoft goes out of its way to be friendly. For men, the uniform is plaid shirts and khakis; with women, informality also prevails. There are frequent parties and beer bashes—on Friday afternoons, when a software product is completed, or when regular employees leave on good terms. On special occasions, Microsoft holds pep rallies, belying its reputation for nerdiness. For instance, in June 2000, the company celebrated its twenty-fifth birthday with a mass meeting at Seattle's Safeco Field, with the burly Ballmer jumping out of a giant birthday cake and racing through the crowd, covered with icing and sweat, to the tune of Kool and the Gang's "Celebration."

Trying to describe the atmosphere at Microsoft, the journalist James Fallows said simply, "The people are nice." A computer buff, Fallows works six-month stints every few years writing software for Microsoft. Although he's a temp worker, Fallows is paid by Microsoft, not by a staffing agency. He's assigned prestigious work—writing word processing programs, not testing software. And as a respected pundit and a Harvard man, too, he doubtless gets celebrity treatment. From this privileged vantage point, Fallows reported, "[Microsoft is] about as collegial and non-backbiting an environment as I've ever been part of. What people considered a sharp exchange about features or strategy (they call such disagreement 'pushback') was nothing compared with the way lawyers, journalists, or politicians snap at one another."[6]

Visiting Microsoft in the spring of 2000 in order to study workplace conflicts, I couldn't help but notice how nicely I was treated and how relaxed the temp workers seemed to be, even though they were talking with a visiting researcher about their problems with their employer. When I worked as a union organizer, I often found it difficult to get into office buildings and even more challenging to talk to workers. Concerned about getting workers into trouble with management, I made sure that their supervisors didn't see them talking to me. But at Microsoft, everything seemed different. A year before 9/11, after signing in, I was welcomed onto Microsoft's campus and shuttled by bus from building to building. When I showed up at the buildings, receptionists asked me whom I wanted to see and why, and, after I answered, "I'm here to interview Ms. Millet," they waved me in. Interviewing workers over lunch or late-afternoon coffee, I often looked nervously over my shoulder to see whether anyone was watching us and listening in on our conversations, but the workers seemed relaxed, even when they were sitting in Microsoft's subsidized cafeteria, drinking Microsoft's free cappuccino, and complaining about Microsoft's personnel policies.

Still, there was trouble in paradise, if only because many temp workers knew that soon they would be thrown out of this Garden of Eden.

"PAYROLL" IS A VERB, "PERMA-TEMP" IS A NOUN

Microsoft's sales grew more than a hundredfold, from $7.5 million in 1980 to $804 million in 1989. But because Gates dreaded having permanent employees almost as much as he did software pirates and computer viruses, Microsoft applied its considerable ingenuity to finding ways to hold down its "headcount."

During the 1980s, Microsoft hired thousands of "independent contractors" every year. While many companies use freelancers for specialized creative or professional tasks—as artists, accountants, or advertising copywriters—Microsoft hired its short-term workers to do relatively routine tasks, such as proofreading, indexing, formatting, and software testing, as well as some work that was considered midlevel, such as developing CD-ROMs, designing Web sites, and writing software manuals. Officially, the company did not consider these workers to be regular employees. Microsoft didn't provide them with health insurance, pension credits, or vacation days, nor did it withhold federal taxes from their paychecks. Instead, the company reported their annual earnings to the IRS with 1099 forms.

In an audit of Microsoft's staffing policies completed in 1989, the IRS found that many freelancers did much the same work as many of Microsoft's full-time workers. Therefore, the IRS ruled, the temp workers had been misclassified as contractors, and many owed back taxes, some of which Microsoft ended up paying. Microsoft would have to change its employment practices. Typically, the company found an unusual way to control headcount without visibly violating the law.

Microsoft offered some of the "independent contractors" permanent positions, but the great majority were moved to the payrolls of temporary employment agencies in the Seattle area that would withhold the workers' taxes from their paychecks. Thus, the staffing agency Volt might write a paycheck for a software tester who went to work every day at Microsoft. This arrangement added another word to Microsoft-speak. "Payroll" became a verb, as in "Volt is payrolling three of the workers on the new tax software project."

On January 17, 1990, Microsoft's then president Jon Shirley sent an e-mail to the company's managers, with copies to Gates and Ballmer, explaining just how this sleight of hand would work. "First do not have your people just make all the freelancers temps," Shirley explained. "That should only happen in the cases where there is a clearly defined end date to a project and a firm commitment to let the person go when that project is completed."[7]

As Sharon Decker, who served as Microsoft's director of temporary staffing toward the end of the 1990s, later explained, the decision to move the freelancers to temporary staffing agencies and the increasing use of these workers flowed naturally from the company's commitment to being nimble and flexible.

"To my knowledge, there was no 'big decision' where people sat in a room and said, 'This is how we are going to staff the company, and this is why we're going to do it,'" she said. "We've just always wanted to maintain flexibility and to avoid big fluctuations in the number of full-time workers."

By the middle of the decade, Microsoft had established a clearly defined, if baroquely bewildering, system for hiring, paying, firing, and rehiring its temporary workers. As with other companies, people who wanted to work for Microsoft would apply to the company and come in for an interview. Usually, they wanted permanent jobs with benefits and career opportunities. But very often, Microsoft had other ideas. If an applicant didn't have impressive academic credentials, didn't do well on the "brain-teasers" in her interview, or didn't come off as a potential superstar, then she was either rejected outright or shunted into a routine job such as software testing. And most workers who were hired for these jobs were placed in temporary positions.

Once she was hired as a temp worker, Microsoft would refer her to a temporary staffing agency—at one time, Microsoft worked with almost a hundred of these in the Seattle area—which would be her formal employer, writing her paychecks and withholding her taxes. She'd have a second job interview with her agency to negotiate—or, more likely, to be told—her hourly wage. Then, she'd report for work at a Microsoft office where the head of her working group would be her day-to-day supervisor. Most often, temporary employees worked alongside permanent employees. But when it came to performance evaluations, the temps would receive theirs from their agency. If they received a raise during their stints, the agency would inform them. And the agency would send them their formal termination notices at the end of their assignments.

Formally, the staffing agencies employed the temporary workers, but this was about as accurate as saying that Queen Elizabeth rules England, Scotland, Wales, and Northern Ireland. Anjani Millet, a temporary software tester, tried to explain to me how Volt, the leading staffing agency at Microsoft, related to her: "They're basically like a payrolling agency pretending to be an employment agency. . . . According to Microsoft, Microsoft doesn't keep records on us. I'm supposed to meet with a Volt rep who barely knows me. Volt decides on your increase, but you know they talked to Microsoft."

Ultimately, there was something in this arrangement for everyone but the temp workers. Microsoft avoided the cost and the commitment of hiring and keeping permanent employees. The agencies got substantial fees from Microsoft without doing much more than sending out paychecks and W2 forms. But the temporary workers were trapped in an economic limbo. During the mid-1990s, most earned between $18 and $25 an hour, with small increases after their first six months on the job. They received no stock options, no pay on sick days, and a pinch-penny health plan that seemed to be based on the assumption that most employees were, and would always remain, young, single, and childless.

Not only didn't the temporary employees work for the staffing agencies that wrote their paychecks, but quite a few of the temporary employees weren't even temporary. In reality, many temps worked on the same project for much longer than their nominal three-month stints, and Microsoft moved many other temps from project to project. After their temporary assignments were over, the temp workers were nominally let go by Microsoft. Then, they were sent back to their staffing agency, which "hired" them once again for a "new" assignment at Microsoft. Thus, these long-term temporary workers angrily but accurately called themselves "perma-temps"—an Orwellian word for a seemingly self-contradictory situation. As Lisa Lewis, a Microsoft temp, told a Washington State Senate Committee hearing in 1999, "In the last two years, I have worked in the same group, with the same agency, on a contract that renewed every three months. When Microsoft hired me, they said I'd have to 'join' an agency."

Although Microsoft is idyllic compared to most workplaces, it does have a caste system—and the temp workers were second-class citizens, compared to the superstars. While at work in Microsoft buildings, the temps were required to wear orange badges to distinguish them from the regular employees, who wore blue badges, and the workers for outside companies, such as the shuttle bus drivers, who wore brown badges. While temps could enjoy the free soft drinks that Microsoft offers its employees, they could not use the athletic fields or attend the annual picnic. "Some people get stock options, training, and a health club," Larsen said. "But if you're a temporary worker for Volt, what you get is free soda."

At a company where the Internet was at least as much of a gathering place as the picnic grounds was, the temps suffered an additional indignity—they had an *a* in front of their names on their @microsoft.com e-mail accounts. Unlike Hester Prynne's scarlet letter, the temps' *a* stood for "agency employee," not "adulterer." Even more humiliatingly, many of the temps found that they weren't invited to the parties to celebrate the completion of their software projects, although, as testers, many worked longer and harder than anyone as the group effort staggered toward the finish line.

More important, though less tangible, was the feeling of being excluded from the intellectual excitement of creating software. While working as a temp, Courtney remembered walking down a hallway and hearing two software developers talking about a new product they were devising. "They saw me, and they saw my orange badge," Courtney recalled, "and they stopped talking."

When WashTech members and other Microsoft temporary employees got together to swap stories about their intense and insecure work lives, their passion was palpable. They had applied for their jobs because they were caught up in the excitement of making software, and they were proud of Microsoft, proud of their products, and proud of their work. But they were frustrated with how Microsoft and the staffing agencies treated them. As Anjani Millet said, "Volt was beyond frustrating—I hate them. I love my job—Volt is my only source of stress on this job."[8] In fact, the phrase "Love the work, hate the job" first occurred to me when I was interviewing temp workers at Microsoft in 2000.

Most of the temps were software testers—the quality control workers of the Information Age. They were proud of the skills and the persistence that they brought to their jobs. Usually, their work combined the most intuitive exercises of imagination and the most tedious drudgery. Often, they would evaluate an entire product by operating it in the ways that a novice consumer would use it, not expertly but following the instructions or their own instincts. And testers would also slog through the rote work of looking for bugs in the lengthy lines of computer code that, taken together, constitute a piece of software. They needed to be intuitive and persistent, and they knew it.

"You just poke at the software any way you can think to poke at it until it breaks, or you conclude that it has no defects or only trivial defects," Larsen explained. "It's detail work, and it takes persistence." As Millet said, "You have to have a mentality, very curious, kind of ruthless. You find something small and say, 'Wait a second.' Then you go on to the next problem. I'm very excited about it actually."

Millet understood that the software testers are the Information Age version of a familiar figure from the Industrial Age—the quality control manager. Because most testers are journey-workers, not geniuses, they are better able than the most expert programmers to determine whether regular consumers will find a software product user-friendly. "We are the advocates for the users—that's what we are," she told me. "Microsoft looks for testers who can use the technology but still, in their habits, are aligned with the user. . . . We're in between the users and the development geeks. . . . The product does not ship until we sign off on it." But most of the higher-ranking employees and the members of Microsoft's high command didn't appreciate the skills that the testers brought to their work and the contributions they made. While Fallows was mostly enthusiastic about Microsoft, he acknowledged, "There was a profound caste division between testers and developers—the latter tended to view the testers as a necessary evil."

Although many of the temps lacked the elite educational backgrounds and math-whiz mannerisms that Microsoft values, they knew they brought essential skills and valuable experiences to a company that produced software for wide-ranging purposes and worldwide markets. A strikingly beautiful woman who could have been cast as a Eurasian intelligence agent in an action movie, Millet has three BA degrees in photography and fine art, women's studies, and psychology. She has worked as a visual artist, a performance artist, a photographer, and an administrative assistant in an office. And she has taught herself computer skills, including two- and three-dimensional graphics and digital-designed illustration. Fluent in several languages, she helped to produce software products that provide interactive instruction in business English for French and Japanese audiences. Full of excitement, she bragged, "It [the software that teaches English to the Japanese] is one of Microsoft's best-selling products." While the temp workers had mixed feelings about Microsoft, they were intensely loyal to the colleagues, temporary and permanent, with whom they worked every day. Most work with teams of anywhere from six to twenty programmers and testers, usually with one or two leaders. For instance, Millet recalled a project where she worked with "six testers, one test leader, and one supervisor above us—the technical guru." As she remembered fondly, "It was a pretty tight little bunch." As their project proceeds and the team members work longer and longer hours together, they frequently develop intense friendships. As the software industry observer McConnell wrote, "Despite their lack of commitment to [their] company, programmers do seem committed to their occupation. Many programmers feel more loyal to colleagues at other companies than they do to their employers."

But Microsoft did little to draw on the temp workers' commitments to their colleagues and their craft. When their software projects were over, the temp workers would be terminated. Often, they were out the door before the parties that celebrated the completion of the task. Rarely, if ever, did Microsoft debrief them about their experiences in working on the software project, what had been done right, what had been done wrong, and how things might have been done better.

Not listening to the temp workers was Microsoft's loss. Some temps had given serious thought to how Microsoft's work processes could be reorganized so that the temps could do their jobs better. Toward the end of their assignments, temps wandered around bleary-eyed, reflecting Microsoft's frequently frantic tempo, with employees working nights and weekends as deadlines approached. A young software tester (who asked me to write about him only by his first name, John, because he was about to be promoted to a permanent position) said that Microsoft's breakneck pace reflected a "buy and burn" personnel policy.

"They get fresh, naïve college graduates and run them into the ground," he said.

Instead of having workers simply plunge into projects and work longer and harder until the dreaded deadline arrives, John said that products should be planned in advance, be carefully scheduled, and be analyzed after they're completed. The result, John said, would be better software, with fewer of the defects that the testers could catch if they had more time to conduct quality control.

John's views were in keeping with McConnell's findings (in fact, he had introduced me to the software guru's works). McConnell contended that about 75 percent of software project teams get going on their projects without planning for how they will schedule the work, test their products, and correct the defects. He calls this "the code-and-fix approach" and compares it to "hurling themselves against the block and trying to move it with brute force." Because of this poor planning, he wrote, "40–80 percent of a typical software project's budget goes into fixing defects that were created earlier on the same project."

When told about John's views, several other software testers, including two leaders of WashTech, agreed. But their immediate problems at Microsoft were so overwhelming—and their opportunities for offering ideas to management were so limited—that when the temporary employees did protest Microsoft's policies, they concentrated on how they could be treated better, not on how they could do their jobs better.

6

"AREN'T WE TECHNOLOGY WORKERS?"

In 1990, the IRS ruled that Microsoft had misclassified its short-term employees as independent contractors. Microsoft responded by offering some of these workers permanent positions. But the company shifted most of the temp workers to the payrolls of staffing agencies, where they would still be working part time for minimal benefits.

Fifty years ago, aggrieved workers would have asked a union to help them. With the decline of unions, however, people with gripes against corporations have been turning to trial lawyers instead. This changing perception of who champions the ordinary citizen is reflected in popular culture. As recently as the 1970s, the attractive young actress Sally Fields played Norma Rae, a courageous textile worker who organized a union in her mill. By the 1990s, the attractive young actress Julia Roberts played Erin Brockovich, a courageous single mom who did the research for a lawsuit that challenged toxic waste dumping in her community. Social conflict, or so it seemed, had moved indoors, from the picket line to the courtroom.

JUSTICE DELAYED

So several Microsoft workers called on a Seattle law firm, Bendich, Stobaugh and Strong, that had recently been in the news for winning a lawsuit filed by temporary employees in the county government. This was a new kind of law firm that resembled a public interest group. It specialized in one issue: the problems of temporary workers. Several years later, it hired a community activist, David West, to study temp workers' issues and locate potential beneficiaries of the firm's lawsuits. Eventually, the firm founded its own think tank, the Center for a Changing Workforce, which did research and advocacy about temp workers' problems and maintained its own Web site, cfcw.org.

When David Stobaugh, a founding partner in the firm, met the temp workers, he soon concluded that they were serious people with legitimate grievances. Their faith in Microsoft had been shaken, first by the IRS decision and then by the company's insistence on finding a new way to keep them off its regular payroll. "When someone in authority tells you that you have been misclassified, it makes you think about things you didn't think about before," he later recalled.[1]

After the firm investigated the temp workers' situation, a strategy suggested itself. The temp workers were performing jobs similar to those of permanent employees, but they were not receiving the same benefits, especially the stock-purchasing plan that had made some Microsoft employees millionaires. In 1992, the firm filed a class action suit in behalf of Microsoft's temporary employees, challenging their exclusion from pensions, other benefits, and the employee stock-purchase plan.

As could be expected from a legal action against a company with enormous resources, the case took eight years to reach a conclusion and even longer before the temp workers received their benefit checks. At first, a district court judge in Seattle "batted down the lawsuit," as Stobaugh put it, requesting further arguments from the law firm and the company. Then, in 1996, another judge from the federal Ninth Circuit ruled in favor of the temp workers. Microsoft appealed the decision, but in 1999, the Ninth Circuit Court of Appeals issued another decision against Microsoft. It was time for Microsoft and the law firm to begin negotiations to settle the case, and on December 13, 2000, Microsoft agreed to pay $97 million to thousands of temporary workers who had been barred from the employee stock-ownership plan.

Then, still more problems emerged. Who were the temp workers who should benefit from the settlement? And where could they be found?

Maintaining the fiction that the temp workers weren't its employees, Microsoft did not keep records of their names and addresses. As for the dozens of staffing agencies that Microsoft had used, most had lost track of the workers. So the law firm ended up working with various private researchers, as well as with WashTech, the fledgling union that some temp workers had founded in 1998, six years after the lawsuit had been filed but two years before it was settled.

Eventually, some eighty-five hundred beneficiaries were located, and in 2005, they began to receive checks, more than $8,000 per person. The temp workers received a total of about $72 million; the law firm, the settlement administrator, the researchers, investigators, and others split some $24 million.

Fifteen years after the temp workers first called on the trial lawyers, many of the temps were displeased with the process and even with the settlement. Some blamed the lawsuit for Microsoft's terminating many of the temps over the years and filling newly created permanent positions with job applicants who were new to the company but did better on their interviews, had better credentials, or simply seemed more like "Bill Clones."

As for the trial lawyers, they hardly fit the stereotype of slick, self-serving shysters who care more about their fees than about their clients. Gaunt and scholarly, Stobaugh was remarkably reflective when he discussed the case with me after the last of the beneficiaries had gotten their checks. When it comes to representing aggrieved workers, he suggested, labor unions and trial lawyers both have a part to play. Since unions should be responsive to their members and concerned with the survival of their employers as well, they are best suited to negotiating with management to improve conditions for workers. But since "unions are future-oriented," the trial lawyer continued, they are "not oriented to rectifying past injustices." Fifteen-year back-pay battles, he concluded, are best handled by outside law firms, while unions help to focus on "the future."

By the middle of the 1990s, while the case was crawling through the courts, growing numbers of temp workers were worrying about their futures. Erin Brockovich's star turn was getting stale, and an unlikely Norma Rae was waiting in the wings.

"THESE FOLKS SHOWED UP AT OUR DOORSTEP"

"These folks just showed up at our doorstep one day," recalled Jonathan Rosenblum, an organizer for the King County Labor Council, which represents local unions in Seattle and its suburbs. "They said they had been to a number of unions, but 'Nobody wants us.'" In his thirties himself, youthful in appearance, and brimming with nervous energy, Rosenblum was intrigued by the prospect of establishing a beachhead in the high-tech industry's flagship company—"the Holy Grail of union organizing," as he later called it.[2]

"These folks" were temporary employees at Microsoft, and on September 26, 1997, they had come to the Labor Temple—an old brick building in Seattle's waterfront district where many unions had their offices—to see whether any would help them organize their coworkers. In their twenties or thirties, the three visitors plied trades that were unheard of decades ago when the Labor Temple started to display photos of unionized craft workers. Mike Blain edited technical manuals about how to use software. Heather McCrae wrote articles for *Encarta*, an encyclopedia that existed only on the Internet. April Grayson tested software. All three were temporary employees at Microsoft.

At that time, except for the class action lawsuit that was then in its seventh year, there was little discussion outside of Microsoft about the problems of its temporary employees. The three workers patiently explained the intricacies of their situations. Officially, they worked for one of forty staffing agencies, not for Microsoft. They were paid between $10 and $40 an hour. They were excluded from Microsoft's picnics, clubs, and discount stores. "Respect, not pay, is the primary issue," Rosenblum concluded.

The visitors to the Labor Temple insisted that many other temp workers at Microsoft were ready to join an organization of some sort. In fact, they'd already collected the names of almost four thousand other workers, along with their phone numbers, e-mail addresses, and the names of their staffing agencies. Although it wasn't clear whether these four thousand workers were as disgruntled as Blain, McCrae, and Grayson or simply were part of a file that the three had somehow acquired, such a "list" is a valuable resource in organizing campaigns. But the three temp workers were by no means certain what they wanted to do with their complaints and their contacts. "Initially, our idea was not to create a union but to create a Web site that would provide technology workers with information about agencies, benefits, training, and so on," Blain recalled several years later.

For his part, Rosenblum understood that it wouldn't be easy for the temp workers to "create a union," even if they wanted to. To the extent that they are enforced at all, the nation's labor laws apply only to workers with a common employer—for instance, the production workers at Boeing. Since the National Labor Relations Act of 1935, most union organizing followed a script that was set forth in the law: Collect "authorization cards" from a majority of the workers in similar jobs at one company, such as blue-collar workers at Kaiser Aluminum. Win an election supervised by the federal National Labor Relations Board for the workers in this "bargaining unit." Negotiate a contract with the company, which improves the workers' pay, fringe benefits, and working conditions.

But federal labor law said nothing about workers like the young people from Microsoft, temporary employees who are paid by staffing agencies. For these workers, the clock had stopped before 1935—or it had fast-forwarded to a postmodern, postindustrial era where no one worked in the same place for too long or even knew for sure who the boss was. Until federal labor law catches up with the modern workplace, the most these workers can do is what angry workers did decades before the formalization of labor relations in the United States—put pressure on whoever can improve their conditions. Often, that means creating a nuisance for the companies where they work, not the companies that sign their paychecks. For instance, janitors are employed by cleaning companies that usually don't have much cash on hand and frequently go out of business. In order to get pay raises, health coverage, and recognition of their unions, janitors have held huge demonstrations against the real estate magnates who own the buildings where they work and who hire the cleaning companies. Rosenblum had worked for the Service Employees International Union (SEIU), which conducted these "Justice for Janitors" campaigns across the country.

So, as the meeting continued, he thought of a more upscale version of Justice for Janitors—Solidarity in Software?—that would embarrass Microsoft into improving conditions for its temporary employees. Because these workers were tech-savvy and eager to create their own Web site, their movement might agitate in cyberspace, not in the streets. With Blain being a former journalist, the agitation might take the form of muckraking about Microsoft. And since tech workers were used to trolling the Internet to find useful information, the Web site could offer useful advice about skills training, career opportunities, and understanding the increasingly baroque employment policies at Microsoft and the staffing agencies.

At this point, the fledgling protest movement at Microsoft might have gone anywhere—or nowhere. Eventually, it would become a new kind of employee organization, long on media savvy but short on actual dues-paying members, that is affiliated with one of the nation's faster-growing and more future-oriented national unions. The direction that the group would take was partly the result of an organizer doing his job so subtly that years later, no one quite remembers whose ideas influenced the group's decisions about its structure, its purposes, and even its name.

After the meeting was over, Rosenblum went to his computer keyboard and tapped out a memo to his boss, Ron Judd, the president of the King County Labor Council. "A campaign to organize Microsoft contract workers would challenge us to think outside of traditional approaches, relationships and legal guidelines," Rosenblum wrote. "For instance, NLRB [National Labor Relations Board] elections would be useless. We would have to organize the contract workers as a group and make common demands on the agencies (and, by extension, Microsoft). . . . New forms of electronic communication, public action, and legal challenges are all tactics that could be applied in an organizing drive." A former tour guide on Mount Rainier who'd found work in the winters as an electrician in Seattle, Judd was interested in new initiatives for the unions, and he asked Rosenblum to keep working with the Microsoft temps.

Soon Rosenblum was playing matchmaker as well as strategist for the Microsoft temps. Before working for the King County Labor Council, he had worked for Jobs with Justice (JwJ), a national campaign that mobilizes union members to support one another's struggles. JwJ was the brainchild of one of the labor movement's most imaginative and eclectic strategists, Larry Cohen, who was the organizing director of the Communications Workers of America (CWA), a union representing workers in the telecommunications industry. A month after the meeting at the Labor Temple, Rosenblum attended a JwJ conference in Chicago. Buttonholing

Cohen, whom he'd known for several years, Rosenblum mentioned that he'd met a group of temporary workers at Microsoft who were interested in organizing. He suggested that CWA help them out in the hope of establishing a presence in the flourishing but almost entirely nonunion high-tech industry.

Most union leaders would have been reluctant to reach out to a group of workers who didn't have steady jobs, weren't covered by federal labor laws, and worked for a large and respected corporation with limitless resources. But Cohen was receptive. With the court-ordered breakup of AT&T in 1984, CWA had been organizing workers throughout the communications and information technology industries. The union had some success in the regional "Baby Bell" companies and the wireless phone industries. Also, CWA had affiliated with the Newspaper Guild, which represents reporters, as well as the National Association of Broadcast Employees and Technicians, which represents TV, cable, and sound-recording employees. But telecommunications, broadcasting, and media were "converging" into new ways of transmitting, processing, and storing information, using computer terminals or even cell phones. Soon, CWA would be up against high-tech companies like Microsoft, with flexible corporate structures that would be difficult to unionize with traditional tactics that relied on federal labor laws.

As CWA's chief organizer, Cohen had experimented with assisting employee organizations at IBM and in Texas's state government. Similar to the new group of Microsoft temps, these organizations had no immediate prospects for winning formal collective bargaining rights and therefore functioned more as advocacy groups than as conventional unions. More than most union leaders, Cohen was fascinated by the challenge of creating new kinds of organizations for workers in emerging industries and unconventional work situations. As he told me in an interview in 1999, "If you strip away what unions are really about, they're about building organizations. At their soul, they're not just about contracts and representation elections, important as those are."[3] So Cohen was receptive to the pitch that Rosenblum made in Chicago: "If the labor movement is ever going to organize in high tech, someone's going to have to invest for years." Years later, Rosenblum recalled, "Larry was very visionary about it. He said, 'There has to be some showing of interest [by the Microsoft workers], but we'll put the resources in to make it happen.'" (In 2006, Cohen was elected the national president of the CWA, one of a new breed of union presidents who had made their reputations as organizing directors. Others in this category included Andrew Stern of the SEIU; Bruce Raynor of the garment and textile workers' union, UNITE; and John Wilhelm of the hotel and restaurant union, HERE. UNITE and HERE later merged into one union, UNITE-HERE.)

Andrea Demajewski, a CWA organizer in Seattle, reached out to Blain and his group. So did several other unions, including the National Writers Union, a group of freelance writers that was loosely affiliated with the United Auto Workers (UAW), and the International Federation of Professional and Technical Engineers (IFPTE), which would soon affiliate with the professional association representing the engineers at Boeing. But neither the UAW nor the IFPTE offered Blain's group the resources that CWA promised to provide, so, eventually, the Microsoft workers went with the telecommunications union. In its characteristically quirky way, the group formally affiliated with the Newspaper Guild, which in turn had affiliated with CWA.

Since its founding, the group had called itself the "Coordinating Committee on High-Tech Labor Issues," a difficult name to pronounce, much less remember. One day that winter, a few of the group's members were sitting around with Rosenblum, trying to come up with a catchier name. Marcus Courtney, a software tester who'd just joined the group, said, "Well, aren't we Washington State Technology Workers?" Then, either Courtney or Rosenblum asked, "Why not WashTech?" Now, the group had a name. By that time, it also had a cause.

WORKING OVERTIME

Late in November, the temp workers learned that Microsoft was quietly convincing Washington's state government to stop requiring that temps be paid time and a half for working more than forty hours a week. Without premium pay for overtime work, most of Microsoft's temporary employees stood to lose thousands of dollars. For instance, if a worker made $30 an hour, time and a half meant that she'd earn an extra $450 for working an additional ten hours in one week—$150 more than she'd get if the new rule went into effect. The temp workers needed the extra money, which usually came in the final weeks of their assignments when their teams worked late into the night to get their software products completed, tested, and out the door. Besides, the temps figured, if they were going to work around the clock just before they were terminated, they deserved some big paychecks in return as a sort of severance package from the world's wealthiest company.

For the temp workers, the process by which the rule was being enacted was almost as infuriating as the money they'd lose. Written in impenetrably legalistic language, the rule was sailing through an obscure state agency at the urging of a little-known lobbying group and without the workers who would be hurt having the opportunity to comment on it. Only when they read the *Seattle Times* on December 5 did the workers realize what was going on behind their backs. The state's Department of Labor and Industry had just closed the "comment period" on a proposed rule change that would exempt from overtime "any employee who is a computer-system analyst, computer programmer, software engineer, software developer or other similarly skilled worker" earning at least $27.63 per hour. The exemption was being proposed by a low-profile trade association, the Washington Software and Digital Media Alliance, whose largest member, Microsoft, just happened to be the state's leading employer of contract software professionals. Supposedly, the rule had been publicized, the public had been invited to comment, and a hearing had been held. But almost all of Microsoft's temp workers had never heard of the proposed rule, and now they were told it was too late to do anything about it.

In just a few days, workers at Microsoft and other high-tech companies deluged the Department of Labor and Industry with angry e-mails, prompting it to reopen the comment period until February 1. Of the first 183 e-mails to the department, 73 were from current or former temporary employees of Microsoft, while most of the other messages were from temp workers at other companies.

Over the next two months, with Blain's group taking the lead, more than 750 Microsoft temps sent e-mails to the department opposing the change in the overtime rules. Coming from workers who had been stereotyped as nerds and geeks, many of the messages revealed remarkable anger, directed not only against the rule and the process by which it was being railroaded through the state Department of Labor and Industry but also against the ways in which Microsoft made the temps work day and night before laying them off and now was making sure that it wouldn't have to pay them at a higher rate for their extra hours.

One temp wrote, "My one, single, only protection against abuse, exploitation, and professional burnout is overtime pay." Another added, "It's a binge-purge kind of existence." Meanwhile, another worker wrote, "Not long ago, a [software] developer in my building was found dead at his desk. The ambulance wasn't called immediately because his workers just thought he was asleep. It's not unusual for somebody to be asleep in their office, having worked all night trying to make some milestone or other. The entire company deliberately operates in a mode of high critical stress."

Dead at his desk after working long hours—the Japanese have a word for it, *karooshi*. Now, the death-by-overwork that afflicted Japanese "salarymen" had crossed the Pacific to legendarily laid-back Seattle. Remarkably, the letter writer, Jay French, hadn't even considered this story remarkable, having told it in the fifth paragraph of a seven-page letter. In conclusion, he warned, "With its famous predatory business practices, Microsoft will immediately begin insisting on 60 or 80 hour weeks from its contractors. Those who refuse will find their contracts suddenly aren't renewed." Underneath his signature, French identified himself as "Online software documentation contractor currently under contract with Microsoft Corporation (contract expires January 10)."

In spite of the outpouring of opposition, on February 1 the department approved the rule change anyway, leaving the temps poorer just before they got their termination notices. Using the Freedom of Information Act, Blain's group collected the names and the e-mail addresses of the people who had protested the rules change, adding them to the list of potential supporters for what would soon become WashTech. While techies traditionally are skeptical of unions, the Washington Software and Digital Media Alliance's influence over state government convinced many Microsoft workers that they needed some kind of organization of their own. As Blain said at the time, "The L&I [Department of Labor and Industry] decision is a symptom of a larger problem. The industry can ask for something else six months from now and they'll probably get it because there is no countervailing voice, no workers' representation."

"I WANT TO BE PART OF SOMETHING"

Over the next two months, the group began to call itself WashTech, affiliated with the Newspaper Guild and the CWA, and prepared for a public debut. Working with the King County Labor Council and with Rosenblum as an organizational guru, WashTech held six public meetings at the Labor Temple, inviting workers whose names were on its original list or who had sent e-mails protesting the changes in the overtime regulations.

Combining old-fashioned labor radicalism and new-fangled Internet activism, WashTech formally waited until springtime to announce that it was beginning a drive to organize tech workers in the Seattle area, starting with the temporary employees at Microsoft. The day was May 1—the international workers holiday, which Seattle's labor radicals had celebrated at the turn of the twentieth century. But WashTech's most important announcement was the launch of its Web site, the new arena for activism at the turn of the twenty-first century. On its first day, the Web site reported on the class-action lawsuit, the overtime pay controversy, and WashTech's goals, which included sick pay, paid holidays, and health coverage for the temp workers.

At a news conference unveiling the Web site, Marcus Courtney explained why the notoriously individualistic tech workers were taking a new look at unions. "When we explored the potential of an organization like this," Courtney said, "we heard people saying, 'I'm not part of a company, and I'm not part of an agency, but I want to be part of something.'" From its first day through the years ahead, however, WashTech had only several hundred dues-paying members. What would keep growing was the number of tech workers in Seattle and throughout the nation who would visit its Web site and subscribe to its e-mail alerts.

By now, WashTech's leaders resembled Microsoft's whiz kids—young, male, workaholic, and intensely competitive. Of the women who had helped to found the group, almost all had drifted away to destinations that hinted at the unusual paths the organization might have followed had they remained. Heather McCrae moved to New York City, where she studied moviemaking. Years later, she directed an award-winning film, *Whatever Floats Your Boat,* about a thirty-two-year-old woman whose husband dies, who wonders whether she would or should ever have kids, and who invites eleven of her friends to get together to talk about the pros and cons of motherhood. April Grayson, who had studied film years earlier, moved back to Mississippi, where she went to work for a project promoting racial reconciliation. Andrea Demajewski quit what she called "the incredibly demanding" work of union organizing to become a postal worker and write fiction in her spare time. Yet another talented woman, Gretchen Wilson, was an organizer for WashTech during its early years but later became a journalist in Africa.

Compared to these renaissance women, WashTech's remaining leaders were more narrowly focused. Of the three temps who wandered into the Labor Temple, only Mike Blain remained. His background gave him a rare perspective on how Microsoft employees could benefit from organizing. After the techies, the second-largest group of temps was the writers and the editors, and Blain's work history reflected their range of experiences. At Microsoft, he'd started as a "content editor" at the online encyclopedia *Encarta* and then became a technical editor, earning $30 an hour. Before working at Microsoft, he'd been a reporter for daily newspapers in the Bay Area in Northern California. As he later observed, the reporters at these papers had not been unionized, and the first time that he belonged to the Newspaper Guild was as a member of WashTech. Early in his twenties, he had been a construction worker, belonging to the Laborers' union and making more money than he'd earn as a reporter. When techies were doubtful about joining WashTech, he told them about his own work history and pointed out, "It says something that I could make as much pouring concrete as working on a newspaper."[4]

Increasingly, WashTech's most visible leader was a relative newcomer, Marcus Courtney. An authentic techie, he had worked in the software industry for four years, including two years at Microsoft. As a temporary software testing engineer, he had helped to develop Windows 98, the most recent edition of the company's flagship product. Blain and Courtney would become WashTech's leadership team, each holding the title of codirector. Although Blain would resign in 2001, leaving Courtney alone at the helm, they worked well together for several years, with their differences in emphasis and style complementing each other.

As Barbara Judd, one of the few women in WashTech's leadership, said several years after Blain left, he and Courtney seemed almost like a TV anchor team or a comedy duo, paired together because they look, think, talk, and behave very differently. Tall and wiry, Blain was "the more quiet, studious, and intellectual" of the two, she observed, as well as being several years older. Shorter, stockier, and already balding, Courtney was twenty-seven in 1998 but was personable, articulate, and organizationally savvy beyond his years. "Marcus is young, driven, and energetic," Judd said. "Mike is the writer. Marcus is the speaker."[5]

For all his experience as a union member, Blain remained a journalist at heart. Having originally intended WashTech to be a Web magazine for information technology workers, he continued to see the organization's role as exposing unfair practices by Microsoft and other employers, causing the companies to change their ways and encouraging employees to sign up with WashTech as subscribers, if not active members. When I interviewed Blain in 1999, he was most animated when discussing WashTech's muckraking and sounded more like a city editor than a union organizer. "We get internal company documents ahead of time and notify people of pending policy changes," he said. "Last July, Microsoft implemented a new policy that said if you were on an assignment for twelve months or longer as a temporary employee, you had to leave for a month. . . . We found out about it before it happened. We posted the story on our Web site. A lot of the staffing agencies didn't even know about it. We broke that story, and it got picked up by the *Seattle Times*."

During the same interview, Blain perceptively pointed out the weakness in WashTech's strategy of building an organization by breaking news stories. "People now think we're a reliable source of news, but they won't join," he admitted. In 1998, more than two thousand workers gave the group their home e-mail addresses so that they could receive WashTech's online newsletter, and this subscription list grew tenfold over the next seven years. Tens of thousands more visited WashTech's Web site, with the largest single flow of traffic coming from Microsoft's own headquarters and many more hits presumably coming from Microsoft workers at home. But little more than two hundred workers joined WashTech as formal members, and their ranks scarcely increased during the years ahead. For all the sense of belonging that was seemingly lacking in the lives of Microsoft's temporary employees, they seemed more comfortable with the virtual community of WashTech's Web site than with the actual community of its meetings. Of course, some temp workers did crave the community of meeting their disgruntled colleagues in person.

As David Larsen said, "Before WashTech, I was a lonely, grumpy guy. After WashTech, I found hundreds of people in the same boat. It wasn't just me."

7

"I KNOW WHAT IT'S LIKE TO
BE TREATED REASONABLY"

By breaking stories on its Web site, planting articles in the
Seattle newspapers, and conducting petition drives among
Microsoft workers, WashTech called attention to some of the
temp workers' worst problems. Remarkably, Microsoft and the staffing agencies changed some of their policies, although they never
acknowledged that anyone had pressured them into doing it and
instead insisted that the changes followed from their concern for
their employees. Was Microsoft really responding to being embar-
rassed in the news media? Or to the class action lawsuit? Or to
pressure from the public officials who were becoming increasingly
attentive to the plight of the growing number of temp workers in
Washington State? Or to the threat of unionization, farfetched as it
might have seemed? Nobody knew, and Microsoft never revealed
its reasons.

The secretiveness of Microsoft and the staffing agencies was
at the heart of two of the temp workers' complaints. The agencies
wouldn't reveal how much they charged Microsoft for "payrolling"
the temp workers, and Microsoft wouldn't reveal whether it kept
personnel files on the temp workers.

Secret Personnel Files: "If Asked, Lie"

The staffing agencies charged Microsoft for the total cost of hiring, paying, and providing minimal levels of benefits to the temp workers. Microsoft knew, but the temp workers never learned, how much the agencies kept for themselves. These mysterious charges came to be called their "agency fees," "billing rates," or "bill rates," with some of the angrier temps favoring the latter phrase because it reminded them of their real boss, Bill Gates. Sometimes supervisors at Microsoft recommended raises for their temp workers, and Microsoft increased its payments to its staffing agencies to cover the raises. Months later, the supervisors often wondered why the temps hadn't thanked them for their pay increases. Awkwardly, they asked the temps how they liked their raises, and it turned out that the temps had never gotten their increases or had received much less than their supervisors had requested because their staffing agencies had pocketed the extra money.

As one of its first campaigns, WashTech conducted a petition drive demanding disclosure of the "bill rates." When Microsoft and the staffing agencies refused, WashTech shared the story with the Seattle's daily newspapers, the *Times* and the *Post-Intelligencer*, each of which ran stories. Early in 2000, several state legislators introduced a bill requiring that the staffing agencies disclose to the workers, with each payment of their wages, how much they are charging companies such as Microsoft for their work.

Meanwhile, the temp workers were also worried about who kept their personnel files—Microsoft or the staffing agencies. For years, temp workers who wanted raises, promotions, or recommendations for other jobs requested formal performance reviews from their supervisors at Microsoft. Almost invariably, the temps were told to get their reviews from their "employers of record"— their staffing agencies. For instance, Barbara Judd, an accountant who worked as a temporary employee in the software giant's new Tax Saver Unit, received this breezy brush-off from someone in Microsoft's Contingent Staffing Group, which managed the temp workers:[1]

Hi Barbara,
Microsoft does not maintain personnel files for employees of temporary agencies. Please contact your agency if you wish to request a copy of any personnel file the agency may maintain.

Thanks! Christina

When the temps contacted their agencies, they were lucky to find someone who knew who they were and, after much hemming and hawing, would pass along some comments that obviously came from their supervisors at Microsoft.

As Courtney explained, here's how the system worked: "Your staffing agency representative would send an evaluation form to your manager at Microsoft. The manager would fill out the form and send it back to your agency. If you asked the agency for your evaluation, then your rep would call you on the phone and read the manager's comments to you. Most agency reps were just regurgitating what the manager had written on the form." In addition to its impenetrability, the process infuriated the temps because it revealed how little Microsoft actually cared about the quality of their work—as far as the company knew, they were interchangeable grunt workers, valued mostly for their high turnover and low wages.

The staffing agencies, after all, would have had no idea how well the temps were doing their jobs unless someone at Microsoft told them. So, understandably, many of the temps suspected that Microsoft was really keeping its own files on their job performance. As it turned out, such secrets are hard to hide from computer-savvy employees at a company where most records are stored in the very computer networks that the workers use on their jobs. In the fall of 1999, while working on the Microsoft corporate network, an employee either stumbled on or hacked into a database that secretly tracked the performance of each temp worker. Soon, the word got out that employees could visit the database and review their records. As Barbara Judd remembered, "There was a heading on each file that read—eligible, eligible with feedback, or ineligible. The workers had no idea that these files were being kept on them and obviously had no way to refute anything in them."

On October 26, in one of its greatest journalistic coups, WashTech's Web site broke the story with the headline, "Microsoft Keeps Secret Personnel Files" and the subhead "Microsoft's 'If Asked, Lie' Policy." Microsoft responded by cutting off access to the database. But this time, the company was unable to persuade the state to uphold its policies. In mid-December 1999, WashTech asked the state Department of Labor and Industries to determine whether the temp workers had the right to examine the personnel records that Microsoft kept on them. On January 25, 2000, the department ruled that the company must show the workers their records because it is "their co-employer," along with the staffing agencies. WashTech rightly claimed that it had won a victory for the temps.

More often, Microsoft would suddenly make small but significant improvements in conditions for the temps, taking care to avoid the appearance that the company was giving in to pressure from the courts, the class action lawsuit, state agencies, WashTech, or anyone else. The timing of these announcements and Microsoft's reasons for taking action were left mysterious. As Blain explained, "Microsoft doesn't tell people what it's doing until it does it, and then it doesn't tell you why it did what it did."

Thus, late in 1998, Microsoft asked its staffing agencies to provide at least a minimal level of employee benefits, including thirteen days of paid annual leave each year, a matching 401k retirement plan, and annual tuition reimbursement of up to $500. The staffing agencies were also encouraged to pay up to half the cost of workers' medical, dental, and vision plans.

For its first two years, WashTech engaged in a type of shad-owboxing with Microsoft, exposing problems in the hope of enlisting support from the temps and prompting the company to improve conditions. Meanwhile, the group's leaders seemed almost too comfortable with their growing roles as media stars, breaking stories on their Web site, spinning sound bites to the newspapers, and being interviewed on national and international outlets. After all, as the 1990s came to a close, it seemed that every media outlet was doing a story about the glories of a new high-tech economy and its corporate poster child, Microsoft. If reporters wanted an opposing point of view—someone who'd say, "Hey, wait a minute, things aren't that great for the worker bees"—there was no one to interview except the malcontents from WashTech. Not only Courtney and Blain but rank-and-file members were becoming practiced quote-meisters. On the day that I first met Larsen, he had already done interviews across the journalistic spectrum, having spoken with the *Wall Street Journal*, which Bill Gates himself might read with his morn-ing cup of Starbucks coffee, and *L'Humanité*, the journal of the French Communist Party.

But functioning like a traditional labor union—winning a fed-erally supervised election to represent the workers and bargaining with Microsoft for better pay and benefits—seemed hopelessly out of reach. Under federal law, Microsoft's fragmented work-force was not a legitimate "bargaining unit." Instead, WashTech assumed, it would have to win separate elections for a clearly defined group of employees: those who worked on one of the company's projects or were "payrolled" by one of its staffing agencies.

To set this process in motion, some workers would have to step forward and risk their jobs to try to bring formal union represen-tation and collective bargaining to Microsoft. Someone did, and she wasn't a typical temp with little to lose—a twenty-something single man. She wasn't a techie, a refugee from journalism, or a disgruntled drifter. She even had an MBA.

NORMA RAE WITH AN MBA

Microsoft's Norma Rae turned out to be in her late forties, married with children, and working in an unlikely bastion of unionism: a new project to develop software to help people do their taxes.

In 1998, Barbara Judd was one of sixty temps who went to work at Microsoft in 1998 to help the company develop a software product that would compete with Intuit's successful TurboTax program. Her skills seemed ideal for the assignment. While working as a financial analyst and, before that, a tax preparer, she had "started learning computer skills twenty years ago" and had taught herself several programming languages. Before coming to Microsoft, she had worked at a tax software company in Bellevue.

She'd taken a temporary position at Microsoft in the hope of getting a foot in the door for a permanent position. "My take on temp work has always been that it's a good way to prove yourself to an employer," she later explained. "Plus, it was a chance to work on a piece of software from the ground up. It's always more exciting to build than it is to fix. I saw that job as a chance for me to be a pioneer."

So she went to work with Microsoft's Tax Saver Unit, a group of twenty temp workers who were mostly financial professionals with computer skills. Judd had a master's of business administration, as did several others. The team also included several attorneys and certified public accounts. Their assignment, as Judd put it, was to "take the federal tax code and interpret it into software."

Despite their formidable credentials and serious responsibilities, they all were temps, "payrolled" through four different staffing agencies. Most of them earned between $30 and $35 an hour. When they started at Microsoft, most of them did not receive sick pay, none of them received stock options, and Judd's health plan cost her $300 a month.

"I figured I'd spend six months as a temp, and then I'd be hired," she later recalled. Like many temps, once she realized "that just wasn't going to happen," she stopped thinking of a permanent career at Microsoft.

Still, there was much that she liked about her work. Munching tortilla chips in Azteca, a popular restaurant near the Microsoft campus, in March 2000, she described her work almost as if it were a kind of play: "One of the things we do all day is solve puzzles. It's a collaborative process—we puzzle out things together."

The work was so interesting and the team members got along so well that it took them a while to become discontented with the ways that Microsoft and their staffing agencies were treating them. When they did become dissatisfied, first they contacted their staffing agencies, then they complained to Microsoft, and only as a last resort did they reach out to WashTech.

Ironically, it all began when Microsoft announced that it was improving conditions for the temp workers. In 1998, soon after the Tax Saver project began, Microsoft announced its new policy that all of the staffing agencies would be required to offer a basic level of benefits.

Judd and several colleagues who were payrolled through Volt Accounting wanted to find out when they would be getting their new benefits. At their request, their manager e-mailed Volt. The staffing agency's answer contradicted Microsoft's announcement and angered Judd and her coworkers. "The testers would be getting some benefits that we wouldn't get—that was the needle," she remembered. Other members of the Tax Saver Unit called their staffing agencies, and most got the same response: their agencies weren't giving them new benefits, either. Then, they started to call and e-mail management officials at Microsoft. Almost all of the officials were friendly but said that it was up to the staffing agencies to improve the temps' benefits.

Soon, over coffee in the cafeteria, the accountants, lawyers, and techies in the Tax Saver Unit started to talk about Microsoft's most unmentionable subject—not sex, but paychecks. "We learned that people were making between $17 and $34 an hour for doing similar jobs," Judd recalled. Their pay scales didn't seem to depend on their credentials, their responsibilities, or their experience, merely which staffing agency they had been assigned to when they started. "We wanted a job classification review," Judd remembered later. "We wanted our jobs reviewed and our pay equalized." Once again, they contacted their staffing agencies and then their supervisor, but nothing seemed to happen.

DO YOU REALLY WANT TO JOIN?

By now, it was March 1999—the height of the tax preparation period but the beginning of a slack season in developing tax preparation software. Fifteen of the temps from the Tax Saver Unit had dinner at Azteca. "There was a general conversation about the benefits being unfair," recalled a young lawyer in the unit with the improbable name Squire Dahl. "We talked about unfair pay scales and people doing the same jobs as others but making twice as much."

"Either that night, or shortly thereafter, we talked about WashTech," Dahl remembered. "Barbara Judd was interested in it. At some point shortly afterward, we decided that someone would connect with WashTech."

"Someone" turned out to be yet another Tax Saver temp, Debbie (not her real name). She called Marcus Courtney, and early in May, twelve of the eighteen temporary employees in the Tax Saver Unit had lunch with him. This being Microsoft, where the supervisors are friendly and the soft drinks are free, the lunch was held in a company cafeteria, and no one remembered lowering their voices or looking anxiously over their shoulders to make sure that management wasn't listening in.

Over burgers and salads, Courtney began to give his usual, low-key, let's-get-acquainted pitch. Noticing that his audience was getting restless, he wondered whether he was coming on too strong.

He began to lighten up on his criticisms of Microsoft and his appeal for the temps to take a new look at joining an organization of their own. Then he noticed a rustling at the table. "Everyone started passing checks down to him," Judd recalled. "He looked shocked."

The checks were made out to WashTech. Some were for $11, WashTech's monthly dues, and some were for $121, the annual dues. Almost unbelievably, Courtney asked, "Do you all want to join WashTech?" The members of the group nodded their heads or answered yes, they did want to join WashTech.

At that first meeting, no one asked Courtney what they should do next. "We had no idea at the time that the National Labor Relations Act leaves temporary workers out," Judd recalled years afterward. "I asked Marcus about that later. He made some remark about, if he told us we couldn't organize, then what would we have done? And he grinned."

In the weeks ahead, several of the Tax Saver employees spoke with Courtney and did their own research on federal labor law. They concluded that their best chance at organizing was to form separate units at each of their four staffing agencies and to ask the agencies to recognize WashTech as their representative. At a second meeting with Courtney, as Dahl recalled, the union leader distributed official cards for the temp workers to sign authorizing WashTech to serve as their representative in collective bargaining. Eventually, sixteen of the eighteen temps signed the cards. Then they selected two of their colleagues to talk to the agencies. Their two delegates were Judd and Dahl.

Years later, Judd recalled that her stint as a union organizer "allowed the adolescent rebel in me to come out." But while she, like Larsen, had come of age in the 1960s, her manner suggested responsibility, not rebelliousness. If growing up in the sixties and seventies had left a mark on her, it was her mellowness. She favored blue jeans, T-shirts, and running shoes; enjoyed a glass of wine or a bottle of beer at lunch; spoke wistfully of moving to Northern California; and treated new acquaintances like old friends. But she also had taken care to do what the gurus of the new economy advised professionals to do: keep learning new skills, acquiring new credentials, and accepting challenging assignments. Her slowly growing disenchantment with Microsoft resulted from her sense that the company wasn't holding up its end of the deal and instead was treating adult employees as if they were adolescents.

"I know what it's like to be treated reasonably," Judd explained. Before temping at Microsoft, she had been a CPA who had regular jobs at various accounting, financial services, and software development companies. Her husband was a member of a craft union, the International Brotherhood of Electrical Workers (IBEW), who had recently retired from the local electrical utility, Seattle Power and Light. Decent salaries, regular raises, health insurance, vacation days, and a pension plan—these were what she expected from her job in return for keeping her skills current and making her best effort.

Judd also understood that at many high-tech companies, the jobs were drifting toward two extremes: temporary positions with low pay and few benefits and superstar perches with six-figure salaries and lavish stock options. While Judd was starting out at Microsoft, her daughter, who was then in her early twenties, worked at a dot-com in San Francisco, often putting in "twenty-hour days and seven-day weeks," as she explained at the time. But Judd's daughter's pay and benefits were no better than her mother's, and after it turned out that "the CEO had lied on the income statement," the company collapsed, and Judd's daughter was out of work, with no savings.

Meanwhile, at the other extreme of the high-tech hierarchy, other young people were on their way toward acquiring wealth beyond their wildest dreams. Judd told the story about meeting one of Microsoft's permanent employees, also a woman in her twenties, near a photocopying machine. By looking at each other's badges, both women could tell where they fit into the corporate caste system. Trying to be friendly, the younger woman complained that she wanted to retire but was tied to Microsoft by "golden handcuffs"—stock options that hadn't yet vested but would eventually make her a millionaire. "Yeah, well," Judd said. "At least, you have health insurance."

Perhaps feeling maternal as well as collegial, Judd mentored a young man who eventually became her fellow worker representative. Named after a motorcycle racer, Squire Tamass, Squire Dahl was a recent law school graduate who took night courses in tax law. Hired as a temporary employee in the Tax Saver Unit and also payrolled through Volt, Dahl had no computer experience beyond doing word processing with a Macintosh computer. Judd took it upon herself to teach him computer skills, forging a friendship that would survive the union drive.[2]

Twenty-seven in 1998, Dahl later recalled, "I was a little intimidated by the whole Microsoft thing and excited to be there." But he soon became disillusioned not only with his pay but also with how he believed that Volt and Microsoft had misled him.

He had started at $16 an hour, with one week of vacation, no sick days, and a health insurance plan that required a substantial contribution from him. "Pretty soon I became really dissatisfied with my pay," he explained years later. When he was interviewed for his job, he said, "Volt told me a higher figure than what I was paid. . . . What I was told when I was interviewed was not the truth about what people were getting paid." When he got his first paycheck and asked his supervisor why he hadn't been paid what he had been promised, he was told, "CPAs get paid that, and you will be paid less." Several months later, at the dinner meeting at the Azteca, Dahl learned that he was the lowest-paid of all the temps at the Tax Saver Unit.

Then, in June 1999, armed with the authorization cards, Dahl and Judd made the rounds of the four staffing agencies that payrolled their coworkers, asking the agencies to recognize WashTech as their representative. "That was a trip all in itself," Judd said years afterward.

Six years later, Dahl still remembered the meeting with Volt, the agency that had payrolled him and Judd. "It was a big glass office," he recalled. "Barbara and I both knew the woman [who was in charge]. She was shocked. She ushered us out of the office." Still, Dahl remembered her being "cordial."

At another agency, Kelly, the reception was even less friendly. As Judd described it, "The man there didn't want to meet with us, so I told him, 'I'll be there on this time and this day.' He did meet with us. He was very angry and basically threatened that if we pursued organizing, we would be jeopardizing our overtime pay. It was very weird." Eventually, all four agencies sent Judd and Dahl letters saying that they did not recognize the temps' right to form a union.

But the organizing drive at the Tax Saver Unit started to attract the attention of other Microsoft workers, the news media, and the company itself. In a twenty-seven-paragraph article on June 4, the *Seattle Times* called the effort "a small but potentially significant breakthrough for organized labor . . . the first time software-company workers in Washington have formed a bargaining unit and sought collective bargaining." At the Tax Saver Unit, one of the supervisors asked Judd, in a matter-of-fact manner, "How much is this going to cost me?" Workers from other units at Microsoft often stopped Judd and Dahl in the hallways and wished them well.

Like Being Punched in the Stomach

Three weeks after the newspaper article appeared, Judd was reminded of how little respect many Microsoft officials had for the temps, their skills, and their contributions to the company. As a certified management accountant with a specialty in financial management, Judd was required to get thirty hours a year of continuing professional education in order to maintain her professional designations. Fortunately for her, or so she thought at first, the Institute of Management Accountants was holding its annual conference in Seattle during the last week in June. She could attend the conference, receive continuing education credits, and maintain her professional certifications.

As it happened, Microsoft's chief financial officer, Greg Maffei, was on the conference program as the keynote speaker. Judd attended his talk, and during questions from the floor, she asked him how Microsoft was responding to the series of lawsuits and court orders demanding that the company improve conditions for its temporary employees. In response, Maffei spoke candidly and contemptuously, first about the courts and then about the temporary workers themselves.

"There are nutty judges in this country to start with," Maffei began. Then he explained that there was a "tension" in converting some temps to full-time status. "We're very tough in hiring in terms of standards, but we weren't as tough on temps. So you [find] that the quality of the temps is not as good as the quality of the full-time people, so we really are having a hard time doing that conversion, even though we have allotted the temps for certain jobs we wouldn't necessarily have said we wanted them for full time."

"When he said it, I felt like I was being punched in the stomach," Judd remembered. "I thought, 'Oh my God, he doesn't know who he's talking to. He has no idea that there could be a temp worker who's a CPA and is attending this conference.'"

Judd obtained a tape recording of Maffei's response and brought it to the *Seattle Times*. For a few days, Maffei's dismissive remarks about the temps were a local news story, and Judd was a celebrity, interviewed in the newspapers and on television. In a news release the next day, Maffei apologized to the judges and the temps, declaring, "Let me be clear: I have tremendous respect for the courts and the employees of contingent staff companies that help us develop great products for our customers." Even in a moment of contrition, Maffei couldn't bring himself to describe the temps as full-fledged professionals at Microsoft. Implicitly, they were subordinates and outsiders, whose role was to "help us."

In July, WashTech supported the Tax Saver Unit with the first union rally ever on the Microsoft campus. That morning, the unit's sixteen union supporters wore WashTech T-shirts to work. At lunchtime, together with about twenty-five other WashTech supporters, they held a rally outside the cafeteria in their building. Courtney spoke first, followed by Judd. "When I was done, someone tapped me on the shoulder for being kind of schmaltzy," she remembered. "You know, we really weren't completely comfortable with this union-organizing thing. It was very difficult for all of us to attend a rally."

The next day, Microsoft sent every employee in the Tax Saver Unit an e-mail explaining that the company had a standing policy against "solicitation" by "outside organizations"—standard language for employers seeking to keep union organizers off their premises.

With this first indication of disapproval by the company, the tightly knit group of union supporters in the Tax Saver Unit began to splinter. "With so much publicity," Judd recalled, "some of the workers felt that WashTech was using us to promote unions in general, when all most of us wanted was just for our situation to get better." Debbie, who had been one of the earliest advocates of organizing, suddenly seemed to change her mind. Judd remembered her telling the others: "You'd better knock it off. If you keep at it, they'll close the project down." Soon, other workers noticed that Debbie was going out and having cigarettes with one of the supervisors.

That fall, the four staffing agencies announced that they were adding more sick days and improving the health coverage and other benefits for the temp workers. Microsoft began a job classification review for the temps in the Tax Saver Unit, and several employees, including Dahl, got substantial pay increases. "They said they were planning it all along," Judd explained. "After the benefits and salaries were adjusted, many of the workers were then, if not totally satisfied, at least partially placated."

The Tax Saver temps didn't conduct any more union activities other than paying dues and attending monthly meetings at the

WashTech offices. By January 2000, "there were rumblings that the project would get shut down," Dahl said. "I already knew this was coming through the grapevine. I had cleaned out my desk the day before we got the word."

On March 22, every employee in the Tax Saver Unit got an e-mail from a supervisor telling them to attend a mandatory meeting the next day. "When we got the e-mail, we just knew— bingo!—the writing is on the wall," Judd recalled. At the meeting, they were told that Microsoft was discontinuing its work on the Tax Saver software product, the unit would close two days later, and all the employees would be terminated.

Intriguingly, even then and years later as well, Judd and her coworkers did not believe that Microsoft had closed the unit because of the organizing campaign. "I really didn't think they closed it because we were organizing," she said five years afterward. "We might have been a splinter in their finger. Intuit really owns the software tax preparation market they wanted to be part of."

With their impressive credentials and varied work experience, the employees had no trouble finding jobs at other software development or tax preparation companies. For years to come, the union supporters would hold reunions at one another's homes. Debbie, however, wasn't invited.

WashTech continued to have several hundred members working for Microsoft and other high-tech companies in the Seattle area. Courtney remained its president and became even more widely quoted as a representative of information technology workers in the years ahead as the news media covered the growing story about the offshoring of technical and professional jobs to India and other countries. Tens of thousands more technical workers subscribed to WashTech's e-mail bulletins and visited its Web site as the group focused more on exposing and opposing offshoring. Especially after Cohen was elected national president of CWA in 2005, WashTech became the structure through which the union expanded its organizing efforts among public employees and workers in telecommunications companies throughout the state of Washington.

But organizing Microsoft was still WashTech's "Holy Grail"— the still unattainable dream that remained its reason for being. Interviewed in 2005, Courtney wistfully remembered, "In 2000, we really were very close to achieving large-scale organizing among the temps."

8

THE LOVE-HATE WORKPLACE

For as long as most journalists can remember, every Labor Day, a peculiar ritual is played out in the nation's newspapers. With the decline of the union movement, Democratic candidates no longer kick off their campaigns with Labor Day rallies in downtown Detroit, many major cities no longer have Labor Day parades, and many local unions no longer have Labor Day picnics. But research, interest, and advocacy groups of all kinds— liberal and conservative, business and labor—release their own surveys about whether working Americans are satisfied with their jobs.

Typically, these studies are released in time for Labor Day, and their findings reflect their sponsorship. For instance, in 2006, the conservative American Enterprise Institute found that "Strong majorities say they are satisfied with their jobs," whereas the AFL-CIO (American Federation of Labor and Congress of Industrial Organizations) found that workers were anxious about their economic situations. Meanwhile, an impartial research group, the Conference Board, came forth with a finding that seems more plausible: Americans are increasingly dissatisfied with their jobs but still are very closely divided, with about half of those surveyed in 2005 saying that they were dissatisfied, compared to only about 40 percent in 1995.[1]

Of course, this finding suggests that when it comes to whether they are pleased with their jobs, Americans as a people report contradictory opinions, depending on our circumstances: during good economic times, most of us say we are happy at work, whereas in worse times, about half of us admit that we are dissatisfied. But something even more complex is at work. When it comes to job satisfaction, Americans are not only closely divided among ourselves—we are closely divided within ourselves.

To be sure, some of our ambivalence reflects the tangled emotions people experience whenever they are asked whether they are pleased with any aspects of their economic situation. For all of our dissatisfactions, we don't want to sound like we're unsuccessful. Professional pollsters have long understood that when people are asked to evaluate their own financial situation, they will usually say that they are doing well, and the best way to get a truthful assessment of their feelings about the economy is to ask how they think their neighbors and coworkers are doing. So, when asked if they are satisfied with their jobs, Americans are also likely to insist that they are happy—people don't want to acknowledge that their life's work has left them feeling like failures.

But there may also be another explanation for why Americans' attitudes about their jobs are so ambivalent. With most Americans achieving higher levels of education than their parents and grandparents did and with the declining number of grueling blue-collar jobs, more people are working in fields that they chose themselves—as teachers, technicians, engineers, computer programmers, and social workers, to name a few jobs that are not only careers but callings. Moreover, many people find reasons for pride and satisfaction in work that others might wrongly consider "unskilled," although the average person would have difficulty doing those jobs himself or herself. Construction craft workers, manufacturing workers, and direct care workers in hospitals and nursing homes all can take pride in performing essential jobs, mastering difficult tasks, and supporting their families.

So if people in many different occupations are asked whether they like their work—or if they are asked about their jobs in ways that sound like questions about the substance of their work—they're likely to answer positively. After all, they do enjoy teaching, nursing, or programming; that is why they went into these fields in the first place. Or they're proud to be able to build cars and computers or care for the very young or the very old, and they'll be damned if they'll let anyone else look down on what they do. But the same people who are proud of the substance of their work may also have serious gripes about the conditions under which they do their work. Yes, Americans are the hardest-working people in any industrialized society. Yes, this reflects our commitment to our careers—our "work ethic," as Richard Nixon would say—as well as economic necessity. However, Americans are also angry about the lack of regular raises and the lack of resources and respect that they need to do their best work. Moreover, many Americans are finding that by devoting so much time, energy, and emotion to their jobs, they are overinvesting in their work in ways that inevitably lead to disillusionment.

The love-hate workplace may have emotional causes, but it has economic consequences. For individual companies and entire countries, their capacity to compete in the global economy depends upon having skilled workforces, fully engaged in their work and actively committed to quality. When the most capable and committed workers lose faith that their judgments are respected and their contributions are appreciated, the quality of the nation's products and services will suffer. Eventually, the world's consumers will be more reluctant to buy what the United States is selling, and the economy will suffer as surely as if our own consumers' purchasing power had declined. So, when Americans love their work but hate their jobs, our future is at risk.

CONSPICUOUS EXERTION

Of course, a foreign visitor might conclude that Americans not only like their work but live to work. After all, Americans are, as Bill Clinton used to say, "the workingest people on earth."

On average, Americans work almost two hundred hours a year more than people in other advanced countries do. Indeed, the average middle-income couple with children now works eight weeks longer than in 1979, and the average working American now gets only seven hours of sleep a night—one hour less than people in most advanced countries sleep every night and also an hour less than most doctors recommend.

"Working families" is not just a political catchphrase but an accurate description of how our households live. In most families, fathers and mothers work outside the home, and so do teenage kids after school. All these hours at work and away from home create gaping holes in Americans' families, communities, and houses of worship. Overly optimistic as the celebrants of self-employment can be, it is easy to agree that families and communities would gain if more working parents worked from their homes and if, as Dan Pink wrote, residential neighborhoods on weekdays did not look as if they had been hit by neutron bombs that eliminated the people but spared the houses.

Lengthening work hours take their toll on our family and community lives, and, through another instance of emotional alchemy, they also take their toll on our work life, as the sociologist Arlie Hochschild wrote in *The Time Bind: When Work Becomes Home and Home Becomes Work*. For people with professional or managerial jobs, being at work can be more enjoyable and even more relaxing than being at home. At work, there are interesting things to do, a ready-made community of people to spend time with, and underlings who are eager to do your bidding. At home, there are unruly kids, an inattentive spouse, dishes to be washed, and diapers to be changed. Not surprisingly, many working parents would rather be at work (I know I've felt that way many times myself), and the less time that working parents spend at home, the more unpleasant their home life becomes.

To be sure, problems at home aren't the only reasons why many Americans would rather be working. Many single or childless people in their twenties and thirties, especially those in high tech, work ten, twelve, fourteen hours or even longer on weekdays and come into the office on weekends as well. Legend has it that a twenty-four-year-old programmer for the now-defunct Internet search company Netscape told a survey researcher that he worked between 110 and 120 hours per week. The researcher was unable to record the response because his computerized questionnaire wouldn't accept a number that big. Indeed, in 2000, the Families and Work Institute found that 73 percent of twenty-five- to thirty-two-year-olds worked more than forty hours per week, compared with 55 percent in 1977. This compulsion to work around the clock, or at least to hang out at the office at all hours, is part of today's youth culture and a central theme of such novels as Douglas Coupland's *Microserfs*. Intriguingly, it is one of the few aspects of youth culture that conservatives admire. For instance, in an article in the neoconservative magazine *City Journal*, the essayist Kay Hymowitz wrote approvingly of what she called young Americans' "ecstatic work ethic," comparing it favorably with the indolence of the hippies of her (and my) generation. Similarly, *Fortune* quoted a thirty-year-old who said, "Work is not work. It's a hobby you happen to get paid for."[2]

Although working too long and hard is hardly the most self-destructive thing that young people have ever done, such habits can damage the physical and emotional health, as well as the family lives, of older people, especially if they are married with children. However, as Sylvia Ann Hewlett and Carolyn Buck Luce wrote in the *Harvard Business Review* in December 2006, many responsible adults accept and even enjoy "Extreme Jobs" that require "sixty hours or more a week, round-the-clock client or customer demands, profit and loss responsibility, and significant amounts of travel." Unlike the twenty-somethings' jobs, which tend to be in start-up companies in emerging sectors of the economy, these positions are in established firms in advertising, investment banking, and the law. Some of these extreme jobholders may simply be earning lots of money in order to save for their families' futures, but many must also love what they are doing.[3]

WHATEVER HAPPENED TO THE RAISE?

Lots of worker discontent, especially among the best-educated and most-skilled workers, results from a simple but mostly unreported fact: while Americans are working harder and smarter than ever, they aren't sharing in the gains of their growing productivity. Because of new technologies, increased levels of education, improved ways of structuring workplaces, and the simple fact that most people are learning more skills and doing their jobs better, Americans are producing more goods and services, with better quality and at lower costs than ever before. But except for the final years of the 1990s, workers' "real wages" (their earnings adjusted for increases in the cost of living) scarcely increased at all. Adding to the frustration of professional and technical workers, while for the most part they did better than workers in more routine jobs, their earnings didn't increase that much, either. In fact, they trailed far behind the wealthiest 1 percent of the population, who may not have done better in college but had the good luck or judgment to inherit wealth, manage hedge funds, or become corporate CEOs.

During the years when the new economy first emerged and the old social contract between corporate America and working Americans eroded, workers suffered a slow-motion depression. From 1979 through 1994, real wages declined by 12 percent, while productivity increased by 24 percent. As the nation's elites never tired of explaining, college graduates generally, and professionals and technicians in particular, were pulling away from working-class wage earners. But the reason wasn't that well-educated workers were rapidly improving their conditions—it was that blue-collar and service workers were fast falling behind.

By the final years of the 1990s, inflation-adjusted wages for most workers finally began to rise, although still not quite as quickly as productivity. Between 1995 and 2000, output per hour grew 2.5 percent per year, while median family income grew 2.2 percent annually—the first real raises that most Americans had received. Still, real wages only recovered their average value by around 1998. Why were wages going up? The economy was approaching full employment for the first time since the late 1960s—unemployment was below 5.5 percent from early 1996 through the end of the decade. Workers' bargaining power was increasing. For the first time in a decade, the minimum wage had increased, pushing up earnings for workers at the bottom of the economic ladder. There was a newly assertive labor movement that won other victories in organizing, bargaining, and legislation. And there was a national administration that balanced the interests of employers and employees, instead of automatically weighing in on behalf of employers.

Starting in 2001, productivity has soared at a rate of about 4 percent per year, but most workers' wages barely increased. Indeed, between 2000 and 2004, the average family's income fell by 3 percent—or about $1,600 in 2004 dollars. By the first years of the twenty-first century, college-educated workers (who tend to be professionals and technicians) found themselves not doing much better than other workers. As *Fortune* reported in 2005, "The skill premium, the extra value of higher education, must have declined after three decades of growing." Indeed, the real annual earnings of college graduates actually declined between 2000 and 2004. While the gap between the earnings of college graduates and high school grads had grown from 1980 through 2000, it began to narrow starting in 2001.

Why was this happening? Just as blue-collar workers had been vulnerable to globalization and automation for several decades, white-collar workers were finding that their jobs could also be digitized and outsourced, and the two trends were often related. Not only workers in call centers but also accountants and radiologists discovered that the information they worked with could be sent to South Asia over the Internet and their jobs could be performed by highly skilled but lower-paid workers in India. As Sheldon Steinback, of the American Council on Education, said, "One could be educationally competitive and easily lose out in the global economic marketplace . . . because of significantly lower wages being paid elsewhere." Since their jobs could be sent overseas, growing numbers of professionals and technicians were in no position to demand raises, and just like factory workers a decade or more ago, they didn't get real raises.

Increasingly, companies were making it a point of policy, instead of only out of necessity, not to award their employees regular across-the-board raises. The new breed of corporate CEOs, exemplified by GE's Jack Welch, believed in "differentiation." Instead of treating all their employees the same, they lavishly rewarded the best performers, fired the worst, and figured that run-of-the-mill workers might as well quit and be replaced by newcomers who were just as good and a little hungrier. New information technologies allowed these companies to measure workers' individual performance more exactly and to reward the high achievers with merit increases and bonuses, while skimping on raises for the rest. As early as 1995, according to a survey of three hundred large companies in 1995 by the Association for Quality and Participation, 74 percent were dismantling traditional pay schemes that awarded annual increases to most employees. That same year, the public opinion analyst Stanley Greenberg, who had polled for Bill Clinton in 1992 and would advise Al Gore in 2000, reported on interviews he had conducted with working-class wage earners. Sixty-five percent of the men and 58 percent of the women said that they had gotten no raises in recent years. "That is now the way the world works," Greenberg wrote. "One does not get raises that matter, unless one works longer hours, a higher paying shift or an additional job."

Together with the full-time, long-term job, the regular raise was becoming a thing of the past. That was one more reason why so many Americans liked the work they did but not the jobs they held.

OVERINVESTING IN WORK?

Working longer hours for lagging pay—this sounds like an investment with a low return. For the great majority of Americans who are working to live, not living to work, their long hours on the job are tolerable only because they have no other way to support themselves and their families.

But what about the ecstatically workaholic young people, the older people in "extreme jobs," and the working parents in flight from their homes? Although they are not typical, they do offer exaggerated reflections of many Americans' attitudes toward work. In the past, as the ethicist Joanne Ciulla wrote, Americans "endowed work with moral value," but now we "dangerously depend on our jobs to be the primary source of our identity, the mainspring of individual self-esteem and happiness." Many look to their work to provide "substitutes for the fulfillment we used to derive from family, friends and religion," she concluded.

Anyone who makes that much of an emotional investment in work is looking for a letdown. In 1999, *Fast Company,* a magazine that focused on high-tech start-ups during the dot-com era, commissioned a survey of college-educated professionals by professors Donald Gibson and Sigal Barsade of the Yale School of Management to explore whether they were becoming disillusioned with the jobs. Reporting on the survey, the magazine observed, "These days more people have higher expectations for work than ever before. People want to bring their whole selves to the job—all of their skills, all of their interests, all of their values." When they took their jobs, many of the professionals who were interviewed had been promised many things, including "the authority to define their work; a role as part of a team; the chance to be a team player; the opportunity to think creatively." Inevitably, most of these professionals ended up feeling disillusioned with their jobs, and 24 percent were "chronically" angry at work. Such feelings are worsened when companies purport to base employees' pay scales entirely on their performance. Workers who lose out on raises feel not only underpaid but also underappreciated.[4]

Just as dependent personalities frequently find abusive spouses, people who seek complete personal fulfillment at work often end up with manipulative bosses who exploit their employees' needs in order to extract ever-increasing amounts of work from them for ever-diminishing rewards. Managers can let you call them by their first names, wear blue-jeans and T-shirts to work, and play rock music in your cubicle, while underpaying and overworking you. In a true story that sounds like it came from a *Dilbert* cartoon, there was a bank that laid off half of its employees and required the remaining workers to take on larger workloads. In order to boost employees' morale, the bank's management played Patti LaBelle's "New Attitude" before meetings and hung "We are a team" banners in the offices. Eventually, the employees realized that management was not their friend.[5]

PROFESSIONAL PARADISE LOST

There's a similar sense of disillusionment among many workers who never allowed themselves to be played for suckers by manipulative New Age employers but who simply accepted the age-old promises of their professions that they would be allowed to serve the public by achieving accepted standards of ethics and excellence.

Although many technical, service, and skilled blue-collar workers are enjoying greater degrees of discretion on their jobs, a great number of physicians, nurses, journalists, and engineers are finding that being professionals no longer shields them from the pressures of the marketplace.

Physicians, for instance, used to be considered "free professionals": self-employed solo practitioners. Now, in this era of managed care, almost half of the nation's more than 680,000 physicians are working as employees of hospitals or health maintenance organizations. Whereas they used to make their own decisions about medical treatments, in consultation with their colleagues and their patients, these salaried doctors now find themselves second-guessed by nonphysicians, including officials of their hospitals, HMOs, and insurance companies. Often, they're required to spend a lot of time completing cumbersome paperwork, while being allowed only limited amounts of time to visit with their patients. As Barry

Liebowitz, a pediatrician who serves as president of the National Doctors' Alliance, a fledgling union with sixteen thousand members, declared, "Doctors are afraid of losing the ability to practice medicine as they were taught, afraid of losing their licenses if they followed corporate decisions they don't agree with, and afraid of being fired if they refuse."

Largely because of such concerns, and at variance with public stereotypes, professionals now are the most heavily unionized sector of the workforce, with 23 percent of professionals belonging to unions, compared to less than 15 percent of the entire workforce. This results in part because unionism is increasingly concentrated in the public sector, and professionals such as public school teachers, state university professors, state highway engineers, and social workers in state and local welfare departments are heavily unionized. Meanwhile, as is less well known, various occupations in the media and the arts, including newspaper reporters, television and radio announcers, and stage and screen actors, also belong to talent guilds.

But now, with the threats to the integrity of professions such as medicine and nursing, the American Medical Association and the American Nurses Association have set up special units to organize members of these professions to bargain with their employers, and many doctors and nurses are joining established unions, such as the Service Employees International Union, which organized workers at Northwest Hospital in Seattle, as recounted in chapter 3. In the years ahead, many of the nation's best-educated workers will be at odds with their employers not because they want to get more pay or do less work but because they want to do their best work.

JOB SATISFACTION: IT ALL DEPENDS ON WHAT YOU ASK

The nation's businesses, as well as academic and advocacy institutions of all kinds, spend millions of dollars every year to study whether Americans are satisfied with their jobs. Many of the most sophisticated studies do describe Americans' ambivalent attitudes. People identify closely with their occupations—and this makes them say they are satisfied with their work. And they also want to overcome the obstacles to doing their best work—and this can make some say that they are dissatisfied with their jobs. But you have to know what to look for because the conclusions that these studies reach depend on the questions that they ask.

For more than a month, I reviewed several decades' worth of news stories about studies of job satisfaction conducted by private companies, government agencies, universities, think tanks, and interest groups. Surprisingly, it seems that back in the 1960s and 1970s, scholars had sophisticated ideas about job satisfaction that today's researchers have ignored, rejected, or never learned.

The founder of job satisfaction studies, the behavioral scientist Frederic Herzberg, believed that workers' needs had two basic dimensions, what he called "intrinsic" and "extrinsic" factors: in other words, "the work" and "the job." Extrinsic factors, such as inadequate pay, incompetent supervision, and dirty working conditions could lead to dissatisfaction, Herzberg maintained. And these complaints could be relieved by raising wages, retraining the supervisors, and cleaning up the workplaces.

Then the workers wouldn't be quite as unhappy, Herzberg explained. But they still wouldn't be happy. Satisfaction depends on "the provision of intrinsic factors, such as achievement, accomplishment, responsibility, and challenging work," Herzberg concluded. During the 1970s, in the aftermath of the Lordstown strike, leaders from business, labor, government, and academia were concerned with the "blue-collar blues." The questions posed and the answers received by job satisfaction studies reflected this concern. For instance, a survey conducted by the University of Michigan found: "What workers want most, as more than 100 studies in the past 20 years show, is to become masters of their immediate environment and to feel that their work and they themselves are important—the twin ingredients of self-esteem. . . . Workers recognize that some of the dirty jobs can be transformed only into the merely tolerable, but the most impressive features of work are felt to be avoidable: constant supervision and coercion, lack of variety, monotony, meaningless tasks, and isolation."

Now that many of the worst factory jobs have been improved, more recent studies tend to combine workers' views about the intrinsic and extrinsic aspects of their situations—their work and their jobs—into one question about whether they are satisfied. Because more people are doing work that they have chosen, because work generally is more pleasant, and because it is human nature not to admit unhappiness with a huge element of one's life, most people say they're satisfied with their jobs. Not surprisingly, surveys sponsored by conservative and corporate groups find that workers say they're satisfied, while surveys sponsored by liberal and labor groups report more dissatisfaction.

Recent studies by institutions with no ax to grind find that there is an increasing conflict between workers' commitment to their occupations and employers and their sense that their employers do not share their dedication. For instance, a study conducted by Harris Interactive/Business and Legal Reports in 2006 found that 56 percent of workers said they are loyal to their companies, down from 59 percent in 2005, while only 25 percent of workers said their company is loyal to the employees, down from 41 percent in 2004. Only 38 percent of employees said that morale at their company is good or excellent, down from 44 percent in 2004 and 40 percent in 2005. Meanwhile, in its 2006 Employee Review, the recruiting firm Randstad found that pressures at work are escalating, job satisfaction is falling, and Americans feel increasingly stressed and dissatisfied about the way their organizations treat them and the gulf between what employers say and what they actually do. Similarly, in another study conducted in 2006, the Pew Research Center found that an overwhelming majority of adult Americans "thinks that workers were better off a generation ago than they are now on every key dimension of worker life—be it wages, benefits, retirement plans, on-the-job stress, the loyalty they are shown by employers or the need to regularly upgrade worker skills."

To be sure, pro-labor studies that are intended merely for the media can be as one-sided and self-serving as studies that business groups conduct for public consumption. Just as business says workers are satisfied, labor says workers are dissatisfied—stop the presses! But much more can be learned from a study conducted by a labor group seeking strategic guidance for organizing campaigns.

In a survey conducted during 1997, the AFL-CIO's Department for Professional Employees interviewed a range of professional and technical workers involved in contested organizing campaigns, including four where the union lost and two where the union won. Surprisingly for a union-sponsored study, the survey found "a very high level of job satisfaction," based mostly on the type of work that people did. "Attachment to the occupation is also unusually high," concluded the author of the report, Professor Richard Hurd of the Cornell School of Industrial and Labor Relations. Seventy-three percent of the employees had worked at their jobs for ten years or more, and 74 percent expected to still be in the occupation five years from now. But, Hurd continued, "This commitment to the work they do does not imply approval of employer actions." Fifty-six percent of the workers gave top management negative ratings, and their greatest complaint was the lack of "freedom to exercise professional judgment."

These findings were in keeping with the results of the Worker Representation and Participation Study, conducted in 1994 for President Clinton's commission on labor law reform, which was chaired by former labor secretary John Dunlop. Surveying a cross-section of American workers, the study found that 63 percent wanted to participate in decision making much more than their companies allowed them to do, 76 percent said that such worker participation would make their companies more successful, and only 38 percent said that their companies kept promises to their employees.

Workers' widespread dedication to their occupations, their dissatisfaction with management policies, and their demand for a greater voice in decisions all suggest that the concerns of the Northwest Hospital workers and the Microsoft temp workers are widely shared. So, how are these discontents being expressed, and what impact will they have?

SILENT STRIKES: WHY WORKER
DISCONTENT MATTERS

To be sure, most professional and technical workers cannot act on their discontents, except by quitting their jobs. The strike at Boeing and the organizing campaign at Microsoft were unusual events resulting from special circumstances. After all, the Boeing engineers were already the largest group of unionized professionals in private industry in this country, while the contingent workers at Microsoft already shared a sense of group identity because their status as long-term temporary workers had attracted the attention of the IRS and the federal courts.

While their problems aren't producing collective action, professional and technical workers are increasingly disenchanted with their jobs. Their discontent takes many quiet but crucial forms that are transforming popular culture, the political process, their own occupations, their workplaces, and, eventually, the economy as well. On the cultural front, alienated white-collar workers like the carton character Dilbert are replacing angry blue-collar workers, such as the sitcom character Archie Bunker, as iconic figures. In politics, professional and technical workers are becoming more liberal in their views and voting patterns, and they have shifted entire regions, such as the Pacific Northwest, into the Democratic camp. Changing the character of their occupations, professional and technical workers are becoming the most heavily unionized sector of the workforce, surpassing factory and construction workers.

At its most intense, white-collar workers' discontent can create the kinds of conflicts that cause business magazines to describe many of the nation's leading corporations as "at war with themselves." In the face of massive layoffs, increased workloads for the remaining employees, and drastic changes in their strategies, structures, and product lines, Boeing, IBM, and Kodak all suffered from internal dissension. But of all these embattled companies' white-collar workforces, only Boeing's engineers and technicians had union representation and could raise their concerns forthrightly in a strike. Unlike Boeing's employees, the professionals at these other companies don't have unions. Instead, white-collar discontents kept simmering, then bubbling over in backbiting, badmouthing, and high turnover rates.

These are extreme examples, but many well-educated and highly skilled workers are withholding their labor less dramatically. Largely because of the low salaries and the lack of autonomy, young college graduates are avoiding professions like nursing and teaching, and even engineering and information technology, while experienced employees in these fields are often switching to better-paying occupations. Thus, the federal government anticipates shortages of two million teachers, one million nurses, and twenty-four thousand physicians in the years ahead.

When there are shortages of professionals and technicians in essential occupations, when high turnover rates make companies pay more to recruit and retrain workers for these positions, and when internal turmoil makes workers less diligent and efficient, the costs are obvious. Less perceptibly but most ominously of all, many professionals and technicians are investing less of their energies, emotions, and intelligence in their current jobs. Some of them subtly subvert decisions with which they disagree, while others are unwilling to offer their own ideas, to assume new responsibilities, or to subordinate their personal priorities to their company's goals.

Such "silent strikes" are most important not for the damage that alienated employees can cause their companies but for the contributions that they don't make. In the new economy, companies achieve a competitive edge with what analysts call "economies of depth"—the ability of employees to solve problems, customize services, improvise effectively, and work cooperatively. Companies whose employees are estranged from their employers and from one another are less likely to achieve these improvements. Indeed, for employees, whether their jobs can be digitized or outsourced often depends on whether they are making an irreplaceable individual contribution and developing personal relationships with their customers and clients.

When Americans love their work, they can achieve this level of performance. When they hate their jobs, their careers and their companies will suffer. How Americans resolve their ambivalence between work they're dedicated to and jobs they're dissatisfied with will shape the economy's future.

For several months before and after the turn of the twenty-first century, this angry ambivalence was on display at bargaining tables and picket lines in the Seattle metropolitan area. The United States' leading exporter, Boeing, still has the nation's largest professional and technical workforce, but for all their pride in their professions and their products, these workers were increasingly angry at their company. So, when they went on strike, their picket signs read, "On Strike *for* Boeing."

9

"A COMPANY THAT HIRES ENGINEERS AND OTHER PEOPLE"

From its founding, Boeing was consumed with a passion for engineering, designing, building, and selling aircraft that would "push the envelope"—a phrase that was originated by test pilots—for how fast a plane could go, how far it could fly, and how many people it could carry. In 1910, a wealthy Seattle lumberman, William Boeing, watched one of the nation's first air races at Belmont Park, New York. He became fascinated by flight and believed he could build a better plane himself. In 1916, with $100,000 in capital—much of it his own money—Boeing bought an abandoned Seattle shipyard, built a one-room factory, and hired thirty employees. After the United States entered World War I, the navy needed airplanes, and Boeing built fifty-five of them—still primitive planes, made of wood and linen—filling its first production order and turning its first profit on a product.[1]

Now Boeing was in business, and from the first, the aircraft business was an act of faith. More than any other aircraft company, Boeing was willing to wager that new technologies could take flight as aircraft and that big buyers—civilian, military, and governmental—could be found for these flying machines.

Throughout the company's history, the recurring theme was "We had this great idea. We bet the company's future on it. And, after we hit a rough patch, our bet paid off—big time."

NATIONAL CHAMPION

Risk-taking, record-breaking, and world-beating, Boeing became the kind of company that former labor secretary Robert Reich calls a "national champion"—a corporation that carries America's banner into international economic competition. By the beginning of the 1990s, other national champions—GM, Bethlehem Steel, and Kodak—had fallen behind foreign competitors. But Boeing's willingness to risk everything for international supremacy helped to maintain the U.S. lead in military and commercial aircraft.

In fact, Boeing often made its biggest gambles when it was hit by hard times. Once World War I was over, there were no more military orders for several years. So, during the 1920s, Boeing pioneered air travel, developing all-metal monoplanes (replacing the clumsy wooden biplanes), pressurized cabins with forced-air ventilation, and retractable landing gear.

Soon the Great Depression began, and Boeing went into another tailspin. The company had only $500,000 in cash; it had few orders for the new planes; and it would soon lay off seven hundred of its seventeen hundred employees. But Boeing responded by thinking big. Beginning in 1934, Boeing drew up plans for a four-engine bomber. When the War Department rejected the idea as impractical, Boeing built it anyway, investing $275,000 of its own money in the project. After the United States was attacked at Pearl Harbor, the military bought the plane after all, and Boeing would build ten thousand of them during World War II. The bomber was named the B-17 but was more commonly called "the Flying Fortress," and it was used in the Pacific and in Europe, where it pulverized military and industrial targets in Hitler's Germany. Meanwhile, Boeing also designed and built another bomber weighing twice as much as the B-17—the B-29—which dropped the atomic bombs on Hiroshima and Nagasaki.

When World War II was won, Boeing hit another rough patch. The military didn't need any more bombers, and soon, thirty thousand Boeing workers lost their jobs. So Boeing made another big gamble—it would develop transcontinental jet travel. With an initial investment of $20 million and no guarantee that the airlines would buy jets to replace their propeller planes, Boeing began to develop what became the 707 jet. After years of work and tens of millions of dollars more for research, development, testing, and production, the 707 went on the market in 1957. It could fly from New York City to Los Angeles in four and a half hours and across the Atlantic in fewer than seven hours, but first Boeing had to find a buyer. After Pan American switched to 707s, other major airlines had to follow—who would want to travel more slowly?—and transatlantic propeller planes and ocean liners became obsolete.

By the end of the 1960s, Boeing once again invested an unheard-of sum—this time, $1 billion—to build a bigger and faster plane. Introduced in 1969 and with Pan Am once again making the first big buy, the 747 jumbo jet soon dominated long-haul routes, such as traveling across North America, the Atlantic Ocean, or the Pacific Ocean. As the first giant passenger plane, it made world travel reliable, comfortable, and affordable, so that middle-class families, not only the fabled "jet-setters," could go overseas more than once in a lifetime.

Meanwhile, the United States was embroiled in an arms race and a space race with the Soviet Union, and Boeing spurred both national efforts. Among other weapons systems, Boeing built the B-52 bomber, the Minuteman missile, the Cruise missile, and the AWACS (Airborne Warning and Control System) spy plane. In the space race, Boeing designed and produced the Saturn launch vehicle that sent the Apollo spacecraft toward the moon, the lunar orbiter that helped NASA to find a safe place for the astronauts to touch down, and the Lunar Roving Vehicle that the astronauts used to get around after they landed.

But shortly after the 1969 moon walk, the economy went into a recession, the market for new passenger planes became saturated, and a newly active environmental movement convinced Congress to cut off funding for yet another ambitious project that Boeing was pioneering—the supersonic transport. Boeing's factories were filled with unsold jumbo jets; the company laid off half of its eighty thousand workers; and someone put up a billboard on a highway leading out of town with the headline: "Will the last person leaving Seattle please turn out the lights?"

Boeing stuck with its wagers on its newest planes, and soon those bets began to pay off. Eventually, the company sold more than fourteen hundred of the 747 jumbo jets and another thousand of the smaller 737s. By 1994, the company introduced updated versions of its jumbo, midsized, and smaller passenger liners. But for the first time, Boeing faced formidable competition from a company outside the United States. Its new rival was Airbus, a consortium of British, French, German, and Spanish companies that was subsidized by their governments. Would Boeing respond as it had in the past by making big investments in new technologies?

An Engineers' Company

Up until the late 1990s, Boeing would have fought back by ordering its engineers to design a new aircraft that would take the world marketplace by storm. Just as newspapers that value their reporters are called "writers' papers" and recording companies that cater to their musicians are known as "artists' labels," Boeing traditionally was the aerospace company where the engineers came first. Boeing was willing to spend money—lots of money—to make long-term investments in new ideas. If those ideas took a while to make money, well, that's how it was because, at Boeing, the engineers, not the accountants, called the shots.

Boeing's philosophy could be summed up as go-for-it-and-damn-the-expenses—but not damn-the-quality. In air travel, quality means safety, and more than any other aircraft company, Boeing understood the necessity of convincing government officials, military leaders, airline executives, pilots, and passengers that the company's planes were not only the world's biggest and fastest but also the best and the safest.

Thus, Boeing became famous for what was called its "suspenders and belt" engineering—it always had a good backup for everything. In the early days, this meant that the planes were prepared for what would happen if an engine failed or the landing gear jammed. By the time Boeing built giant jetliners, the engineers made sure that instead of the two backup systems on most jets, there were four separate fail-safe systems. When the 747 jumbo jet was introduced in 1970, the insurance companies predicted that there would be three crashes in its first eighteen months of flight. Instead, in the 747's first ten years, there were only five accidents, and two were determined to be due to pilot errors, not to problems with the planes. As an executive of Germany's national airline, Lufthansa, told *Time* magazine in 1980, "There is no secret at all about Boeing's success. The company just keeps coming up with the right plane, at the right time, at the right price." In that same article, *Time* observed that "Engineering remains the secret of Boeing's success in the commercial aviation market" because "the company's engineers are the most innovative and imaginative."[2]

During its Golden Age, which lasted, with only a few interruptions, until the late 1990s, Boeing became known as "a company that hires engineers and other people." Much like high school football stars being courted by college coaches, the top graduates of the nation's engineering schools were wooed by Boeing and were promised exciting careers, designing the future equivalents of the Flying Fortress, the 747, and the Space Shuttle. Their opportunities for advancement were limitless—most of Boeing's chairmen and presidents were engineers themselves. In fact, of William Boeing's first thirty hires in 1916, three were engineers. Two of them, Claire Egtvedt and Phil Johnson, were future presidents of the Boeing Company.

By the year 2000, Boeing had about twelve thousand engineers and eight thousand technicians in the Seattle area, compared to some twenty-seven thousand blue-collar workers—an unusually high ratio of professionals to production workers for a manufacturing company. The engineers were a well-educated workforce; 98 percent had bachelor of science degrees in mechanical, electrical, or civil engineering, and many had master's degrees or doctorates in mathematics or science but were considered part of the engineering team. For their part, almost all of the technicians had at least an associate's degree in technical fields such as design, and some also had earned bachelor of science degrees while working at Boeing.

As one engineer explained, the chain of command had been the same for decades: "The engineers develop the specifications for a project, the designers (technicians) interpret it, and the blue-collar workers build it." Traditionally, there had been some tension among the units (each of which is represented by a union), with some engineers claiming that they did all the brain work, some technicians contending that they made the engineers' plans practical, and some machinists complaining that they were the only ones who had to get their hands dirty, and, besides, their knowledge of how the planes really work helped to salvage some faulty designs.

While the engineers called the shots at Boeing's huge factories and office complexes, their own working conditions were less than luxurious. As recently as the middle of the 1980s, the leader of the engineers' and technicians' union, Charles Bofferding, recalled, "There used to be a sea of desks, with power cords coming down from the ceiling, so it looked like a garment shop. The cords were connected to the lights and the calculators and the computers."[3] With the advent of personal computers, the engineers had their work stations in cubicles, small private offices, or large work areas that several engineers shared.

Nor were engineers and technicians paid nearly as well as the most successful software developers on the fast track at the dot-com companies that were springing up in Seattle in the late 1990s. Most of these software developers were young enough to be the Boeing employees' kids, and many of them actually were. By 2000, the engineers' salaries ranged from $37,000 to $128,000, with an average of $63,000—good money, to be sure, but nothing like the salaries and the stock options that the dot-commers were receiving as they jumped from job to job in what turned out to be the final years of the 1990s boom. For their part, the technicians earned from $21,000 to $81,000, with an average of $45,000—more like the wages of skilled blue-collar workers.

As the buzz about the booming dot-com economy kept getting louder and Boeing kept talking about cutting costs, the engineers and technicians became increasingly discontented. But the organization that spoke for them was an unlikely instrument for their discontent: a professional association that had staged only one strike, which lasted just one day.

"WE ARE PROFESSIONAL MEN"

Along with having invented the passenger plane, the fighter plane, and the jumbo jet, Boeing used to hold one more world record—the company had the largest white-collar "independent union" in the entire world. "Independent unions" are employee organizations that exist only at one company. Indeed, another phrase for "independent union" is "company union." The latter phrase has become a term of contempt, reflecting the fact that unions that represent workers at only one company tend to be unusually attentive to that company's interests, sometimes to the point of neglecting the needs of the workers themselves.

But even in its earliest days, the engineers' union wasn't beholden to Boeing. It just reflected the views of the engineers who, in many ways, were truer believers in the free market than the Boeing Company was. After all, Boeing depended on government contracts and had learned to live with its blue-collar workers' union, the Machinists. But Boeing's engineers believed that they would do just fine in the free market; after all, they were educated, talented, hardworking people whose skills were very much in demand.

Early in 1944, feeling that they were losing out on improvements in pay, pensions, and health insurance—a recurring anxiety for Boeing's white-collar workers—a group of engineers founded the Seattle Professional Engineers Association, or SPEEA (Spee-uh), as it has been called ever since (although it later changed its official name to "Society of Professional Engineering Employees in Aerospace"). Reluctant to call itself a union, SPEEA split hairs to explain exactly what it was. Its first president, Trygve Hoff, said that SPEEA was "a bargaining agent for the engineer, rather than a union, per se," and saw its role as "stressing the professional ideas of its engineers."[4]

In its first contract talks with Boeing in 1946, SPEEA confounded the company by showing just how unpredictable "the professional ideas of its engineers" could be. By then, Boeing had worked out a stable, if often stormy, relationship with the Machinists, and the management negotiators expected that the basic features of the Machinists' contract would be replicated in the white-collar employees' contract.

But Boeing hadn't reckoned with the fact that the engineers were reluctant to accept several basic features of most union contracts. First, the company proposed across-the-board salary increases for all the engineers—an idea that most unions would gladly accept, and many employers would initially oppose. But the engineers' association rejected the idea, insisting that the engineers who had earned the best evaluations from their supervisors should receive the biggest raises—a concept called "merit raises" that unions usually resist.

Then, the company suggested that years of service to the company—what most union contracts call "seniority"—should be a decisive factor in deciding which engineers should be promoted and which would keep their jobs in the event that some employees had to be let go for economic reasons. Once again, the engineers' association balked at an idea that most unions would embrace. "We want advancement to be based on ability, not seniority," the engineers' chief negotiator, Trygve Hoff, declared.

Having reached a deadlock on two important issues, Boeing's chief negotiator began to expect the worst. "Will you be going on strike?" he asked Hoff. Hoff responded that even if the bargaining bogged down indefinitely, the engineers would not strike, but they just might encourage their most capable colleagues to find jobs outside Boeing. "We are professional men," Hoff said, "And what we'll do is this—we'll set up an office to comb the United States for engineering jobs, and we'll hire away from Boeing every single able engineer we can find jobs for."

Hoff's unusual ultimatum—that the union would set up an employment agency, not picket lines—alarmed Boeing's chief negotiator at least as much as a threat to conduct a conventional strike would. The Boeing's engineers' faith in a free market for their own talents was well-founded. They were the best aircraft engineers in the world. They knew it. Boeing knew it. And a permanent exodus of engineers would hurt Boeing much more than a walkout would, in which the engineers would eventually return to work.

So Boeing took the threat to its board of directors, and they agreed to offer the engineers pay increases averaging 29 percent per person, a huge sum that would be awarded on the basis of each engineer's performance ratings. This was the first of many times that the engineers got their way by doing things differently from most unions.

In its early years, SPEEA spent much of its time fighting off the Machinists and the Teamsters. Ultimately, SPEEA went its own way, representing the interests of an individualistic workforce whose talents were in great demand as postwar prosperity fueled the popularity of air travel and the Cold War generated military contracts for bombers, fighter planes, and missiles. Reflecting the engineers' sense that the free market valued their skills at least as much as Boeing did, SPEEA conducted a campaign to eliminate a government restriction that prevented a company from offering a job to an aircraft engineer without the consent of his current employer. This rule had made sense when it was written during World War II, and the war effort required that major contractors such as Boeing have stable and loyal workforces. But by the 1950s, there was no reason for aircraft engineers to be the only civilians still laboring under wartime restrictions on their employment opportunities, and in 1956, SPEEA obtained a letter from the assistant secretary of the air force declaring that the policy no longer existed.

In the years ahead, SPEEA became an ever-more-respected part of the Boeing Company and the Seattle community. For engineers, being active in SPEEA actually advanced their careers by building their professional networks and bolstering their professional reputations. For instance, in 1948, an ambitious young engineer named T. A. Wilson joined SPEEA and soon was elected to serve on its executive committee. Boeing took notice of him, too, and, in 1951, he was promoted into management; he resigned his leadership position in SPEEA but retained his membership. Climbing steadily through the management ranks, Wilson became Boeing's president in 1968 and served until 1985. While Wilson served as second in command, another SPEEA member, Phil Condit, was working his way up the executive ladder until he became Boeing's president in 1992 and its chairman and chief executive officer in 1996.

Meanwhile, SPEEA won an election in 1971 to represent Boeing's technicians, once again defeating the Machinists. For all their pride in their profession, the engineers welcomed the technicians into their ranks. In a gesture of inclusion, SPEEA's leaders stopped boasting about "the engineering community" at Boeing and started to talk about "the technical community," a phrase that encompassed the techs as well as the engineers.

But the next two decades were SPEEA's last gasp as a purely professional association that didn't call itself a union and wanted nothing to do with other labor organizations. By 1992, with the U.S. economy mired in recession and stiff competition from Airbus in the global marketplace, Boeing took a hard line in contract negotiations with SPEEA. More than 70 percent of the engineers and technicians voted to reject Boeing's offer, and on January 19,

1993, SPEEA members staged a one-day strike. They returned to work the next day, and at the end of the month, they accepted an agreement that strengthened their protections against layoffs but did not improve their pay and benefits.

In the years ahead, SPEEA continued to consider itself a professional association, but, in its own way, it became more of a union as well. One charismatic and controversial leader exemplified SPEEA's evolution. With a master's of science degree from Michigan State University, Charles Bofferding had been an engineer at Boeing since 1980. As he reminded anyone who would listen, he had twice been honored by the company as "a distinguished technical contributor" and once was selected as a "high potential employee." But he turned his talents to SPEEA, and in 1991, he became the executive director. More than six feet tall, stocky, and bespectacled, Bofferding was an imposing presence who dominated most gatherings. Often using an engineer's lingo of analyzing systems and solving problems, Bofferding advocated European-style codetermination for Boeing, with the engineers partnering with management to set the company's course. But while he preached labor-management cooperation, Bofferding also loved to take potshots at the company, priding himself on his ability to coin pithy and quotable phrases—"my sound bites"—which he used in personal conversation, public speeches, and frequent interviews with Seattle newspapers, local TV stations, and aerospace trade journals. Sometimes, it seemed that he would rather coin a phrase than cut a deal. But at a time when Boeing's engineers felt that they were being ignored by the company, most appreciated having a leader who gave voice to their gripes and their dreams. Only later would many turn against a man whose very largeness—his public prominence, his overwhelming personality, and his domination of the organization—eventually generated resentment.[5]

In the late 1990s, though, most engineers resented Boeing, not Bofferding. Looking back at that one-day strike in 1993, they vowed that the next time, they would do it right. Boeing was becoming a less friendly place to work, and the engineers would soon wonder whether the free market and what had been a weak professional association were enough to protect them from changes beyond their control.

THE NEW BOEING

Boeing's chief executive officer, Phil Condit, was behaving strangely, and it was as jarring as if the unassuming airplane designer down the street had morphed into Hugh Hefner.

Like most of Boeing's CEOs before him, he was an engineer by profession. Of average height and increasingly paunchy as he climbed the corporate ladder, with horn-rimmed glasses and an unassuming manner, his bulk made him look like a friendly bear. Boeing people often came to him with their problems, and he listened carefully, asked intelligent questions, and offered sensible advice. If anyone had a gripe against him, it was that he tended to be noncommittal, not domineering. Condit had a booming voice, but he rarely used it.

Even his wardrobe marked him as a laid-back "Boeing guy," a meld of the engineer's indifference to fashion and the emerging style of Seattle grunge. While he'd wear suits for formal occasions like board meetings, he was Boeing's first CEO to wear open-collar shirts with sport jackets at internal meetings and in his office. Whenever he could get away with it, he seemed even more comfortable in a sweater and blue jeans. That's what he was wearing when he showed up, unannounced, on the Machinists' picket lines in 1995 to ask Boeing's blue-collar workers what was bugging them. Good old Phil, they thought, not an ounce of arrogance in his ample body.

As with so many at Boeing, Condit had been consumed as a youngster with the mystique of flight. Growing up in San Francisco, he liked to go to the airport and watch the planes. He was recruited by Boeing in 1965, just after he had earned his master's degree in aeronautical engineering at Princeton. While working at Boeing, he discovered a way to make jumbo jets safe for other aircraft flying near them. He figured out how to calculate the size of the "vortex"—the whirlpool of air that sucks everything nearby toward its center—that jumbo jets cause when they take off. Condit's formula allowed the Federal Aviation Administration to develop rules for how much distance jumbo jets should keep between themselves and smaller aircraft. Later, Condit led the teams that designed two of Boeing's most successful planes, the midsized 757 and the wide-body 777. When Condit became the company's president in 1992, his selection seemed like a well-deserved reward for Boeing's best engineer ever. But by the time he became chairman and chief executive officer in 1996, there were whispers that Condit was starting to act less like a Boeing guy and more like the free-spending CEOs at other large companies. In his late fifties, good old Phil was starting to live large.

The workhorse had become a playboy. His long hours at the office wrecked his first two marriages. And having been unusually hard working as a younger man, he may have felt that he was finally entitled to some fun. He married twice more and developed a reputation as a womanizer. During one of his stints as a single man, he moved into the company's suite at the Four Seasons Hotel in Seattle and had Boeing pick up the tab for building a bedroom there. When he remarried, he built himself a mansion outside the city, which was designed to reflect a medieval motif and where he hosted parties whose theme was King Arthur's royal court.[6]

Condit's Camelot was a far cry from the unpretentious image that his predecessors had carefully cultivated. Traditionally, Boeing's top executives had lived modestly, and if they weren't model family men, no one ever heard about it. Their adventurous spirits were channeled entirely into their work; the rest of their lives seemed as drab as a Seattle winter. For instance, in 1969, Boeing's chairman and CEO T. A. Wilson flew to Washington, D.C., to testify before a congressional committee. Most corporate CEOs would have had a limousine waiting for them at the airport. Wilson was met by Geoff Stamper, the son of Boeing's president,

Mal Stamper. The younger Stamper was a student at American University, and he drove Wilson into town in a rusted jalopy. Years later, Geoff Stamper became Boeing's chief negotiator in contract talks with the engineers, and he would miss the days when the company's egalitarianism endeared it to its employees.[7]

So, when Condit started living large, many engineers thought that his midlife crisis mirrored the company's confusion about its own future. Instead of the collegial company where engineers collaborated on new technological breakthroughs and the top executives figured out how to finance and market these marvels, Boeing was becoming more like other businesses. As the financial analyst Pierre Chao would explain, it was an era when investors were looking to make as much money as they could as quickly as possible, and companies were catering to them by emphasizing profits over long-term growth. The aerospace giant's last new airplane—the jumbo 777—had gone into production in 1989. Now there were no ambitious new projects under way—no jets, missile systems, or space shuttles that would cloak their creators in glory, just as the 777 had become Condit's calling card. Rather than make big investments in new generations of aircraft, the company was saving money by trimming its payroll and seeking other opportunities with large potential returns, such as servicing airplanes and doing more defense work, with its guaranteed profits and cost-plus contracts.

As part of its strategy to expand its work for the military, Boeing acquired one of its major competitors for defense contracts: McDonnell-Douglas. On paper, the two companies seemed to complement each other. Boeing did three-quarters of its business with commercial airlines and the remainder with the Pentagon and the space program. McDonnell-Douglas had recently gotten out of the commercial aircraft business and worked entirely on defense or space projects.

During 1996, Boeing and McDonnell-Douglas negotiated a merger, with the tacit approval of the Defense Department, which was encouraging its contractors to consolidate. The two companies officially joined together on August 1, 1997, and although the entire merged company was called Boeing, the engineers who had always been part of Boeing soon felt that it was their company, not McDonnell-Douglas, that was fading away.

An awkward but revealing phrase soon entered the engineers' vocabulary. Employees and executives who had been with Boeing before the merger came to be called "Heritage Boeing." Meanwhile, the only representatives of McDonnell-Douglas whom Boeing's employees ever encountered were the top executives who started trooping into Seattle; since McDonnell-Douglas's factories and offices were in St. Louis and Southern California, few of Boeing's engineers, technicians, and machinists ever met their counterparts from their merger partner. As Boeing's employees met managers from McDonnell-Douglas, a culture clash developed.

"I call the merger 'the Boy Scouts meeting the mercenaries,'" Bofferding explained. "Boeing's culture was polite and professional. But McDonnell-Douglas was more aggressive and business-based. People would stab each other in the back to advance. That company was not ruled by engineers, but rather by ruthless bean counters." Like many other engineers, Bofferding believed that the "mercenaries" were overpowering the "Boy Scouts." "Any time a more aggressive culture meets a more passive culture," he said, "the more aggressive culture comes out front first."[8]

For the Heritage Boeing loyalists, the culture clash was symbolized by the differences between Condit, who remained the merged company's chairman and CEO, and Harry Stonecipher, who had been McDonnell-Douglas's CEO and had moved to Seattle to become second in command to Condit, with the title of president of Boeing. With slicked-back gray hair, a heavily lined face, and rimless glasses, Stonecipher seemed like Condit's polar opposite. Where Condit hesitated to resolve difficult issues, Stonecipher was blunt, brutally candid, and decisive. He had spent most of his career at GE, directing its commercial and military transport division and becoming a favorite of the CEO, Jack Welch, who was famous for eliminating entire operations that didn't turn a profit. Moving to McDonnell-Douglas, Stonecipher quickly climbed to CEO and closed the company's civilian aircraft division.

That history was enough for Boeing's engineers to be wary of Stonecipher, and he solidified his standing as ogre in chief with his constant questioning of Boeing's established ways of doing things. He sent urgent e-mails to his subordinates, typed out entirely in capital letters—the electronic equivalent of having your boss pick up his phone and scream at you. "An awful lot of people in 'Commercial' [Boeing's commercial airplanes division] believe they don't have a 'Harry Stonecipher' problem," he told a reporter. "I can tell you that, until we find a solution to the performance out there, they will have a Harry Stonecipher problem."[9]

For all his faults, compared to Stonecipher, Condit began to look like Sir Lancelot from the lavish Camelot-themed parties in his mansion. As Stan Sorscher, who led the engineer's negotiating committee in 1999 and 2000, explained, "A lot of people think, 'Phil old buddy, come rescue us from Harry.'"[10]

But Stonecipher was right about some things. Boeing's "performance" had to improve. For Boeing, 1997 and 1998 had been the years from hell. For the first time in a half century, Boeing was losing money, having run up a deficit of $178 million in 1997. The value of its stock declined by 32 percent in 1998. Worse yet, there was no one to blame but Boeing itself. The U.S. economy was booming. Demand for commercial aircraft was increasing. Had Boeing been better managed, it might have had one of its best years ever—the orders for new planes had reached record levels. But Boeing had been unable to meet its delivery schedules because it had shortages of parts and a production system that couldn't keep up with its customers' demands.[11]

Boeing was in trouble with the stock analysts and institutional investors who were the gatekeepers to the investment capital it needed. By the end of 1998, a news article in the *Seattle Times* reported what Boeing's executives had been hearing from the financial community and their own board of directors. Leading investment gurus were getting ready to downgrade the company's common stock to "neutral" or even "hold." These ratings warned potential investors that if they bought shares of Boeing, they would have to wait a long time before their holdings would increase in value. The naysayers included such opinion leaders as Joseph Campbell of Lehman Brothers, Cai von Rumohr of S. G. Cowen and Company, and George Shapiro of Salomon Smith Barney. "The believers have given up," explained Pierre Chao, who was then with Morgan Stanley. Alone among those quoted, he predicted that Boeing could still rebound and he dismissed calls for Condit's removal, saying that they would do little more than "satisfy the bloodlust" of angry investors.[12] (Chao's balanced view of Boeing gave Sorscher and Bofferding the idea of reaching out to him in 1999. Shrewdly, they sensed that someone who was critical of the company but hadn't given up on it entirely could be their emissary to a corporate management that they feared was losing its way.)

When Boeing had hit rough patches in the past, its CEOs had announced that they were securing the company's future with new breakthroughs—a jumbo jet, a fighter plane, or a spacecraft. But at a time when Wall Street moved money at warp speed to the investments that offered the largest and fastest returns, the most ambitious plans that the company considered were for cutting the company's spending and staff.

On August 5, 1998, there was a top-level management meeting, whose details eventually leaked out and came to symbolize Boeing's efforts to return to health through bloodletting. More than two dozen of the company's top executives sat around a table in the board room. At first, Condit held forth. He spoke about how he'd been humiliated at recent meetings with large investors. He said they'd berated him about how much money they'd lost on their holdings of Boeing stock. They'd even called him a liar. Never again, he declared, would he suffer such indignities—Boeing had to get its act together. And, then, or so the stories went, the usually phlegmatic Condit had started crying, leaving the floor to Stonecipher, who went on to promise all kinds of cutbacks.[13]

To be sure, the story played into the stereotypes of the two men and the corporate traditions they represented—Condit, the sensitive "Boeing guy," and Stonecipher, the martinet and McDonnell "mercenary." But soon the rumors were confirmed by bad news. Within weeks, at least six senior executives, including Ron Woodard, the head of Boeing's commercial airlines division, were fired—the first management purge in the company's history. Then, in December, Boeing announced that it would eliminate forty-eight thousand jobs throughout the company, including management, engineers and technicians, and blue-collar workers. Some of those who received layoff notices had been hired only a year earlier.

In an effort to win back Wall Street's confidence, Condit traveled to Orlando, Florida, on February 24, 1999, to meet with many of the same Wall Street analysts who had badmouthed Boeing in its hometown newspaper only two months earlier. Condit said that Boeing was reviewing all of its operations and would try to sell or, if that failed, eliminate every part of the company that didn't turn a significant profit or stand a good chance of doing so. "Nothing escapes scrutiny here," he said. "There are no sacred cows."[14]

To emphasize his cost-consciousness, Condit wasn't accompanied by the heads of Boeing's civilian or military aircraft divisions. Instead, he brought Boeing's new chief financial officer, Deborah Hopkins, who had previously worked for Ford and General Motors. She said that the company had conducted a study of its finances and found that 10 percent of its equity—$1.3 billion out of $13 billion—was tied up in activities that lost money. But not for much longer, she promised. Boeing would fix, sell off, or simply eliminate what she called these "value-destroying operations." Back in Seattle, Hopkins's remarks got people talking. Only forty-six, she was being mentioned as a potential successor to Stonecipher or even Condit. For the engineers, the financial officer's ascendancy was one more sign that the new Boeing valued number crunchers more than airplane builders.

10

THE MAX PLANCK INSTITUTE
FOR CYNICISM

To the engineers, it seemed that Boeing was going out of its way to make them anxious and angry. Starting in the mid-1990s, the company tried to explain its new strategy of scaling back new investments and cutting costs, leaving the engineers either bewildered or enraged. In 1996, there was an "all-hands meeting" for about three hundred people who worked in Manufacturing Research and Development. To accommodate all the engineers and technicians who had to attend and to signal the meeting's importance, the meeting was held at a movie theater in the Seattle suburb of Renton. Increasingly discontented with the company, Stan Sorscher still remembered the meeting years later: "A management person gave a vision. He explained how we could become more profitable by cutting costs. When we walked back to our office afterward, everyone asked, 'What's going on in this company?' 'What's my future?' 'What's my role?'"[1]

"A TEAM, NOT A FAMILY"

By 1999, the engineers were so upset that the trade journal *Aviation Week* published a series of articles about how Boeing and other aviation aerospace companies were "surrender[ing] to the

185

bottom line," displaying "a mindless preoccupation with cutting costs," and losing "the adventurous engineering that made the U.S. aerospace industry dominant and innovative."[2]

Perhaps because the magazine also attacked "a lack of vision at the top," the series stung Condit, who responded in an e-mail message to Boeing employees on June 25, 1999. Claiming that the articles reflected a "confused bit of nostalgia" for "the good old days," he explained why Boeing was wooing Wall Street: "We care [about Boeing's stock price] because we compete in the market for the capital that is necessary to launch new projects. . . . Our shareholders are, for the most part, not loyal to Boeing but looking for the best returns. If we do not perform, they can easily take the money and invest in other companies."[3]

Not only was Boeing making its corporate strategies less adventurous, but it also began to boast that it was making its workplaces less friendly. In 1998, it conducted a "cultural audit" to explore why it was having such a hard time getting things done properly, on time, and within its budget. The audit concluded that it was time to toughen up.[4]

Soon, Boeing's top executives began to use new buzzwords that set the engineers on edge. Proclaiming that the company was evolving into "the New Boeing," Condit and Stonecipher both spoke of moving "from a family culture to a team culture." In an interview with a reporter, Boeing's press spokesman, Peter Conte, explained, "In a family, you continue to take care of everybody, whether they contribute or not."

Meanwhile, many engineers were reaching the uncomfortable conclusion that Boeing was cutting corners on quality and even (although this idea was almost unmentionable outside of closed meetings) on safety as well. Some of the angriest engineers were the best-educated and best-paid scientists. They might have been expected to move ahead at Boeing, but their careers had stalled in the new era of cutbacks. Instead, they channeled their energies into SPEEA, with the result that many of the association's officers seemed more like the senior faculty in a physics department than the leaders of a labor union.

Sorscher, for instance, has a PhD in physics. Short and slender, he described himself as "physically unthreatening—the kind of guy no one's afraid to ask for directions." But he began to challenge Boeing's management by speaking up at public meetings and also, or so Boeing claimed, by leaking embarrassing information to the Seattle newspapers (an alleged infraction for which he was disciplined by the company).

In 1998, the company held another meeting for about three hundred employees in Manufacturing Research and Development. Once again, a management person presented the vision of how the company could cut its way to recovery. This time, when the meeting was opened up for questions, Sorscher stood up. "This is a shrinking company with shrinking prospects," he said. "We all want to make products that the customers want to buy. But with all the cuts in research and quality control, I don't see how we can do this."

As a scientist speaking to other professionals, Sorscher was reluctant to present his opinions as established facts. So he concluded by saying, "What I have just said is one possible interpretation of events. Convince me I'm wrong." As Sorscher remembered later, "The supervisor who conducted the meeting said, 'There's a plan, trust me.'"[5]

Sorscher's specialty at work was testing aircraft parts by using ultrasound. This technology uses reverberations at frequencies that are too high for humans to hear. Because these vibrations can shake loose anything that isn't absolutely unmovable, ultrasound can help workers to inspect the graphite in an aircraft's wing-skin to make sure it isn't coming apart—an imperceptible defect that could produce other problems that just might cause a crash.

One day, Sorscher got a call from a fellow physicist who had been working with a team of engineers to figure out ways to test the prototype for a new product and improve how it would be designed and built. There had been a brainstorming session about a new aircraft. The physicist had made the sort of suggestions that a scientist would be expected to offer: "Let's produce laser-based ultrasound testing" and "Let's do process improvement, so we can do a better job." Ordinarily, these ideas would have been routinely approved. Traditionally, Boeing believed in testing and tinkering with everything over and over again. But this time, while the engineers at the meeting nodded sagely in approval, the management person overruled them, saying, "The important thing is to cut costs." Long after the incident took place, Sorscher still couldn't control his rage: "What the management guy was really saying was screw quality, screw [Boeing's] competitive advantage in the future."[6]

Sorscher's own working group consisted of nineteen scientists, engineers, and technicians who did nondestructive testing of aircraft, rockets, and other Boeing products. They shared a private joke. Among one another, they called themselves "the Max Planck Institute for Cynicism." One of the greatest physicists of the late nineteenth and early twentieth centuries, Max Planck had invented the quantum theory, which explains the behavior of small packets of energy such as heat and light and was a forerunner for Albert Einstein's theory of relativity. Planck remains a hero for scientists, and throughout Western Europe, there are Max Planck Institutes for physics and other fields of research. Linking Planck's name to cynicism was a bitter joke, but by the end of the 1990s, it took more than that to shock Boeing's best-educated employees.

No More "Boys and Toys"

Sorscher and his working group weren't the only people who noticed that Boeing was becoming less interested in exploring new frontiers in aeronautics. Few observers understood the industry better than Pierre Chao, the Wall Street stock analyst who had been almost alone in 1998 in predicting that Boeing might rebound from its disastrous predicament. Chao had been quoted in news stories about how Wall Street stock analysts were giving up on Boeing, which had lost money for the last few years even though the economy was booming. Understanding that an influential Wall Street figure could be a valuable contact, Sorscher called Chao to introduce himself and to see whether they could start to exchange information. Chao responded agreeably—he could always use more sources in the industry—and the two men kept in touch. Eventually, Sorscher invited Chao to address a meeting of SPEEA's stewards (the union's elected leaders in each workplace) early in 2000.

On the evening of the meeting, Chao delivered an overhead presentation consisting of fifty separate slides, each with charts and graphs. He explained why companies like Boeing were retrenching. He brought bad news: this downturn was being driven by the airline companies, the Defense Department, the investment community, and the aircraft manufacturers themselves—and there was little the engineers could do about it except adjust to it.

For most of their history, Chao said, the airline companies and the aircraft manufacturers had shared a passion for airplanes—the bigger and faster, the better. But now the aerospace engineers who were dedicated to building the world's best planes and who, like Boeing's executives and blue-collar workers, were mostly men in their forties and fifties, had to face an unpleasant fact. "The old era of boys and toys is over," Chao said. "There is a new era of conservatism and a focus on profits and growth."

Boeing's leading customers, the commercial airlines, were scaling down their orders of new airplanes. Airlines in the United States had been deregulated, and in a fiercely competitive environment, several companies had gone out of business, others were in trouble, and the most successful newcomers offered the lowest fares. Meanwhile, around the world, national airlines that used to be owned by governments were being privatized, with the result that they, too, were concentrating on cutting costs. To make things even worse, the Asian economies were in crisis, further depressing the demand for new airplanes. And unlike in the past, the Pentagon wouldn't make up for the slack; the Cold War was over, and U.S. defense spending was declining, too.

So, now, the airline companies would rather repair their existing airplanes than replace them with new aircraft. When they had to buy new planes, they would order very few at a time, and they wanted planes that were as small as possible, so that they could keep their costs and their fares as low as they could. And they were less interested in new technologies, unless these cut costs.

As for Wall Street, Chao declared, showing one of his over-head slides, "The stock market is focusing on the efficient use of capital, exacerbating many of the trends." At firms like his own, he explained, "The rule of thumb is, 'Never invest during an industry downturn.'"

How were aerospace companies like Boeing responding? Chao explained that they, too, would be changing their goals "from performance/technology to efficiency/costs." Manufacturers were trying to trim 15 to 25 percent of their costs, so trailblazing research and new product development were being cut back. As with the airline companies, the new breed of executives were "MBA weenies, not goggle-heads," as Sorscher summed it up later. By "goggle-head," he meant an executive or an engineer smitten with the romance of flight, just like the first pilots who wore goggles—in other words, the boys who loved their toys.

Every player—the airlines, the manufacturers, and the investors—was pursuing a strategy to slow down the development of new and better planes. Not surprisingly, several of Chao's slides were headlined "Paradigm Shift!"

What would be the role for engineers in this bland new world? Chao knew that Boeing's engineers had been the heroes of Boeing's history, as the company developed the first passenger planes for civilian travel, fighters and bombers for the military, and launch vehicles for the space program. Now, he told them, they should prepare to play a new part. Instead of inventing exciting new technologies, they should "revamp basic design and development processes to be cheaper." He called this new role "the Renaissance Engineer," but he understood that most engineers would not find it inspiring to be cost cutters, instead of trailblazers.

The engineers didn't like the news Chao brought them. But, as Sorscher remembered later, "Everyone loved him" because he gave the kind of fact-filled report that the engineers had delivered many times themselves. Although Chao's talk had been scheduled months in advance, he was speaking at an important time—the second night of the engineers and technicians' strike against Boeing.[7]

UNLIKELY REBELS

Why were the engineers and technicians, including scientific superstars like Sorscher, willing to believe that Boeing was forsaking its own best traditions and betraying its own best employees? After all, these skilled professionals were unlikely rebels. Most of the engineers and technicians were family men in their forties and fifties who had worked for Boeing most of their adult lives. They still seemed like grown-up versions of the kids who had aced their math and science exams in high school and had dreamed of designing jumbo jets that would take travelers to faraway places and rockets that would carry astronauts to the moon, Mars, and beyond.

By the beginning of 2000, the engineers' experiences exemplified why so many of the best-educated, most-skilled, and highest-paid workers in the United States were deeply committed to their occupations but increasingly resentful of the conditions under which they tried to function every day. They loved their work, but they were beginning to hate their jobs, and the things that they loved and the things they loathed were all tangled up together.

On the positive side, which they still preferred to talk about, the engineers understood that they were doing some of the most exciting work imaginable, the pioneering projects they had dreamed about as kids who built model airplanes at home or joined the science club in school. They were designing jumbo jets, missile systems, or even spacecraft—the stuff of science fiction when they were adolescents but all in a day's work at Boeing. They knew that the security of all Americans and the safety of airline passengers depended on how well they did their jobs. As Doug Smith, a bearded, wiry man who led the Boeing technicians' bargaining team, said shortly after the strike, "We believe that we are working for the people who buy the seats on the airplanes, not just the airline companies who buy the planes."[8]

Not only did they find their work exciting and important, but the engineers and technicians still cared about their company. They considered themselves devoted to Boeing's best traditions, especially its willingness to make big investments—big gambles, really—in new ideas for building bigger, better aircraft. In their love for their life's work and their loyalty to their employer's mission, they resembled other dedicated workers at the turn of the twenty-first century.

On the negative side, as with many other Americans who were devoted to their work, the engineers were disappointed with the circumstances under which they did their work. Having no ambitious new projects to engage their ambitions and being second-guessed by cost-cutting managers, Boeing's engineers and technicians worried whether the company's top executives shared their own commitment to quality. Here, too, the Boeing engineers had the same attitude toward their employers that many other professionals had, such as nurses who worried that their hospitals were cutting corners on patient care.

During the autumn of 1999, as Boeing and the union representing its engineers and technicians tried to negotiate a new contract, the engineers saw the company's insistence on holding the line on salary increases and cutting back their health coverage through the prism of the larger question of whether the company still respected them and valued their work. "When the company started to treat us as a cost, not a partner, people took great offense," explained Tom McCarty, an engineer who helped to design AWACS surveillance planes for the U.S. Air Force.[9]

That fall, while the negotiations were deadlocking, SPEEA made an important decision that would make it easier to stage a successful strike—the association joined a national union that was part of the U.S. labor federation the AFL-CIO. Always considering itself a professional association, SPEEA had in the past rejected approaches from the Machinists, who represented

Boeing's factory workers, and the Teamsters, who had a strong presence in Seattle, believing that both unions were too blue-collar for their tastes. During the late 1990s, SPEEA turned its attentions to a very different kind of union, the International Federation of Professional and Technical Engineers (IFPTE). Like SPEEA, IFPTE was relatively small, with just about fifty thousand members, including professional employees of the federal government and engineers in private industry.

Instead of being swallowed up by a larger union, SPEEA would account for more than a quarter of IFPTE's membership. But as part of IFPTE, SPEEA would enjoy the advantages of being part of the AFL-CIO. Members of other unions, like the Machinists and the Teamsters, would be more likely to honor its picket lines, and if they ever struck at Boeing, the engineers and technicians could receive financial and political support from the huge labor federation. After a mating dance that lasted several years, SPEEA's members voted by an 80 percent margin in October 1999 to join IFPTE and thus to become part of the AFL-CIO as well. Newly assertive and now part of a national union, many were calling the engineers' association "the New SPEEA"—a worthy antagonist to "the New Boeing."[10]

THE BROKEN BARGAIN

Early in 2000, just before the strike began, the federal mediator, C. Richard Barnes, said, "The social contract at this company has broken down." Many of the issues at Boeing were typical of conflicts at workplaces all across the United States, where the old social contract—steady jobs with regular raises and stable benefits in return for years of faithful service—was coming apart, and nothing new had emerged to take its place.

But for the engineers and technicians at Boeing, their social contract with their company extended well beyond the traditional bargain of trading loyalty for security. As with well-educated and highly skilled employees throughout the United States, they believed that they had attained an implicit but all-important understanding: if they poured their intelligence, their energy, and their emotional commitment into their company, they were entitled to receive respect, recognition, and the opportunity to do their best work in return. When they felt that their commitment to the company was being ignored, they responded not only as angry workers but almost like jilted lovers.

The Boeing engineers strike was the twenty-first century's first major battle about defining a new social contract for the U.S. workplace. The strike cast such a large shadow because the protagonists and the problems all were larger than life, just like the jumbo jets that Boeing built. As the world's leading aerospace company and the nation's leading exporter, Boeing had been unusually dedicated to excellence; its engineers and technicians were so angry at their company because they held such high expectations for it. For its part, Boeing's engineering and technical workforce was the largest and, almost certainly, the most talented anywhere in the world; in happier times, no company could count on more devoted professionals.

Now, the engineers and technicians were so disillusioned with the company to which they had dedicated their careers that they were ready to go on strike. This time, they would rack up a record that Boeing never wanted. Boeing became the battleground for the longest and largest strike by professional employees of any private company.

11

"ON STRIKE *FOR* BOEING"

At a rally in October 1999, just as SPEEA's negotiations with Boeing were beginning to bog down, the union's executive director, Charles Bofferding, posed a simple question to the more than eight hundred engineers and technicians: "How many people think that our negotiations will be a joint effort with Boeing to find common solutions to mutual problems?" Not a single hand went up.[1]

On that October evening, few of the assembled engineers and technicians hooted in derision against Boeing. After all, it wasn't their style—at least, not yet—to chant "Strike, strike, strike!" even at mass meetings. But neither did a single hand go up to support the view that the company was treating its professionals properly.

By then, most of Boeing's twenty thousand engineers and technicians were becoming convinced that they would have to do what they had never done before—conduct a serious strike. But Boeing's top management, including its representatives at the bargaining table, were just as confident that the majority of their professional employees would never walk off the job, or, if they did, they would straggle back, drenched, demoralized, and defeated, after only a day or two of pounding the pavements in the chilly rains of a Seattle winter.

WHEN THE CEO SOLD A CONTRACT

Earlier that fall, Boeing had negotiated a contract with workers whom it really did fear, the more than twenty-five thousand production workers who belonged to the Machinists union. The Machinists had successfully struck for sixty-nine days in 1995, and Boeing didn't want its production lines shut down again. So the company offered its blue-collar workers pay increases totaling 17 percent over three years, as well as $1,000 bonuses, just for agreeing to the new contract. The pay, the benefits, and the bonuses seemed so generous, and the company seemed so eager to avoid a strike, that Bofferding told friends, with uncharacteristic crudity, "Boeing wet their pants and emptied their wallet."

When they bargained with the Machinists, Boeing's management most of all wanted labor peace: no deadlock in negotiations, no strike, and no delays in delivering jumbo jets to the major airlines and in sending jet fighters, AWACS surveillance planes, and radar systems to the Pentagon. So, in order to make sure the Machinists understood how much Boeing needed them, the company's CEO, Phil Condit himself, had been at the bargaining table with the Machinists during the final days of the contract negotiations.

After the blue-collar workers' bargaining committee accepted the contract, Condit helped the Machinists' leaders to sell it to their members. "This is the best contract ever," Condit declared in newspaper advertisements and even in television spots. When the Machinists' members voted to accept the contract, Boeing's top executives figured that they had saved the company from a costly strike until the Machinists' new contract expired in 2003.

So, as they turned their attention to the engineers and technicians, Boeing's executives weren't concentrating on avoiding a strike. They wanted to begin what they saw as a difficult, drawn-out, but necessary process of slowing the growth in salaries and controlling the cost of health care and other benefits. They had devised a three-point strategy: First, impose these pay cuts and benefits for the clerical staff and other employees who weren't represented by unions of any kind. Then, force the engineers and technicians in SPEEA, who hardly seemed formidable adversaries, to agree to similar changes. And then, in the next round of negotiations, force the Machinists to agree to what every other major group of Boeing employees would have accepted by then.

In keeping with the tough, technocratic rhetoric of the "New Boeing," the company's number crunchers came up with a concept they called "total compensation." Taken together, the total pay and benefits packages of each major group of employees would not exceed the levels that the company had predetermined before the bargaining began. It was a surefire formula for conflict with the engineers, who never accepted any solution as predetermined—after all, didn't Boeing pay them to find new and better ways of designing aircraft?

"NO RESPECT" FOR ENGINEERS AND TECHNICIANS

Even under the best of circumstances, Boeing's wish list would have been a hard sell. But as bargaining began that fall, everything seemed to go wrong. The engineers and technicians were already anxious about every aspect of "the New Boeing"—the merger with McDonnell-Douglas, the talk about not being a "family" any more, and the incidents of accountants overruling engineers. Then it became clear that Boeing had no intention of matching the generous pay and benefits package it had given its blue-collar workers. And instead of the CEO, Phil Condit, who had attended the Machinists' negotiations, Boeing was sending underlings to the bargaining table, led by their director of union relations, Geoff Stamper, and their vice president for engineering. As the engineers would say on their picket lines, it all boiled down to a lack of respect for them.

Ironically, Stamper was the last person anyone would accuse of disrespecting engineers or anyone else. His father, Mal Stamper, had been Boeing's president and an advocate of humane employee relations; his idealistic nature became apparent when he devoted his retirement years to developing programs designed to help youngsters from poor families to learn to read. Following his father, Geoff Stamper went to work for Boeing, acquiring a self-effacing manner that was designed to dispel any resentment of his being the boss's son. As had his father, he would reveal some long-suppressed impulses after he retired from Boeing. When I interviewed him in 2005, with his long hair, blue jeans, and T-shirt, he looked more like an aging drummer for a rock group than a former management negotiator. He was working on a novel after having run a quixotic campaign for the state legislature in which he presented himself as a pro-life liberal, reflecting his commitment to Catholic moral and social teachings.[2]

Sitting at a Starbucks in Redmond, Stamper said that he saw it all coming—the engineers' bitterness, the growing antagonism between SPEEA's bargaining team and their management counterparts, the deadlock in negotiations, and the lengthy strike—but that he was powerless to stop it. "Boeing had a great deal of angst about whether the Machinists would go on strike," Stamper recalled. "So they oversold the IAM [International Association of Machinists] contract. This complicated things for the SPEEA negotiations. Having the CEO run around and say, 'This is the best contract ever.' What it did for SPEEA was that equaling the IAM contract became the only thing they cared about." As Stamper saw it, even Condit's presence at the Machinists' contract talks and his absence from the SPEEA negotiations insulted the engineers. "It became that comparison thing," Stamper said, years later. "You don't love us as much as them."

Equaling or even exceeding the Machinists' contract became an overriding concern for Bofferding. The engineer-turned-union-leader was offended by how Boeing and the Machinists had arrived at the settlement, which he would describe years later as "a classic power negotiation." As the negotiations began—and Boeing's bargainers told him they would not be offering SPEEA what the Machinists got—Bofferding told a reporter, "We'll see if Phil [Condit] respects all his employees or merely fears some of them."

Condit was nowhere near the bargaining table. Like almost everyone at Boeing, Bofferding was personally fond of Stamper, whose very diffidence signaled the fact that he wasn't calling the shots. But Stamper was outranked by two other executives at the bargaining table with SPEEA: his immediate boss, the vice president for employee and union relations, Jerry Calhoun, and Calhoun's boss, Jim Dagnon, who had been hired as "vice president of human resources" but soon changed his title to the grandiose appellation "vice president of people."

Dagnon got on fine with the Machinists, but the engineers hated him, and Stamper thought he understood why. Before coming to Boeing two years before, Dagnon had been in charge of labor relations at the railroad company Burlington Northern, where he had dealt with blue-collar unions. He had learned how to bargain the old-fashioned way: both sides pounded the table, cursed each other out, and threatened to fight on the picket lines until, having validated each other's manhood, they could come to an agreement without either the union's members or the company's management feeling that their interests had been sold out.

Having bargained with the engineers and the Machinists, Stamper believed that the Machinists were from Mars, while SPEEA was from M.I.T. Like their blue-collar brethren at the railroads, the Machinists understood and thrived on conflict. But the engineers believed in dispassionate inquiry, drawing conclusions from the data, arriving at a consensus about the best way to do things, and then working together to get it done. "When you negotiate with SPEEA, they want to be stroked," he explained. "You begin with your philosophical framework, and you move forward from there."

If management ever was foolish enough to try that collegial approach with the Machinists, Stamper said, the blue-collar bargainers would say, "Get to the fucking numbers." Summing up the differences between the two groups, Stamper said, "SPEEA wants to be loved. The Machinists want to get down to business."

Clearly, there was a personality conflict between Dagnon and Bofferding and eventually with the entire engineering workforce. In 1997, when Dagnon came to Boeing, he and Bofferding had a get-acquainted lunch. As Bofferding remembered their first meeting: "He said he would work with the unions. He said he would notify me of any notices going out to the employees from Boeing before they were sent. I told him I wasn't interested in getting a jump on the press. I was interested in our people being brought into the process that makes decisions."

For two years, Dagnon and Bofferding warily circled each other. Then, early in the fall of 1999, with Dagnon taking the lead, Boeing announced that it would cut the health coverage for its white-collar employees outside the SPEEA units. Without union representation, there was nothing these workers could do to challenge the company's decision.

But SPEEA held a rally to protest the cuts in benefits for the nonunion workers. As Dagnon often would, he wondered why the hell the engineers weren't playing the labor relations game by the traditional rules. "Why do you care about the non-reps?" Dagnon asked Bofferding. "You have a contract that protects your benefits." Bofferding replied, "The important thing I don't think you appreciate is that the Boeing Company is our company. This is like your going into my neighborhood and burning down every third house and telling me, 'Don't worry I'm not going to burn your house.' You are still burning my neighborhood." Once again, Dagnon and Bofferding were talking past each other.

"You Misunderstood"

As the negotiations with SPEEA began in October 1999, Boeing's bargainers told the engineers and technicians' team that they wouldn't be getting what the Machinists had won—no guaranteed 17 percent pay increases, no 10 percent signing bonus, no continuation of their costly medical plan. That was bad enough. But what really infuriated the SPEEA negotiators was that management tried to force them to accept the "total compensation" concept of cutting health insurance and other benefits, *without even letting the engineers offer their own ideas.*

SPEEA's negotiators were asked to choose among three unattractive options: the Machinists' plan, which traditionally had been less generous than what the professionals enjoyed; a trimmed-down version of the engineering and technical employees' long-standing plan; or a new system that Boeing management had just devised and that seemed to the engineers, who figured they were better at math than the management negotiators were, to be the stingiest of all three choices.

Still, something about the way management told them to *Decide what you want with health coverage* made the engineers think they were being asked to solve a problem—which, after all, was what they did for Boeing every day on their jobs.

So, working with their bargaining committee and eventually with benefits experts from Boeing, several engineers came up with their own proposal. "We came up with a new plan that met their specifications," Bofferding boasted several years later. "It met their total dollar limit and was a repackaging of existing plans." The last thing Boeing wanted was for the engineers to put an entirely new proposal on the table, but, as Bofferding said, "Their mistake was: never challenge engineers to come up with a new and creative proposal. They'll do it."

Stamper was bemused. *Charlie and his boys were doing their thing again, acting like they should be running Boeing.* Dagnon was indignant. He told the SPEEA negotiators, "You misunderstood. We didn't want you to design a new plan, you were supposed to pick one of the three plans we gave you. Since you didn't pick a plan, we are going to assign you the non-rep total comp package."

Health insurance wasn't the only benefit that Boeing wanted to cut back. For years, the company had provided a generous life insurance policy for the engineers and technicians, paying out one and a quarter of employees' annual salaries to their survivors. For an engineer who earned $100,000 a year, this meant that his family would receive $125,000 if he died while still on the job. In the 1999 negotiations, Boeing wanted to put an end to that formula and replace it with a maximum payment of $36,000.

Lots of engineers did the math. They concluded that $36,000 wouldn't cover much more than their caskets, their funerals, and several months' mortgage payments. Ordinarily, life insurance isn't the most important issue for companies and unions, but it had a special significance for one member of the SPEEA executive board, Dave Patzwald, who had cancer and thought that he might be mortally ill. Patzwald brooded that Boeing was going to take $70,000 from his family, and as he shared his worries with friends and colleagues, the engineers got angrier. "Why is Boeing nickel-and-diming families like Dave's?" they wondered aloud. "How much money could they possibly save by cutting the benefits they pay to the families of people who die before they retire?"

By early December, Boeing's bargainers weren't budging from their position. Recommending that they reject it, the SPEEA negotiating team put the offer to a vote, mailing ballots to all of the engineers and technicians, whether or not they were members of the union. When the ballots were counted on December 12, 98 percent of the employees in each unit had rejected Boeing's contract offer.

NOT THE CENTER OF THE UNIVERSE

When asked to comment on the vote, Dagnon told a reporter from the *Wall Street Journal* that Boeing could do little to sweeten its offer because the company had resolved that the settlement with SPEEA could not cost more than a fixed sum that he would not reveal. Gracelessly, he added, "The engineers have to understand that they are no longer the center of the universe."[3]

Right after he made that remark, Dagnon told Boeing's public relations director, Peter Conte, about it. "Don't you think that needed to be said?" he asked. Conte replied, "I think you're going to get a huge backlash."

For the engineers who posted photocopies of the *Wall Street Journal* article on dozens of Boeing bulletin boards, Dagnon's tactless statement added insult to injury. Their anger against Boeing was like an onion: beneath each layer of bitterness was a new and more emotionally charged anxiety about Boeing's future. Being offered less than the Machinists had been given meant that Boeing didn't respect the engineers and technicians.

And the lack of respect suggested something even more disturbing: maybe the "New Boeing" envisioned a future where it wouldn't need the world's best engineers because it would no longer make that many of the world's best planes.

In a column that the physicist Stan Sorscher, the chairman of the engineers' negotiating committee, wrote for the SPEEA newsletter and in talks he gave to groups of engineers and technicians, he masterfully linked the professionals' sense that they were being slighted and shortchanged with deeper worries about Boeing's future and their own.

He began with what every engineer knew: Boeing was losing out in the global marketplace to rivals like Airbus. Observing that Boeing could choose to either compete or retreat, he continued, "If Boeing's leaders choose to compete, then engineers and technicians will be critical contributors to that effort." He connected this unarguable observation to Boeing's contract offer, contending, "If the technical community is important, then we would see a good contract offer. A good contract offer is one that sends the message that management respects and depends upon our contributions as employees." More in sorrow than in anger, he concluded, "When I look at this offer, I see the message that Boeing's leaders have no commitment to compete; nor resolve to restore our position in our markets; no place for us in Boeing's future."[4]

Sorscher's logic was so impeccable that the only remaining question was *What do we do now?* Regretfully, he said, "I must acknowledge that our business strategy is not negotiable in our contracts. Our business strategy will not suddenly change based on favorable terms and conditions in the contract." But, fortunately, the engineers and technicians could take a stand in other ways, by rejecting Boeing's contract offer and preparing to strike.

Sorscher declared, "This is our one public collective opportunity to make a statement to Boeing's leaders. When we vote on this contract, I want us to send a message back: No confidence in our leaders. No confidence in a business plan to retreat. No on this contract."

Sorscher made a powerful appeal for his colleagues to vote down the contract, as they overwhelmingly did, and to prepare to strike, as they eventually would. But for the next few weeks, he would be asking his increasingly restive constituents not to march but to wait.

Catching Up with the Troops

As the holiday season began, Stan Sorscher had a recurring nightmare. In his dream, he and one other worker were picketing in the parking lot of a Boeing building. And everyone else was walking by them on their way to work.

In his waking hours, though, Sorscher and other SPEEA leaders were experiencing something very different. Their coworkers were saying that they were ready to strike and were asking, with increasing impatience, when the union would give the word to walk off their jobs. Early in January, Sorscher got a call from a woman who worked as an engineer in the critically important flight test area, where planes received the safety certificates they needed before they could be sold to the airline companies. She told him that she was ready to strike. He asked her to talk to everyone in her work area and find out whether they were also ready to strike. Later that day, she called him back and said, yes, everyone in her area was ready to strike.

As Sorscher hung up the phone, he had a sudden insight that foretold the success of the strike. "I thought—this is flight test,"

Sorscher recalled later. "I started to realize that we don't need everyone to strike. Critical functions such as flight test, and many others as well, are so important that they could choke off production overall."

Soon after the phone call from the woman in flight test, Sorscher spoke at a meeting at a Boeing facility in the Seattle suburb of Renton. "These people were steaming" against Boeing and even against SPEEA, Sorscher recalled. "This was a meeting where I made sure I had a door behind me, so I could get out alive if they rushed me."

A woman asked, "If we go out on strike, will you [SPEEA] support us?" The question stung Sorscher. "I was amazed that she would question whether SPEEA leaders would support the members' decision," he remembered.[5]

For Sorscher, Bofferding, and other leaders of SPEEA, there were sound strategic reasons behind their seeming reluctance to call a strike, even though the contract had expired on December 1.

First, while SPEEA's members sounded mad and militant, they accounted for only 60 percent of the engineers and technicians. Forty percent of the professional workforce hadn't even bothered to join the union. Under ordinary circumstances, these employees would not be expected to strike, and, together with management and the Machinists (whose contract forbade them from honoring another union's picket lines), they could keep Boeing running while the company waited out the striking technicians. So, in order to win over this substantial silent minority of engineers and technicians, who presumably were much less disaffected from Boeing than the most militant members of SPEEA, it was important that the union establish that it was forced to strike. "We had two groups of people in SPEEA—the fighters and the philosophers," Bofferding explained after the strike was over. "The fighters were ready to go from day 1. The philosophers said we just have to present our case better and they'll yield. We had to persuade the philosophers that we had tried everything possible to persuade the company."

Second, Boeing's business depends on the decisions of a relatively small number of influential people in the Pentagon, the Federal Aviation Administration, the major airlines, the Wall Street investment houses, and the leading institutional investors. These decision makers aren't comfortable with conflict, and, just as with the most cautious engineers, it was important that the record show that Boeing's intransigence had forced SPEEA to strike.

So SPEEA agreed to extend the contract past December. As the engineers' and technicians' frustrations began to boil over, it meant that the inevitable strike would stand a greater chance of succeeding.

By the second week in January, Boeing presented a new contract offer that was little different from what the engineers and technicians had rejected two months before. This time, the leaders of SPEEA submitted the offer to the engineers and technicians, without recommending that they either accept or reject it. But this was clear: if they rejected the offer, there was nothing left to do but go on strike.

Both units voted to reject the contract, but by very different margins. The engineers voted no by only 3,308 to 3,173—a majority of only 51 percent. But the technicians rejected it by 3,374 to 2,039—a much more substantial margin of 62 percent to 38 percent.

So now SPEEA faced an even more difficult decision. Little more than half of the engineers had even bothered to vote, and barely more than half of those who did vote had rejected the contract and thereby chosen to strike. National labor leaders became aware that the Boeing engineers were about to conduct a strike. For better or worse, the strike would make headlines and would be seen as a harbinger for the future of unionism among professionals.

High-ranking labor leaders streamed into Seattle, asking questions and offering advice, much of it direct and downbeat. As Bofferding remembered, several labor leaders asked him, "Are you *out of your mind*? You have only 60 percent of the workers paying dues. You have only 50 percent support for a strike. You would only get 30 percent of your people out on the picket lines. The company would leave you there to die."

But there were more promising signs that large numbers of engineers and technicians would walk out and stay out. For some time, SPEEA had been polling its members by telephone every night, and by January, there was growing support for a strike. Meanwhile, more than seven hundred new members had joined SPEEA during January.

Soon after announcing that the contract had been voted down, SPEEA called upon the engineers and technicians to go on strike, starting at nine in the morning, Thursday, February 3. But in a last-minute effort to avert a strike, the director of the Federal Mediation and Conciliation Service, Richard Barnes, called Bofferding and asked to be allowed to intervene in the negotiations. So SPEEA called off its strike, and the union and Boeing agreed to meet together, with Barnes mediating between them.

To many engineers and technicians, it seemed that SPEEA, once again, had sounded an uncertain trumpet. On the afternoon that SPEEA postponed the strike, there was a scuffle in the parking lot of the union's headquarters in suburban Tukwila, with union negotiators and shop stewards shouting at each other. One frustrated engineer, Donna Gaskill, declared, "We should have been out on strike in December. Now our union is saying, 'Well, you're not going out on strike this time, either.'" At the Boeing plant in Renton, where Sorscher had feared that he would be physically attacked several weeks earlier, employees chanted, "Strike, strike, strike," every half hour. At Boeing's main plant in Everett, engineers, technicians, and some production workers held a lunchtime rally, chanting, "We are Boeing."

From Sunday, February 6, through Tuesday, February 8, Barnes made a marathon effort to forge an agreement, meeting with both sides, separately or together, for as long as ten hours a day. But neither side budged, and the talks broke down late Monday night. Meanwhile, at lunchtime on Monday, hundreds of engineers and technicians held protest marches in Everett, Renton, and

Tukwila, chanting slogans and waving signs. Expressing a sentiment shared by many, Thomas McAndrews, who had worked at Boeing as an engineer for twenty years, declared, "It's almost like they [Boeing] are trying to provoke a strike. This is not a militant union."

"EIGHT THOUSAND NOBODIES"

With every other option exhausted, SPEEA called a strike for nine o'clock in the morning on Tuesday, February 8. As always, SPEEA did things its own way. If most unions called a strike for nine in the morning, they would ask their members not to go to work that day and instead to picket the buildings where they worked. But SPEEA devised a distinctive form of street theater and pulled it off.

Engineers and technicians reported for work early that morning, and at nine A.M., all across Boeing-land, they shut off their computers, filled their carrying cases with their personal belongings, and marched out of the buildings.

The engineers' leader, Sorscher, had observed what Boeing's production workers did when they walked off their jobs: "When the Machinists strike, traditionally, they pack up their tools and close up their toolboxes. The toolboxes are all collected and often wrapped in plastic in one part of the shop floor. Machinists' tools are their personal property, and it's considered extremely provocative to use a striker's tools. That would be more insulting than simply scabbing."

So Sorscher devised a walking-off-the-job routine of his own that was modeled after the Machinists' and was followed by many other engineers. He shut down his computer, backed everything up from his hard drive onto Zip disks, packed up his personal materials, and walked out of the building. "The point was that I would be gone for a long time," he later recalled, "and a quick backup seemed a prudent thing to do before walking out."

From Boeing plants and office buildings all across the Seattle area, engineers and technicians marched or drove to a rally at Renton Memorial Stadium, attended by an estimated eight thousand employees. Bofferding remembered that morning: "There were traffic backups getting to the stadium. At first, the company said nobody had walked out of work. I was at the rally on the phone with a reporter who had just told me Boeing told him that 'no one walked out,' when the more than eight thousand people there roared about something. The reporter asked me what that noise was, and I told him, 'That's the sound of eight thousand nobodies.'"

In other indications that the strike could be effective, UPS drivers, who were members of the Teamsters union, refused to cross SPEEA's picket lines and deliver packages to Boeing's offices and plants. Railroad workers at Burlington Northern, where Dagnon had worked before, refused to deliver two 737 fuselages to Boeing's Renton plant. But the Machinists' contract forbade them from honoring another union's picket lines, so the scene at Boeing's plants was the opposite of earlier strikes: the blue-collars kept working, while the engineers and technicians picketed outside.

No Nerds, No Birds

Now, they were out on the street, doing what they, their employer, and their blue-collar coworkers never expected them to do: conducting a strike. It was all so new for them, walking back and forth on the streets in front of Boeing's sprawling factories and office buildings. Weren't they supposed to carry picket signs? What should those signs say? Should they chant some slogans? Sing songs? And how would they keep warm? They weren't sure what to do or how to do it.

Long strikes usually become bitter battles, with strikers cursing out those who keep working. But the Boeing engineers and technicians tried to conduct a different kind of strike, one without rancor toward their company or even toward colleagues who crossed their picket lines.

Always proud of his "sound bites," Bofferding went into overdrive as he gave interviews to television, radio, and newspaper reporters from the Seattle area and all over the nation and the world. "We're not trying to hurt Boeing," he said early in the strike. "We're trying to save Boeing." Later on, he developed a snappier saying: "We're not trying to bring Boeing to its knees—we're trying to bring it to its senses."

But while Bofferding, Sorscher, and several other strike leaders were polished public performers, much else about the strike was improvised. Unlike the Machinists, the engineers didn't have a strike fund to make weekly payments to workers who were now going without paychecks. Many engineers had set some money aside, as veteran union members will do during difficult contract negotiations, but others had not and found themselves short of money to make mortgage payments and even to feed their families. Instead, some engineers became regular, if sheepish, visitors to food banks in the Seattle area, and some of the more enterprising set up food banks of their own.

Picket signs, too, were works in progress. At first, along with the standard-issue signs that said "SPEEA on Strike," the engineers had handwritten signs with the slogan "No Brains, No Planes." But the Machinists understandably objected—*"What's the matter, you think you're the only ones with brains?"* So the engineers drew on the self-mockery that many must have used years earlier to avoid getting beaten up in their schoolyards and rewrote their slogan. Soon, their signs said, "No Nerds, No Birds."[6]

Another slogan, however, revealed what was really on many engineers' minds. In a deliberate switch from the usual picket-line slogan that says something like "UAW on Strike against Ford," some engineers carried signs that declared, "SPEEA on Strike *for* Boeing." This slogan gave voice to their feeling that reluctantly but resolutely, they were striking to preserve Boeing's traditions and protect its future against managers who ran the risk of losing many of the company's most dedicated employees and surrendering lucrative commercial aircraft markets to competitors such as Airbus.

Just as the engineers kept insisting on their loyalty and even love for Boeing, they rarely expressed any anger toward those of their colleagues who crossed their picket lines and went to work. There were no shouts of "scab," no angry strikers surrounding the cars of their nonstriking coworkers, and no public statements by SPEEA leaders denouncing disloyal engineers and technicians.

The result was a rarity in long strikes: instead of hardening divisions between strikers and nonstrikers, growing numbers of engineers and technicians refused to report to work as the strike continued. Paul Almeida, the president of the national union that SPEEA had recently joined, had seen many strikes but had never seen so little bad feeling within a workforce. "This was different from what happens with blue-collar workers," he said. "If they cross a picket line one day, they usually scab throughout the strike. One reason was that there was little rancor, no threats against those who crossed the picket lines, so they felt comfortable joining the strike later."[7]

Meanwhile, there were surprisingly few incidents of violence or vandalism. At the Boeing facility in Renton, always a center of militancy, the picket captain found nails on the ground near the building's entryway, which were apparently intended to puncture the tires on non-striking workers' cars or suppliers' trucks. Although the picketers had been eager to go on strike, they were not interested in going to jail, and they picked up the nails, one by one. No cars or trucks were damaged, at Renton or elsewhere.

From Designing AWACS to Building Better Burn Barrels

Although striking was something new for SPEEA, the engineers approached the task with the same careful planning and diligent teamwork that they brought to their jobs. When national union leaders who had marched on their share of picket lines visited with SPEEA to show their support, they were impressed, even amazed. The second in command at the AFL-CIO, Richard Trumka, had previously been president of the United Mine Workers, for whom striking is a sacrament. But he had never seen anything like the SPEEA pickets—"the most high-tech picket line I have ever seen" with "the pickets deployed with almost military precision."[8]

If the picket lines seemed to be coordinated as carefully as U.S. military operations, it was because some of the same people were planning both endeavors. For instance, negotiating committee member Tom McCarty, who had helped to devise the health insurance proposal that Boeing summarily dismissed, had spent twenty-seven years designing radar systems for the air force.[9]

When the strike began, McCarty organized a system of supply runs that provided picket lines with coffee, snacks, firewood, and cell phones. Forty-eight engineers and technicians were divided into three crews, each working eight-hour shifts, who got the supplies and loaded them onto vans. Sixteen people shared the responsibility for driving four vans and visiting each picket line location at least three times a day. "We created our own miniature society," McCarty said.

Married to his high school sweetheart and the father of six grown children, McCarty was hardly a hothead. He had a degree in electrical engineering and had worked for Bell Labs in his native New Jersey before moving to Seattle in 1973 to take a job with Boeing. Over the years, he had designed radar target simulation units for the AWACS surveillance planes that Boeing produced for the air force, as well as various military communications systems. His fellow engineers looked to McCarty to find new ways to design sophisticated projects. Even his hobby involved repairing and retooling things; on weekends, he fixed old cars.

During the strike, McCarty finally designed something he could boast about in public: an energy-efficient, environmentally responsible version of the "burn barrels" that striking workers in the Seattle area use to keep warm in the winter.

If workers went on strike during Seattle's winters, which lasted roughly from December through March, they set up several burn barrels on each city block, filled them with scrap wood, and set the contents afire to keep themselves warm. The city police and the firefighters were familiar with the burn barrels; they used these themselves if they ever struck. Over the years, the burn barrel had assumed classical dimensions, much like an official major league baseball, a Super Bowl football, or the boxing gloves used in a heavyweight championship fight. "Burn barrels were usually fifty-five-gallon fuel drums, with the tops cut off, like you see in the movies about strikes on the waterfront or people keeping warm in the Great Depression," McCarty said. "You throw wood in there, and it generates heat and light, but it also gets smoke in your face."

When McCarty started to supply the picket lines, strikers at every site told him that they needed burn barrels. Thinking that the burn barrels were merely one more item to obtain and distribute, he went to a scrap metal dealer in the nearby town of Kent and bought forty fifty-five-gallon steel drums, which are usually used to carry oil or paint. He punched holes in their sides for air, piled them into his pickup truck (which could carry only six of the steel drums at a time), and started to deliver them to the picket lines. "That worked fine for three days," he recalled.

But three days into the strike, as McCarty later explained, "From what I heard and pieced together from informants, [Boeing's president] Harry Stonecipher looked out his window at Boeing headquarters, saw the burn barrel and people standing around it, and realized that if people didn't have it, it would be much less pleasant. He called someone in the state Environmental Protection Agency [EPA] and put pressure on them to look at the burn barrels and determine whether they could have open fires."

Soon, a letter from the state EPA arrived at SPEEA's headquarters. Not knowing what it was about, someone in the mailroom gave it to Maria Nelson, a contract administrator who opened it, saw that it had something to do with supplying picket lines, and gave it to SPEEA's volunteer quartermaster, McCarty. Reading it carefully, he saw that the state officials were advising SPEEA that the burn barrels, which did emit smoke, were in violation of the environmental regulations for the Puget Sound area. If SPEEA continued to use the burn barrels, the state would set a fine for every day.

For a minute or two, McCarty was furious. But then, he calmed down and approached the notice as an engineering challenge—how to build a burn barrel that would meet environmental standards.

"I was struck when I read the letter that we would be allowed to burn wood as long as the stove completely enclosed the fire and it emitted the smoke at a height of six feet or more," McCarty said. Visualizing how such a burn barrel could be built, he went back to Binford's Scrap Metal yard in Kent, looked at the fifty-five-gallon steel drums, and came up with a more detailed plan. "I could make a wood stove out of the drum by putting a lid on it, cutting the lid in half, hinging it in front, putting a load of wood in back, and adding a stove pipe on top," he explained.

He loaded a few of the steel drums onto his pickup truck; stopped at a Home Depot, where he got wood, hinges, and a stove pipe; went home; and got to work in his backyard. Experimenting with "a couple of configurations," he settled on one that was easy to build and use. He put it together, started a fire, and watched with pride as the smoke came out of the stovepipe, six feet above the ground.

Pleased with his handiwork, he took the first new-model burn barrel to the picket line nearby in Kent, where the engineers and technicians were delighted to see a more sophisticated, environmentally sound, and, they hoped, entirely legal contraption to keep them warm.

At McCarty's suggestion, SPEEA invited the state EPA to send an inspector to examine the new burn barrel and determine whether it met the most stringent environmental requirements. The next day, an inspector arrived at the picket line in Kent, observed how the burn barrel worked and emitted smoke, took a careful look at how it was constructed, and pronounced it fit for outside use near the Puget Sound. "He told me I did a great job," McCarty said.

Reassured that the new burn barrels had the state's seal of approval, McCarty and another engineer, Morris Adams, went to work building sixty of them and distributing them to the picket sites. The strikers used them not only to keep warm but also to cook meals. "They became the social center of the strike," McCarty said. "There is something primal about people gathering at night around a warm fire."

As the strike continued, the burn barrels became a legend, locally, nationally, and even internationally. Machinists, truck drivers, and other union members stopped by the sites and said they'd want some of the new burn barrels themselves the next time they went on strike. The national AFL-CIO's two top leaders, John Sweeney and Richard Trumka, toured picket lines and said they'd never seen anything like the burn barrels. Long after the strike was over, SPEEA and its parent union received requests from engineers around the world, asking how to build the burn barrels. McCarty produced a brochure, complete with instructions and photographs, which he e-mailed to people who asked how to build the environmentally friendly steel stoves for outdoor use.

THE ULTIMATE LOGJAM

Most long strikes become wars of economic attrition. The outcome is determined by whether the union can shut down the employer's operations so effectively that it costs the company more to allow the work stoppage to continue than to reach a settlement.

It took a while for both sides to realize how the engineers could cripple Boeing. Boeing originally thought that it could survive an engineers' strike for several weeks, while its blue-collar workers continued to meet the company's production orders. But this optimistic assumption forgot a fact that the engineers remembered: they were uniquely positioned to prevent Boeing's airplanes from ever reaching the airline companies.

That was because the Federal Aviation Administration (FAA) required that airplanes be certified as safe for flight before they could be "released," as the federal regulations put it, to the commercial airlines.

And who did the certifying?

None other than an elite corps of about five hundred of the best-educated and most highly skilled Boeing engineers whom the FAA had deputized as "designated engineering representatives" or "D.E.R.'s," as they called themselves. These were engineers like the angry woman from the flight test unit who had called Sorscher in January, demanding to know when SPEEA would go on strike.[10]

Separate certifications were required for many of a plane's parts, systems, and functions, so one aircraft might need signoffs from as many as fifty D.E.R.'s. Yet all but twenty-three of the almost five hundred D.E.R.'s were on strike, so it became nearly impossible for Boeing to obtain the necessary certifications for its planes so that they could be delivered to the airline companies.

The result was a bottleneck that was a manufacturing company's worst nightmare and a striking union's wildest dream. After the engineers and technicians walked off their jobs on February 8, it took nine days until Boeing delivered its first airplane since the strike began. By the end of the month, it had fallen short of the forty-two it had promised the airlines. Planes that had been built but that couldn't be delivered were clogging Boeing Field.

Meanwhile, Boeing's defense work was slowing down because the engineers and technicians weren't there to devise and design new projects. By early March, Boeing admitted that it was falling behind schedule on important defense contracts, including on its proposal to develop a new joint strike fighter jet, an effort where it was competing with its longtime rival, Lockheed Martin. Suffering similar problems with its civilian aircraft projects, Boeing temporarily halted its research work for developing a new fleet of commercial jetliners known within the company as the 20XX, where it was competing with Airbus.

12

ONE OF BOEING'S BEST
YEARS EVER

Several weeks into the strike, Sorscher and Bofferding left Seattle for Sacramento, then rented a car and drove to a golfing resort hotel in the town of Silverado. The physically imposing Bofferding and the wiry Sorscher made an unlikely-looking duo— imagine George Goodman and Woody Allen traveling together.

This was no pleasure trip; they were there to make their case to the investment community. Boeing's top executives were going to deliver a presentation at an annual meeting of investment analysts in the Napa Valley, deep in California's wine country, and when Sorscher and Bofferding heard about the meeting, they decided that they should go, too.

When they arrived at the hotel, they mingled with the people in the lobby, movers and shakers from Boeing's top brass and the financial community. Alan Mulally, the president of Boeing's commercial airline group (six years later, he became the president of Ford), was there. If he was surprised to see them, he didn't reveal it and greeted Bofferding and Sorscher with a noncommittal, "Hi, how ya doing?"

Later, the two engineers hosted a floating bull session in their suite. "We were amazed to have key financial people come to our suite and talk to us," Sorscher said, "people who represented the mutual fund shareholders who owned a lot of shares of Boeing."[1]

AN INTERLUDE IN SILVERADO

Trained to analyze how systems work, the engineers kept trying to find the pressure points through which they could influence Boeing's decision makers. Having concluded that, as Sorscher put it, "Boeing was embarking on this weird business model, dictated by pressures from the financial community," the engineers became intrigued with whether they could make their case to the power brokers on Wall Street. That was why Sorscher had reached out to the investment guru Pierre Chao years earlier, and why they now had left the picket lines in Seattle to lobby a meeting of investment analysts at a vacation spot.

By then, with the engineers' strike beginning to take its toll, investors were alarmed by Boeing's failure to deliver its planes to the airlines and its falling behind on projects for the Pentagon. Although Wall Street didn't like old-fashioned "integrated manufacturers" who made products from start to finish with unionized American workers, the financial community also didn't like conflict, instability, and unpredictability—and the continuing strike seemed likely to bring nothing but turmoil. So the financial analysts sought out Bofferding and Sorscher, listened to them respectfully, and always seemed just about to pop the inescapable but as-yet unspoken question, "What do you guys want?"

For their part, Bofferding and Sorscher began to realize that the investment analysts and fund managers were reasonable, analytical people like themselves, not the greedy ogres of so much union rhetoric. "The financial analysts were well-meaning, conscientious people with their own interests and values," Sorscher said. "They wanted to see the strike settled."

"Some of these guys were in so deep with Boeing, they couldn't liquidate their holdings," Sorscher continued. "They wouldn't want to contribute to a sell-off."

Finally, with several other stock analysts in the room, Cliff Ransom, the vice president of State Street Research and Management Company, asked the question that Bofferding and Sorscher were waiting for: "What would it take to settle the strike?"

Bofferding explained what SPEEA would settle for in terms of pay and benefits, sketching out something very close to the eventual settlement. The big issue, he said, was health insurance—the engineers and technicians would never agree to pay part of their premiums when the Machinists weren't. The compensation package had to be increased, with a little more going to guaranteed increases, not to merit raises determined by management. And Boeing needed to express an intention—Bofferding understood there could be no guarantees—to provide job security for the engineers. When he isn't spouting "sound bites," Bofferding sounds like the sober number cruncher that he is, and the analysts thought to themselves, This guy isn't asking for the moon.

As Bofferding spoke, Ransom and the other analysts listened quietly and wrote quickly in their notebooks. When Bofferding was done, they snapped their notebooks shut, and Ransom said quietly, "That's not very much." The point had been made; after that, the aerospace engineers and the stock analysts tried to make small talk about how lovely the Napa Valley was.

"The impression I had was, this is not a hard deal to make," Sorscher said. "Two weeks later, we were back at work."

Sorscher is certain that Ransom and perhaps other analysts and fund managers told Boeing what would be required to settle the strike and urged them to make the deal. But first, SPEEA made one more effort to use the financial community to send a message to Boeing.

Another leader of the financial community whom Bofferding and Sorscher had met at Silverado, Joe Campbell of Lehman Brothers, hosted a conference call for them on March 9 with fund managers and stock analysts. A reporter from the *Wall Street Journal* heard about the call and wrote a story that appeared the next day.

"Interviews with analysts and some individual investors said they are increasingly wary of the impact of a long strike," the *Journal* reported. The analysts were likely to reduce their estimates for Boeing's earnings for the first quarter of 2000 by 20 percent or more because of the decline in jetliner deliveries, the article continued, and "estimates for the remaining quarters are likely to drop if the strike isn't settled by March 31."

Campbell was mentioned by name, and so was Chao, who had been impressed by the engineers when he met them at the stewards' meeting. They were mostly "a rational, intelligent bunch," Chao said. "Frankly, the more love and respect the engineers receive, the easier it will be to settle this strike."

A week later, negotiators from Boeing and SPEEA were meeting with federal mediators in Washington, D.C., to settle the strike. The "love" would come later.

"A Very Political Company"

In addition to financial analysts and fund managers, SPEEA also lobbied public officials and political candidates. These efforts were important because Boeing relied heavily on Defense Department contracts and rulings by the FAA, and, as Bofferding put it, "The Boeing Company is a very political company, and this is a very political year." Washington State's Democratic primary was scheduled for February 29, and Vice President Al Gore and former New Jersey senator Bill Bradley were both eagerly wooing union members.[2]

Even before the strike was called, leaders of SPEEA and its parent union, IFPTE, met with people on the staffs of Gore, labor secretary Alexis Herman, and FAA administrator Jane Garvey. They made contacts that served them well when negotiations broke down and SPEEA started to look for anyone with the clout to get Boeing to budge from its bargaining stance.

While SPEEA was lobbying Clinton administration officials, Gore's challenger came calling for SPEEA's support. During the first week of the strike, Bill Bradley, who was trying to present himself as more liberal than Gore, joined five hundred picketers in front of Boeing's corporate headquarters. Calling the strikers "brothers and sisters"—the way that union members traditionally address one another but a whole new way of talking for most aerospace engineers—Bradley urged them to "Hold out for what you believe."[3]

While SPEEA was joining the rest of the AFL-CIO in supporting Gore, their leaders understood that Bradley's support for the strike was a valuable bargaining chip to get Gore and the entire Clinton administration to put pressure on Boeing. Shortly after Bradley's appearance, Gore's office called IFPTE to ask it to help arrange an event where he would shake hands on a picket line. Fortunately for Gore, the union's staffers remembered that when the vice president went to Seattle, he would usually land his plane at Boeing Field, the company's property and the very place where its new planes were now piling up uninspected. "We told him, if he landed at Boeing Field, he would have to cross one picket line to shake hands on another picket line," IFPTE president Paul Almeida later recalled. Instead, Gore flew into Sea-Tac Airport, like any other traveler.

Democrats weren't the only politicians wooing the Boeing engineers who, under ordinary circumstances, were potential Republican voters. One week after the strike began, Washington's Republican senator Slade Gorton released a statement urging the company and the union to go back to the bargaining table. While his wording was ostensibly evenhanded, many engineers heard something they liked. "My observation is that Boeing's success has always been due to the fact that everyone is working together almost like a family," Gorton said. "I would like to see that rapport restored." Since the company's top executives first announced the emergence of the "New Boeing," they'd proclaimed that Boeing had become "a team, not a family." Now a U.S. senator—and a Republican, at that—had declared that Boeing should become a family again.

Meanwhile, SPEEA walked a tightrope with the FAA. Despite what Boeing's management suspected, the engineers insisted that they never violated the ultimate taboo in Boeing-world—publicly warning that the planes might not be safe—but they did insist that the FAA maintain and enforce its strict rules that new planes had to be inspected by the D.E.R.'s, almost all of whom were on strike.

Thus, early in March, about 230 D.E.R.'s signed a letter to FAA administrator Garvey urging her to hold Boeing to the normal inspection standards, despite the strike. Although the letter didn't say that Boeing's planes weren't safe, it did imply that Boeing might try to deliver some improperly inspected planes to the airlines.

Several days later, the president of Boeing's commercial aircraft division, Alan Mulally, sent a letter to the engineers and technicians that, in turn, exaggerated the extent to which SPEEA was suggesting that there might ever be safety hazards with the company's planes. He pleaded with employees "not to become one of the few who are maliciously attacking our company and deliberately trying to destroy our reputation." In an interview with the *Wall Street Journal*, he charged that some members were being "destructive" to Boeing for allegedly telling the FAA, members of Congress, and several airlines that Boeing wasn't able to help them troubleshoot the seven thousand of its planes that were already in use or to assure the safety of its newly manufactured planes. He said that Boeing's planes were "absolutely" safe and that safety was Boeing's "number one priority."

Years later, union leaders still denied that they had ever bad-mouthed Boeing's safety practices. "We knew we couldn't have sidebar discussions with Jane Garvey," Almeida said. "There were engineers who wanted to present information about why certain planes weren't ready to be delivered. But we never blew that whistle."

"Moving the Packages Around"

The picket lines, the publicity stunts, the pressure from financial analysts and politicians all were intended to get Boeing to move from a position that it had repackaged once and the engineers had rejected twice.

But getting Boeing to budge wouldn't be easy. Far from saying that they would meet SPEEA halfway, Boeing's leaders declared for several weeks that they had made a generous offer, SPEEA was foolish to reject it, and they would not make a proposal that cost more money than they had already offered. Moreover, they insisted that the company could survive a long strike and, if necessary, would find ways to produce and deliver aircraft without relying on the engineers and technicians in the Seattle area. So, for the first few weeks of the strike, it became what Almeida called "a war of attrition, like the Ali-Frazier fights—the question was, who would fall down first?" Would Boeing buckle under the pressure of being unable to deliver its airplanes and watching its stock price decline? Or would the engineers and technicians, who were losing a total of $3.4 million in pay every day, give up and give in?

Almost a week after the walkout began, on February 15, Boeing held its first press conference of the strike. Saying that the company could continue to function almost indefinitely, Condit declared, "We can do it a long, long time. They [SPEEA] have to come say they are willing to talk." If necessary, he continued, Boeing might try to do the work on its planes and other products at locations other than the Seattle area, presumably at the old McDonnell-Douglas factories in St. Louis and Southern California, where the white-collar workers were not on strike. Responding to this threat, Bofferding called it an "old school" management tactic that was designed to "remove all hope." He said SPEEA was "ready to talk" with Boeing.

But, maintaining the company's hard line, on the day after the news conference, Stonecipher told reporters that Boeing didn't plan to put more money on the table. Comparing the negotiations to "moving the packages around," he said that Boeing would "stay within the box" of the total cost that the company was willing to pay for a settlement.

By the beginning of the next week, Monday, February 21, federal mediators returned to Seattle to try to get the company and the union to start talking to each other again, even if they wouldn't meet with each other and would exchange offers only through an intermediary. Before meeting separately with each side, one of the mediators, Rick Oglesby, said, "We haven't gotten any signs from either side that they've got a different position than they've got on the table."

Still, by Tuesday, both sides were saying that they would meet with each other again. But once they started talking face-to-face, they were reminded of how far apart they were, and talks broke down again by Saturday night, February 26. As Condit himself had warned, Boeing had indeed moved some economic proposals around, while staying within the box of the total price it was willing to pay. On the most controversial issue of the entire strike—who would pay for employees' health insurance—Boeing continued to insist that the engineers and technicians share the cost, but Boeing scaled the demand back a little. Similarly, Boeing still didn't promise the white-collar employees a bonus for signing their contract but did offer each employee the option to buy a hundred shares of stock over five years, which would be worth $1,000 for each worker. In addition, the company offered to have a higher share of the raises be guaranteed, rather than awarded at the discretion of the managers.

Boeing had moved the money around, but not to the satisfaction of the engineers and technicians. By Saturday night, picketers were telling anyone who would listen that Boeing's latest proposal was a "shell game." For both sides and for the federal mediators, it seemed that Boeing and its white-collar employees were ready for a long strike.

Just as SPEEA had been trying to exert leverage on Boeing, Boeing now tried to put pressure on SPEEA, with a seeming favor and several new threats. Right before contract talks broke down again on February 26, Boeing made a surprising offer to SPEEA. Picking up on a proposal that the union had routinely made at the beginning of the negotiations but that had a low priority for its members, the company offered to allow the engineers and the technicians to vote on whether to have an "agency shop"—a system that exists in most union contracts, requiring all employees to pay a fee to the union to cover the costs of negotiations and grievance handling, even if they don't join the union.

"I was astonished," recalled Almeida, who saw the apparent concession as a clever ruse by Boeing. If SPEEA had accepted the offer of an agency shop, especially if it had also given ground on an issue of more importance to individual employees, such as pay increases or health insurance, Boeing could have leaked the story to the news media and presented the union as more interested in collecting dues money than in improving conditions for the engineers and technicians. "They wanted agency shop to be a 'wedge issue,' between the union and the workers, just like in politics," Almeida said. "They wanted the union to grab it. Fortunately, we didn't take the bait."

Just a few days later, on March 1, Boeing threatened to declare that the negotiations had reached an "impasse"—a stalemate that could not be resolved. Under federal law, the company could then impose its own contract terms on the engineers and technicians. In a letter to SPEEA that followed the requirements of the nation's labor laws, Boeing cited "substantial differences" over the issues and asked the union to respond.

This was a no-win proposition for SPEEA. If it formally agreed that there were substantial disagreements, this would make it easier for Boeing to impose its terms for a contract. If the union tried to establish that there was still some give-and-take in the bargaining, it would have to make a concession. And if the union publicly disputed that there was a deadlock, it would be denying the obvious and would appear ridiculous. Instead, Bofferding used another one of his sound bites, calling Boeing's latest move "a temper tantrum." Meanwhile, the union put out the word that it might ask the FAA to suspend Boeing's authority to certify the safety of its new airplanes.

Rather than impose its entire contract proposal, which included items that the employees didn't like, such as having to pay 5 percent of their medical premiums, Boeing announced that it would put its most attractive proposal into effect. In a news conference on Sunday, March 5, Mulally, who headed the company's commercial aircraft division, said that engineers and technicians who went back to work would receive the salary increase that Boeing was offering for the first year. Still respected by many of the engineers, who saw him as one of their own, Mulally appealed to the engineers to return to their jobs. In the days ahead, few would take him up on his offer.

As the strike entered its second month, it was a standoff. After four weeks without paychecks, the engineers and technicians continued to lose more than $3 million a day. Many were having a hard time making their mortgage payments, paying their utility bills, or even affording groceries and other necessities. As professionals who were used to dealing with numbers and other inescapable realities, the engineers and technicians understood that the longer they stayed out of work, the less likely it was that any contract settlement would recover the money they were losing.

For its part, Boeing was also hurting. By the end of February, the company had delivered only 9 commercial aircraft since the start of the strike—just one-third as fast as it should be producing planes, in order to meet its goal of delivering 480 aircraft that year. In addition, Boeing was falling behind on engineering and design work on commercial and military projects, including the competition to develop a new joint strike fighter jet for the Defense Department, where the company was going up against its longtime rival, Lockheed Martin, and its work on the F-22 fighter jet for the air force. As the *Wall Street Journal* reported, the same large shareholders and financial analysts who had put pressure on Boeing to hold the line on its personnel costs were now worried that the strike would plunge the company into a downward spiral of production delays and lost contracts.

While Boeing and SPEEA grew increasingly angry at each other and determined not to be the first to back down, the actual differences between them were surprisingly narrow. When Boeing made its third offer, SPEEA was offended, but, in fact, the two sides' bargaining positions were only $107 million apart.

Yet how would that gap be bridged?

MAKING THE DEAL

In the end, there was only one way to get Boeing and SPEEA to move from their bargaining positions: move them all across the continent.

After failing to prevent the strike or to reach a settlement after two weeks, the chief federal mediator, C. Richard Barnes, had kept in touch with both sides. Even after SPEEA rejected Boeing's third offer, he continued his "shuttle diplomacy" between the company and the union.

As an experienced mediator, he understood that settling a long strike was often a matter of time, location, and personalities. Clearly, the engineers and technicians needed to prove that they could conduct a successful strike. Similarly, Boeing felt that it couldn't make substantial concessions after the weaker of its two unions had gone out for only a week or two. But after the strike had dragged on for more than a month, both sides had proved their points.

Still, Barnes understood, the negotiators needed a new location, if only to escape from their coworkers and the energetic reporters from Seattle's two daily newspapers and its radio and TV stations, all of whom were watching their every move and would have waited in the lobby, the coffee shop, and the barroom of any local hotel where meetings were taking place. So Barnes summoned both bargaining teams to the FMCS (Federal Mediation and Conciliation Service) headquarters in Washington, D.C., where few journalists knew who they were and where the strike was not the main news story in town.

"He [Barnes] moved the negotiations to Washington, D.C., to get them [the Boeing and SPEEA negotiators] out of their normal environment," Almeida recalled. "The strategy was to isolate them and make them work out their own problems."

Then, with the encouragement of Barnes and the agreement of the leaders of Boeing and SPEEA, both sides reshuffled their negotiating teams. In place of the unwieldy bargaining teams that had deadlocked three times in Seattle, Boeing and SPEEA each agreed to bring only five negotiators apiece to Washington, D.C. Boeing brought Dagnon, Calhoun, Stamper, and two others. SPEEA brought Bofferding, Buckham, Sorscher, Smith, and their attorney, Phyllis Rogers.

Even far away from familiar surroundings, Dagnon and Bofferding would still be at loggerheads, so Barnes tried to introduce a new and, ultimately, pivotal personality into the talks. Since Condit and Stonecipher could not personally participate in the negotiations—imagine the chief officers of a major corporation bargaining with a small union—the change would have to come on the union's side of the table. With Barnes's encouragement, SPEEA and its parent union, IFPTE, invited a national labor leader to the talks.

That leader was Richard Trumka, the secretary-treasurer and second in command at the national AFL-CIO. By then, he was familiar to and trusted by SPEEA's leaders and activists. Initially skeptical that a white-collar union with scarcely more than half of its constituents signed up as members could pull off an effective strike, Trumka had visited with the strikers several times, become a believer, and raised funds from other unions to support the engineers and the technicians.

Sporting a Zapata mustache and with the bulky body of a one-time athlete trapped in a desk job, Trumka straddled the blue-collar and white-collar worlds. Born and raised in the small coal-mining community of Nemicola, Pennsylvania, Trumka had worked summers in the mines while attending college and earning professional degrees both as a lawyer and in accounting. He became an attorney for the United Mine Workers and, in 1982, at the age of thirty-three, was elected president of the union. The miners gambled on a well-spoken young man who campaigned in a business suit and had earned the educational credentials they wanted their own kids to have.

As with many of the younger labor leaders who emerged in the 1990s, Trumka was fascinated by the workings of major corporations. In October 2000, I found myself sitting next to Trumka on a shuttle flight from Washington, D.C., to New York City. Continuing his role as the AFL-CIO's emissary to professional employees, he was going to a meeting in Manhattan about the royalty payments for unionized actors who appear in television commercials. I was about to meet with a record company president who had hired me to help write a speech. Trumka was visibly exhausted, and, thinking that he wanted to talk about the presidential campaign, I asked him how it was going in the coal-mining states of West Virginia and Pennsylvania. But Trumka was much more interested in asking me about the record companies and how they were trying to discourage the pirating of their music.

So Trumka, the coal miner's son who became a labor lawyer, found himself leading a negotiating team of aerospace engineers and technicians. Unlike Bofferding, he could get along with Dagnon. Both men were accustomed to traditional labor negotiations—cursing out the other guy in public, understanding that there was nothing personal about it, and then meeting privately and cutting a deal.

When Trumka and Dagnon finally held the inevitable private meeting, the deal wasn't too difficult to make—the two sides, after all, had become estranged emotionally but never really were that far apart substantively. Dagnon scrapped the demand that the engineers and technicians pay part of the cost of their health coverage. He also agreed to the same $1,000 cash bonus that the Machinists had received upon signing their contract, as well as another $1,500 if the engineers and the technicians helped the company to meet production quotas for designing, producing, and delivering new planes in the year ahead—a real priority for Boeing now that the strike had caused severe bottlenecks. As for pay raises, Boeing agreed to spread them more evenly—"peanut-buttering them," as Stamper put it—with guaranteed increases of 3 percent annually over three years for the engineers and 4 percent, 3 percent, and 3 percent for the technicians. With additional potential merit increases and other raises, the economic packages for the engineers and technicians were roughly equal to what the Machinists had received.

Before discussing it with Trumka, Dagnon had cleared his offer with Boeing's top brass, who were anxious to put the strike behind them. For his part, Trumka had little trouble selling the settlement to SPEEA's negotiators. Far from home, they understood that they had no chance of winning more than the Machinists had and were fortunate to have won about as much.

In a nod to the engineers' fears for the future of Boeing and their anger that management didn't respect their opinions, the agreement also created a joint labor-management Leadership Council. Co-chaired by Condit and Almeida, it would discuss issues that included corporate strategies, health-care costs, the efficiency of the company's operations, and the quality of its products.

By the time both bargaining teams had met together and formally approved the agreement, it was four in the morning on Monday, March 20. While both sides' leaders said the things negotiators usually say when they've settled a strike, Condit offered an important insight into why Boeing had finally tried to accommodate the engineers: "One thing Wall Street does not like is ambiguity. Now that agreement is there, it is beginning to make the future less cloudy."

After a few hours' sleep, the SPEEA team, together with Trumka and Almeida, took a transcontinental flight to Seattle, where they would explain the agreement to the engineers and technicians, persuade them to ratify it, and conclude the strike with one more dramatic gesture.

On Sunday morning, the engineers and technicians met in Seattle's futuristic Space Needle, an observation tower that overlooks the entire city and the Puget Sound. With some SPEEA members saying that the agreement wasn't good enough but most realizing that it was the best they could get, each unit voted to accept the contract by about the same 70 percent margin.

At nine on Monday morning, the engineers and technicians went back to work with the same flair for drama that they had used when walking off their jobs six weeks earlier. At many of the larger buildings, SPEEA members held outdoor rallies before they walked through the doors. Trumka, Almeida, and Bofferding stood in front of Boeing's headquarters in Everett, like politicians greeting likely voters, and shook hands with engineers returning to their jobs. At many worksites, when the engineers walked in, management, Machinists, and nonunion clerical workers applauded them.

A HEALTHY CATHARSIS?

The engineers and technicians felt much better about themselves, their jobs, and even their company than they had before the strike. For years after the walkout, most engineers and even many management types believed that the strike had been a good thing not only for the engineers and technicians but also for Boeing.

First, the quiet men and women who designed airplanes and defense systems had proved that they wouldn't be bullied. They had shown Boeing and the Machinists that if necessary, they could strike successfully for six weeks. As Bofferding put it after the strike, "The ninety-pound weakling just grew some muscles."

Second, they had expressed the anger that many had bottled up for years. "It was good for morale to have had the strike," the former management negotiator, Geoff Stamper, said years later. "It would have been a disaster if they had stayed at work dissatisfied, all the frustration not released. I almost think the catharsis was a good thing." The remainder of the year would be one of Boeing's best ever—productivity, sales, and profits were all on an upswing.

Third, strange as it sounds, the engineers demonstrated their loyalty to Boeing by staging the strike. From the signs that said "On Strike *for* Boeing" to the SPEEA negotiators' insistence on trying to solve the company's problems even when their management counterparts clearly wanted them to keep quiet, there was no mistaking the engineers' passionate concern for Boeing. From Condit on down, many executives realized that the engineers and technicians cared about their jobs, their products, and their company. After the strike, Boeing tried to tap that commitment once again.

To be sure, tapping that commitment could be awkward. At the first meeting of the Leadership Council, its two co-chairs, Condit and Almeida, realized that they had never met each other before. Trying to break the ice, Condit said, "It's nice to finally meet you. I've only seen you on television. You kept on saying you were trying to save Boeing. What exactly were you trying to save it from?"

"I just kind of laughed," Almeida recalled. "I couldn't have said what I was thinking: 'I was trying to save it from you.'"[4]

Afterword

"NO ONE KNOWS WHERE"

Six years after the Boeing engineers' strike and the abortive organizing campaign at the Microsoft Tax Saver Unit, several leaders from these struggles once again found themselves arguing with their adversaries. This time, the setting wasn't a picket line or a bargaining table but rather the University of Washington's sprawling and woodsy campus in northeast Seattle. The occasion was a conference conducted by the university's Labor Studies Department about "knowledge workers," a term that may be difficult to define but, by any definition, includes aircraft engineers at Boeing, software writers at Microsoft, and many other workers in the Seattle area.

Charlie Bofferding and Stan Sorscher of SPEEA and Marcus Courtney of WashTech were at the conference, as were executives from Microsoft and Boeing. In panel discussions at the university's Seattle campus, they continued the arguments that had resulted in emotionally charged conflicts in 2000 and had kept simmering ever since. I'd also been invited to address the conference, and after I spoke, people from the audience asked questions that were more like speeches about the conflicts at Boeing, Microsoft, and other companies. One Boeing official was so indignant about what I said that he buttonholed me later with a lengthy handwritten response. For all the relaxed atmosphere

233

at the event, the passionate disagreements that rocked the area's workplaces in the aftermath of the WTO protests still had not subsided. The underlying questions remained unanswered: If skilled and dedicated "knowledge workers" are so essential, then why aren't they paid better and offered the opportunities to do their best work? Or had Microsoft, Boeing, and other leading companies decided that expensive and assertive American workers were too much trouble after all, so why not farm out their jobs to India and China? And what kind of employee organizations could help these "knowledge workers" make their voices heard and their jobs better?

Several of the sessions resembled a cross between provocative academic seminars and deadlocked contract negotiations. At a panel discussion about information technology workers early on a Saturday morning, Courtney was in what, as he later admitted, was a new situation for him. At last, he was sitting next to a top Microsoft executive, in a position to demand improvements in how the company treated its employees. That may have discomforted the management person on his panel, a Microsoft vice president named Tom Gruver, who took an unusual approach during his presentation. Rather than talk about the tens of thousands of knowledge workers at Microsoft, Gruver played the surprisingly candid stand-up comic, joking about how Microsoft was no longer the hot company in the IT industry. Suggesting that he was glad to have an audience at all, Gruver deadpanned, "People don't talk that much about Microsoft. They don't think we're innovative anymore. Everyone likes to talk about Google instead." Turning to his company's less-than-successful marketing campaigns, he recalled that Microsoft had tried the slogan "More productive all the time" but dropped it because "people thought we meant that they would be working all the time."

In his one moment of boastfulness in his opening presentation, Gruver declared that Microsoft had coined the phrases "information worker" and "knowledge worker," and whatever the origins of those terms, there was a sense in which he was indisputably correct.

With the fading of IBM, Microsoft was far and away the nation's leading employer of IT professionals and it had been the first company to grasp that the greatest opportunities in the industry were in a field that was pure intellect—creating software—rather than in designing and manufacturing the hardware, as IBM had done.

Then it was Courtney's turn. Speaking slowly and calmly, with none of the pent-up rage that might be expected of a union leader at long last confronting his employer, Courtney made Microsoft sound more formidable than Gruver had presented the company as being. Like earlier radicals, Courtney explained how Microsoft had created opposing institutions in its own image— the virtual company training cyber-agitators like Courtney and a virtual union like WashTech. Courtney told the story of how he had tested the software for two successful products—Windows 98 and Outlook 2000. But he had remained a temp worker and was paid only $18 an hour, with no health insurance. "I was one of the people who can claim to have been radicalized while working at Microsoft," he declared. Joining and soon leading WashTech, Courtney said he used the technology that he had helped to develop at Microsoft—Web sites and list-serves ("mailing" lists consisting of e-mail addresses)—to organize dissatisfied colleagues at the company. While WashTech had not succeeded in organizing any appreciable numbers of Microsoft employees, its presence in the news media and its growing list-serve had attracted attention to the plight of temporary workers throughout the industry and had prompted Microsoft to change some of its policies. Moreover, Courtney continued, WashTech's use of the Internet for advocacy and organizing had inspired several Internet-based political movements, including the liberal pressure group MoveOn.org and Howard Dean's insurgent presidential campaign in 2004.

Gruver maintained a forced smile during Courtney's remarks. But during the question-and-answer portion of the panel discussion, he was forced to frown. The liberal journalist Robert Kuttner, who had traveled from Boston to attend the conference, asked Gruver what seemed like a softball question but turned out to be subtly subversive: "What kinds of political values are promoted by the environment at Microsoft?" The executive responded that Microsoft devoted "a lot more thought to social change than people give us credit for." He explained that the Bill and Melinda Gates Foundation was promoting better education in the United States and improved health care in Africa, among other causes. Predictably, Courtney then asked whether Microsoft's charity should begin closer to home, improving wages and benefits for its lowest-paid employees. In response, Gruver again tried to change the subject, explaining how many charitable donations Microsoft and its employees contributed every year.

Courtney and Gruver were talking past each other and so, at another panel, were Boeing and its critics.

Owen Herrnstadt, the international affairs director of the Machinists union, which represents Boeing's blue-collar workers, explained how the aerospace giant is farming out the design and the production of parts of its planes to workers in other countries. Increasingly, Americans were doing only the original design and the final assembly of the entire plane. Thus, Machinists', engineers', and technicians' jobs were all being eliminated, either through layoffs or attrition.

Boeing was represented by John McMasters, a veteran engineer on the staff of the Ed Wells Initiative, a skills development program jointly operated by Boeing and SPEEA. In his presentation at the panel and in a later discussion with me, McMasters vehemently defended what sounded like Boeing's viewpoint on outsourcing, the engineers' strike, and the company's future. In a PowerPoint presentation titled "Thoughts on the Engineer of 2020," McMasters explained that the U.S. engineers of the future would be less like their forebears who designed new airplanes from scratch and more like coordinators of the efforts of engineers and technicians around the world. Acknowledging that Boeing and the entire industry "need to replenish and sustain a rapidly aging technical pool," McMasters did not explain how his profession would attract the next generation of engineers who, after all, tend to be young people who dream of designing more advanced airplanes, rockets, and other flying machines. Years earlier, the physicist-turned-engineer Stan Sorscher had explained to me that he had been infuriated by a similar presentation by a Boeing official.

For his part, McMasters seemed intent on arguing with anyone who questioned his views. During the panel discussion, McMasters patronized Herrnstadt as a "young man" who didn't understand the long-term globalizing trends in the aircraft industry. Balding, unflappable and in his late forties, Herrnstadt didn't take the bait and instead simply restated his statistics about how much work Boeing was outsourcing and how many U.S. jobs were being lost. Later that afternoon, when I gave a talk about how the Boeing engineers' strike reflected workers' aspirations to do their jobs better, McMasters was scribbling furiously. When the session was over, he approached me, declared that I had "gotten everything wrong," and gave me several pages of neatly handwritten notes explaining his views about what the Boeing engineers' strike had really meant.

"The SPEEA strike in 2000 was essentially reactionary," he wrote. "Heritage Boeing (pre-1996) was effectively a rather provincial (regional) company off the main road of the rest of the industry that happened to [sell] a substantial number of products overseas, thus contributing to our national balance of trade. While management made no effort to promote the idea, the workers felt like part of a (sometimes dysfunctional) family. People seemed to have a strong desire for a 'sense of community' and it worked for us." While the engineers wanted to remain the leading citizens of a corporate community, McMasters continued, Boeing had to adapt to new developments, including globalization, energy shortages, and the airlines' financial problems. The engineers thought that they were striking to "save the company," but saving Boeing required bolder changes that would discomfort everyone. Abrasive as he appeared, McMasters was making important points that were borne out by Boeing's history after 2000.

Indeed, McMasters and Gruver seemed to symbolize some of the differences between Boeing and Microsoft. McMasters was socially awkward, unfashionably clad in a business suit on a Saturday afternoon. But there was something admirable about his willingness to engage his company's critics in forthright discussions about Boeing's corporate strategies and personnel policies. In contrast, Gruver, like most of the conference participants, was informally dressed. His manner was friendly, ironic, and self-deprecating. But he refused to respond to critics of Microsoft's employment policies—Courtney, Kuttner, or my own presentation at the conference. Both men's personal styles reflected their companies' practices: Boeing said and did many things that its employees despised, but it bargained with unions representing its blue-collar and white-collar workers and sponsored joint labor-management projects such as the Ed Wells Initiative. Microsoft, however—despite all its free coffee and beer bashes—had structured its workforce so that one-third worked for staffing agencies, and every worker would find it almost impossible to win union representation. At Boeing, mavericks such as Stan Sorscher could make themselves heard if they were willing to take the heat. At Microsoft, mavericks tended to quit and start their own competing companies.

In the years since 2000, Boeing, Microsoft, Kaiser Aluminum, and Northwest Hospital went their own, sometimes surprising, ways, still raising the questions that rebels had raised about how each company could continue to engage the energies of its most dedicated employees.

HELLO, I MUST BE LEAVING

Did the engineers' and technicians' strike signal a new partnership between Boeing and its professional workforce and a renewed commitment to commercial aircraft? Or did the strike contribute to

Boeing's determination to be less dependent on skilled U.S. workers, such as the engineers and technicians and the machinists, who were not only capable but costly, assertive, and inclined to challenge the company and to try, every few years, to shut it down?

Years after the strike, it seems that Boeing has been pursuing both paths.

In its own way, Boeing continues to value its workforce, and, once again, it is number one in the worldwide market for commercial aircraft. In the aftermath of the SPEEA strike, Boeing declared that it appreciated the engineers' and technicians' commitment to the company and would work with them on several projects. A new Leadership Council, with officials from Boeing and SPEEA, discusses Boeing's long-term strategies, and the Ed Wells Initiative has expanded its efforts to provide continuing education, professional development, career counseling, and mentoring for engineers and technicians. Long after 2000, there were lively debates about whether the engineers' new assertiveness had encouraged Boeing to renew its commitment to commercial aircraft. But Boeing did become even more vehement about beating Airbus, although it would pursue the goal in unorthodox ways.

Since the difficult negotiations in 1999 and 2000, Boeing has been eager to accommodate the engineers and technicians on economic issues. In 2005, Boeing agreed to what the *Seattle Times* called "a lush contract," including salary increases of 17 percent for the engineers and 15 percent for the technicians over the next three years. Average salaries would increase from $82,060 to $95,884 for the engineers and from $61,744 to $71,134 for the technicians, at a time when most workers, white-collar or blue-collar, were barely staying even. The contract was settled a day after Boeing announced that it would begin to develop a new plane—a stretch derivative of the 747 jumbo jet. Clearly, the company wanted its engineers and technicians to remain motivated, not mutinous.[1]

On the other hand, Boeing was also striving to become, in the business buzzwords of our era, more flexible and global. Early in 2001, the company announced that it would be moving its headquarters from Seattle for several reasons. First, it wanted its top executives to be able to think strategically and allocate capital among Boeing's three divisions—defense, space, and commercial aircraft. Being in Seattle, insiders explained, had predisposed Boeing's leadership to give priority to the company's oldest, largest, and best-known business: building airplanes for civilian travel and freight transportation. But the second reason suggested that producing commercial aircraft still was closest to Boeing's heart. Moving to a larger metropolitan area would bring its corporate headquarters closer to its main airline customers. When Boeing selected Chicago as its new corporate home, executives explained that their central office would now be near O'Hare International Airport, not far from United Airlines' headquarters. Also, they pointed out, O'Hare is a major hub of American Airlines.

The headquarters of Boeing's Commercial Airlines Division, as well as the factories and the offices where the engineers worked, all remained in Seattle. No Machinists or SPEEA members lost their jobs as a result of the move. In fact, the division's chief, Alan Mulally, gained stature inside and outside the company now that he was the leading, and most visible, Boeing executive in Seattle. A former engineer beloved by his former colleagues in SPEEA (but not nearly as popular among the Machinists), Mulally never became the CEO of Boeing, but an ailing Ford Company selected him as its president in 2006.

Still, local residents saw Boeing's relocation of its headquarters as a signal that the company wanted to reduce its reliance on uppity union members from the Seattle area. In an article in the *Seattle Times*'s *Sunday Magazine*, "Sadie Seattle" and "Bill Boeing" pour out their hearts to a marriage counselor to explore why Bill had left home after eighty years of marriage. "It was so you could lay off anyone . . . and not have to run into them in the grocery store," Sadie tells Bill.[2]

Sadie Seattle did have reason to resent Bill Boeing's roving eye. Especially after the move to Chicago, Boeing outsourced much of the design work and parts manufacturing to subcontractors all over the world. Indeed, by some estimates, the company was farming out 64 percent of the work on its current models. This practice raised questions not only among engineers, technicians, and machinists but also among some of Boeing's own advisers and consultants. As early as February 2001, John Hart-Smith, a senior technical fellow at the Phantom Works research unit in Southern California, delivered a lecture at Boeing's Leadership Center in St. Louis. "The most important issue of all," Hart-Smith declared, "is whether or not a company can continue to operate if it relies primarily on outsourcing the majority of work that it once did in-house." Hart's paper became an underground classic among Boeing engineers.[3]

Moving out of Seattle—and outsourcing much of its work—weren't the only controversies at Boeing. In 2003, Boeing's CEO Phil Condit was forced to resign amid allegations that the company had been involved in a corruption case at the Defense Department. No one had linked the scandal to Condit personally, but it had happened on his watch. Then, the soft-spoken Condit was succeeded by the man whom veteran Boeing employees feared the most, the tough-talking former McDonnell-Douglas chief, Harry Stonecipher. Two years later, Stonecipher was forced to resign after having an extramarital affair with a Boeing executive. Contributing to the confusion at Boeing was the sense that each CEO had been caught in the sort of scandal that would have been expected to entrap the other. The rumors of womanizing had always swirled around Condit, while Stonecipher was seen as the hardnosed boss who would do anything to get more defense contracts.

But despite all the turmoil, Boeing was doing something right, after all. Its European rival, Airbus, was pursuing Boeing's old strategy: keep building larger, faster airplanes. But in the aftermath of the September 11, 2001, terror attacks and with jet fuel becoming costlier, the airlines were no longer eager to buy huge, high-flying aircraft. For once, Boeing was listening to its customers in the airlines and among the traveling public, and the aerospace giant made an important discovery. Instead of hub-to-hub travel (flying from New York City to Atlanta, then switching to a smaller plane to a smaller city), passengers were favoring and airlines were beginning to provide point-to-point travel from one midsized city to another. Such flights required midsized planes, not jumbo jets, and Boeing gambled, correctly, that its future was with redesigning older midsized models and building new ones.

By 2005, Boeing was having its best year since 1988, surpassing Airbus in commercial jet sales for the first time in five years. In 2007, it rolled out its newest model, originally called the 7E7, a midsized, wide-body, twin-engine jetliner that will carry between 210 and 330 passengers. In place of the old Boeing mantra of "bigger, faster, higher," this plane could be described as "leaner, cleaner, greener." The first major airplane to use "composite" material for most of the plane's construction, it is made of aluminum, titanium, steel, and carbon-reinforced plastic. Lighter in weight than other planes, it is expected to be at least 20 percent more fuel-efficient than current aircraft. When it goes into service in 2008, it will be called the Dreamliner—a branding that suggests Steven Spielberg more than William Boeing and reflects Boeing's ability to adapt to new economic realties and cultural trends.

But Boeing still has problems regarding the issues raised in 2000. The Dreamliner is way behind schedule largely because of the difficulty in assembling a plane, of which many of the parts are produced overseas. Boeing's corps of engineers is rapidly aging: a Boeing engineer's average age is forty-five. As with other essential professional, technical, and craft jobs, the question is, how to make this work attractive for future generations?

Meanwhile, the organization that advocates for Boeing's engineers and technicians, SPEEA, has also been undergoing turmoil. Its longtime executive director Charles Bofferding was a resilient, effective, and highly quotable leader during the strike. Tall, heavyset, and ever-present in the local news media, he takes up a lot of space in every way, and, eventually, he generated his own antimatter within SPEEA. Starting with SPEEA's 2002 elections, he was charged with one-man rule, and his critics within the organization controlled a majority of the executive board. It was a matter of time before they voted him out, and in August 2007, when Bofferding was at his daughter's wedding and his ally, SPEEA's recently elected president Cynthia Cole, was on vacation, Bofferding's critics ousted him, effective immediately.

But the drama didn't stop there. SPEEA members who supported Bofferding or, at least, opposed his opponents founded their own Web site and set in motion a recall of his adversaries on the executive board. In October, a membership referendum recalled these board members, and the remainder of the board selected Cole as acting executive director. Early in 2008, the board hired a new executive director, Ray Goforth, who had been a senior official and contract negotiator with IFPTE Local 17, which represents engineers, technicians, and computer professionals who work for government agencies in the state of Washington. Heading into the 2008 contract negotiations, SPEEA was in disarray—suffering, some would say, of the very democracy that the engineers insisted upon in their organization.

BEYOND THE BUBBLE

During the late 1990s, when WashTech was founded, some professional workers at companies such as Boeing and Microsoft were afraid that their wages would be undercut or they might even lose their jobs because of the H1-B program, which provides temporary visas for skilled workers requested by U.S. companies. Growing from sixty-five thousand visas granted for the year 1997 to two hundred thousand in 2007, the program brings in technical workers who are tied to one company and cannot demand pay raises or organize unions.

Shortly after 2000, U.S. information technology workers became afraid of something much scarier. Instead of importing tens of thousands of skilled workers from countries like India with large numbers of well-educated but low-paid workers, their companies were beginning to export hundreds of thousands of jobs to the same countries from which they used to recruit workers. The very technologies that IT workers had helped to develop—the digitization of information and its transmission over the Internet—now allowed their employers to farm out their work to people in other countries on other continents.

With its muckraking tradition and its sources throughout Microsoft, WashTech was among the first labor, journalistic, or research organizations to expose this new development. In 2002, someone from Microsoft leaked a sensational document to WashTech: a PowerPoint presentation by Windows executive Brian Valentine. The presentation was titled, "Why Think about India Now?" Its answer was clear: "Quality work at 50 to 60 percent of the cost—that's two heads for the price of one."

WashTech publicized the story on its Web site and in e-mailings to its members and subscribers. Courtney and his colleagues also reached out to their contacts in the news media, and soon the *New York Times*, the *Wall Street Journal*, *Business Week*, and CNN, as well as the *Seattle Times*, the *Post-Intelligencer*, and the *Seattle Weekly*, were all running stories about what came to be called "outsourcing" or "offshoring."[4] While WashTech's membership remained about the same, the subscribers to its updates grew well beyond twenty thousand. Its parent union, CWA, founded a new national Web-based organization called Techs United, which linked to WashTech's site and received WashTech's e-mails. As it was doing in various states and cities where public employees did not yet enjoy the rights to organize unions and bargain with their employers, as well as at IBM, where workers were upset about changes in their pension plan, CWA was positioning itself to conduct a large-scale organizing campaign in the information technology industry sometime in the future.

But what about now? As a highly visible organization entirely dedicated to workers in the high-technology industry, WashTech is potentially attractive to many workers in the industries and the occupations that CWA currently represents. Over the years, WashTech has successfully organized workers in several small software and video game companies and local governments throughout the state of Washington. Then, in 2005, WashTech organized more than 900 employees of the Cingular wireless telephone company and an additional 125 information technology employees in the city of Bothell, not far from Seattle.

Meanwhile, IT workers were having a harder time holding onto their jobs and getting ahead in their careers. Throughout the Seattle area, more than ten thousand jobs were eliminated in information technology between 2001 and 2006, as a result of the collapse of the "bubble" in the industry, the recession, and the offshoring of jobs. For all the talk of Microsoft millionaires, most information technology workers earned in the mid-five figures.

At Microsoft, as Bill Gates prepared to retire from an active role, the company acknowledged that it was having difficulties in recruiting and retaining workers. At a town hall–style meeting with employees on May 18, 2006, Microsoft executives promised to offer a slew of new benefits, including dry cleaning, grocery delivery, and to-go meals from Wolfgang Puck. For all its accomplishments, Microsoft still faced the sort of problems, including missed product deadlines and what *Information Week* magazine called "the bugginess of Windows," that suggested that its low- and midlevel employees weren't doing their best work.

Could WashTech help these employees to improve their own conditions and the quality of their work? Although the group had helped to compel Microsoft to change its policies, company executives had never formally met with Courtney until he sat next to a corporate vice president at the conference. The virtual union had never brought the virtual company to an actual bargaining table.

HENRY KAISER'S HEIRS

After the lockout concluded and the workers returned in the fall of 2000, Kaiser Aluminum was flat-out broke and unable to pay its bills, much less meet its obligations to its retirees. The financier Charles Hurwitz lost control of the company to its largest creditors: various funds providing pension and health benefits to several generations of retired workers. In a sense, these retired workers were Henry Kaiser's heirs—people who had gone to work for Henry J. decades earlier and had traded years of sweat for years of security. As the benefit funds and the Steelworkers Union assumed leadership of what remained of Kaiser Aluminum, they created a company that, under the most difficult of circumstances, reflected his vision of well-treated workers making world-class products.

Once again, Kaiser Aluminum downsized, but this time, there was a larger purpose than simply saving money and boosting stock prices. In Washington State, the company closed its smelters in Tacoma and Mead, concentrating instead on making its rolling mill at Trentwood competitive in the global marketplace. Producing fabricated aluminum parts—sheets, plates, and coils—Kaiser has sold its products to Boeing, Airbus, and other companies in aerospace, transportation, and related industries.

Over the years, Kaiser has invested more than $130 million in the Trentwood plant, adding two heat-treatment furnaces, which strengthen aluminum. Eventually, the company added several hundred new workers at Trentwood for a total of about eight hundred.

When Kaiser emerged from bankruptcy in 2005, it chose a new board of directors, half of whose members were selected by the Steelworkers Union. In addition to retired Steelworkers president George Becker, the board included a former Republican member of Congress from New York State and several corporate executives and academic experts. As Bert Caldwell of the *Seattle Spokesman-Review* declared, "Overall the group will be a significant upgrade from the sad gang that delivered Kaiser to its creditors."[5]

Although most grueling smelting jobs had been eliminated and new equipment had been installed, making aluminum products still isn't an easy job. But, as Dan Wilson, the president of Steelworkers Local 338, explained, the company is experiencing "the best conditions" since he was hired during the 1980s. "It is going to be a pretty good company," said Jim Woodward, a Steelworkers union staffer and a former Kaiser worker.

Most likely, Henry J. would have agreed.

A LONGER TABLE?

If it had been relatively routine for the workers at Northwest Hospital to organize a union in 2000, the years that followed were anything but easy. During the negotiations for a second contract in 2005, the hospital management pursued a goal that is ironic but increasingly commonplace for health-care institutions: cutting back health benefits for the employees, especially the part-time workers and their families. Eventually and reluctantly, the union agreed to having the workers pick up the first 10 percent of the increase in the dependent care premium.

In fairness, Northwest Hospital wasn't being greedy; it was as hard-pressed by rising health care costs as any other large institution. "This is the issue we fight about with all the employers—who's going to pick up the increase in health-care costs," explained Emily Van Bronkhorst, the vice president of SEIU Local 1199NW.

Meanwhile, a group of employees at the hospital was trying to vote out the union. The hospital's management did not seem to be helping the workers who were citing materials and, some claimed, receiving assistance from two anti-union groups, the National Right-to-Work Committee and a conservative state-wide think tank, the Evergreen Freedom Foundation. In 2006, the workers in the service-maintenance bargaining unit voted by a margin of 270 to 145 to keep the union, while the workers in the professional-technical bargaining unit reached the same conclusion by the narrower margin of 51 to 38.

When I interviewed Local 1199NW president Diane Sosne in December 2005, with the negotiations concluded and the decertification vote looming, she was relaxed and optimistic. It was just before the holiday season, and we were sitting in the cafeteria at Swedish Medical Center, where she was preparing to attend a graduation ceremony for workers who were moving up to better-paying jobs through a training program negotiated by the union.

Looking forward, Sosne spoke of bringing Northwest Hospital, Swedish Medical Center, and other local health-care facilities into regional contract negotiations, similar to those that SEIU's flagship health-care union, Local 1199, has conducted in New York City. At least at first, wages would still be resolved hospital by hospital, but the union would help the hospitals create area-wide training, health care, and pension funds for all their workers. Workers would gain from having portable benefits that they could take with them from job to job. The hospitals would gain from having better-trained workers and reducing the risk of strikes resulting from disputes over rising health-care costs. To the extent that hospitals competed for patients, it would be more by improving the quality of care and less by cutting labor costs. To hear her explain it, it sounded like a win-win deal for everyone. She said that she had broached the idea with Northwest Hospital's CEO, Bill Schneider—a transplanted New Yorker, like Sosne—and he didn't dismiss it.[6]

Compared to the quirkier WashTech and SPEEA, Local 1199NW stuck to a proven model for unions representing workers of any kind: professional, technical, service, or blue-collar. A strong statewide union affiliated with a large national union, Local 1199NW sought to organize every health-care facility, one by one, until it could raise standards for wages, benefits, training, and patient care throughout the entire health-care industry. The union had come a long way from its origins as a group of discontented nurses at Group Health in Seattle, and it had a clear sense of where it wanted to go next.

When it came to improving conditions for "knowledge workers," others could look ahead with just as much clarity and perhaps even more imagination. But this much was hard to deny about SEIU and its emphasis on industrial unionism that eventually evolves into labor-management cooperation: *their way works.*

WHAT NEXT?

By 2007, U.S. workers' wages accounted for the lowest share on record of the nation's gross domestic product (the total value of the goods and the services that the economy produces). Wages had declined 5 percent from their highest level just before the recession of 2001—a level that, in fact, had been reached just before the conflicts described in this book. College graduates' hourly wages, adjusted for inflation, were declining, too, and a disproportionate number of the long-term unemployed were professionals with advanced degrees.

Many of the nation's leaders from the worlds of business, government, and academia continued to insist that a better-educated workforce was the only answer to the problems of stagnant living standards, increasing inequality, and growing worker dissatisfaction. But while no reasonable person questioned the importance of education and training, it was becoming more difficult to maintain that well-educated, highly trained, and intensely dedicated workers would inevitably find and keep rewarding and fulfilling jobs.

As if to remind workers that experience and dedication weren't enough, early in 2007, the retailer Circuit City laid off thirty-four hundred of its most senior employees, maintaining that they were overpaid. These workers had earned between $10 and $20 an hour—about average for U.S. workers. The laid-off workers were free to reapply for their old jobs at lower wages, the company announced.

Nonetheless, the business community continued to complain that it was having a hard time hiring and keeping skilled workers.

Shortages existed or were anticipated in scores of occupations, including doctors, nurses, aircraft engineers, highway engineers, teachers, machinists, computer programmers, and software writers, to name only a few. Writing on the Web site of one of the most conservative business magazines, *Forbes*, Bernadette Kenny warned, "Deepening job dissatisfaction, together with the potential shortage of 'knowledge' workers and management talent, makes for an explosive combination, a perfect storm that could spur further waves of voluntary job moves and heighten job turnover."[7]

How could business recruit, retain, and bring out the best in these workers? How could working Americans, including the best educated, improve their condition? When asked a similar question in his final debate during the 2004 presidential campaign, President George W. Bush returned to his two favorite nostrums, cutting taxes and improving education from kindergarten through grade 12. Cautioned by his advisers to drop populist applause lines like his earlier attacks on "Benedict Arnold CEOs" who sent U.S. jobs overseas, the Democratic nominee, Senator John F. Kerry, offered the usual Democratic proposals, including raising the minimum wage and expanding health insurance. These were well worth enacting, but, especially coming from a candidate as privileged as Kerry, they did not compel large numbers of blue-collar or white-collar workers to reconsider their presidential preferences.

With the 2008 elections approaching, in the midst of increasing economic anxieties and an unpopular war in Iraq, the Democrats were heavily favored to retake the White House and hold onto the Congress that they had captured in 2006.

But the Democrats still seemed uncertain about how to discuss the new economy and the new American workplace in ways that made sense to low-wage service workers, insecure industrial workers, and the increasing numbers of professional and technical workers with their own anxieties and aspirations.

In 1992, the economy was nearing the end of one of the first recessions that wiped out white-collar as well as blue-collar jobs.

Bill Clinton campaigned as a populist policy wonk, famously "feeling the pain" of workers who had suffered corporate downsizings or wage freezes. At a time when professional and technical workers first found themselves competing with their counterparts overseas and losing seemingly secure jobs, Clinton appealed to the American faith in education, training, and continuous self-improvement. "How much you earn depends on how much you learn" he would declare, promising people that he would provide lifelong education and training to prepare them for new and better jobs. While Clinton favored controversial trade agreements that were unpopular with working class voters, his instinct was to present them as part of a grand bargain: Corporate America would get the free trade that it wanted. Working Americans would get the education and training they needed to qualify for better-paying positions than the jobs that were being wiped out.

Over eight years, the Clinton administration did expand student aid for four-year and two-year colleges and improved and consolidated several job-training and job placement programs. More important, the economy approached full employment, and, as labor markets tightened, workers finally got raises. But workers across the occupational spectrum, including professional and technical employees, still felt that they were at the mercy of a global marketplace that increasingly saw them as disposable. Meanwhile, the administration's leading advocate of training and upgrading programs, Labor Secretary Robert Reich, resigned in 1997 and later claimed that his projects had been starved for funding in order to balance the federal budget.

After 2000, the Democrats were out of office, and even the most centrist among them reconsidered the support for free trade and the exclusive emphasis on education and training as a cure for its consequences that the Clinton administration's economic policy-makers had promoted during the 1990s. At a time when computer programmers were almost as anxious as autoworkers about having their jobs moved overseas, there was no mass constituency for unregulated globalization and diminishing faith that education and training alone could guarantee job security. But, if the policy consensus of the past two decades was no longer persuasive, what prescriptions would make sense? And how could anyone present them to increasingly anxious American workers?

As the 2008 campaign approached and the economy slid toward a recession, the leading candidates certainly wanted to appeal to working Americans, presumably including professional and technical employees as well as manufacturing and service workers. In their own manner, each of the leading candidates kept trying to find the right ways to address today's workers.

Former North Carolina senator (and 2004 vice presidential nominee) John Edwards campaigned as a populist. He seemed nostalgic for the days when his home state was known for textile mills, not research centers. At first, he spoke mostly about poverty. Then he focused on industrial workers. By the time he broadened his appeal to include technicians threatened by outsourcing and nurses overruled by insurance companies, many voters had tuned out.

The early front-runner, Senator Hillary Rodham Clinton, recalled the good economic times during her husband's administration but also repudiated some of his centrist policies. She called for a "time-out" on new trade agreements and offered detailed proposals for improving education and training and creating new jobs in environmentally conscious industries. But she suffered from the sense, especially among college-educated professionals, that she was the sort of establishment candidate whom they had rebelled against for decades. During the primary season, she came to rely on working-class voters, especially women, but many manufacturing workers still associated the name Clinton with unpopular trade deals like the North American Free Trade Agreement. The passions that had hit the streets of Seattle in 1999 were finding their way to the polling places in the primaries and caucuses of 2008.

As the campaign continued, discontented voters turned to an insurgent candidate, Senator Barack Obama of Illinois. The first

African American with a serious chance to win the presidency, he had begun his career as a community organizer in a Chicago neighborhood where the steel mills had closed. But he had also been the president of the *Harvard Law Review*, had authored two books, and enjoyed his earliest popularity among the voters with the most formal education—people who tended to work in professional and technical jobs. At first, he seemed the latest in a line of cerebral candidates, such as Adlai Stevenson, Morris Udall, Gary Hart, Paul Tsongas, and Bill Bradley, who mostly lacked mass appeal. But, as the campaign continued, Obama was increasingly successful in breaking through the lines of color and class, seeking to become the sort of modern populist that Bill Clinton had been in 1992 and Howard Dean had briefly become in 2004.

While Obama's roots are usually traced to Kansas and Kenya, his family background is so eclectic that he is tangentially connected to communities, companies, and concepts described in this book. His mother, Stanley Ann Dunham, attended high school in the Seattle area during the late 1950's, a time when the social and intellectual ferment that had been present since the 1919 general strike was beginning to emerge once again. One of her teachers assigned the book *The Organization Man* by William Whyte, which criticized the corporate conformity of that era and foreshadowed the discontents of today's white-collar workers. Obama's maternal grandmother, Madelyn Dunham, worked for Boeing in Wichita during World War II.[8] Obama carried the Democratic caucuses in Washington State, with support from the SEIU and many members of WashTech and SPEEA. While he spoke more about changing the political system than challenging corporate policies, his outsider's approach appealed to professional and technical workers who felt mistreated by large institutions of all kinds.

Like its Democratic allies, the labor movement was uncertain how to appeal to a changing workforce. Unions declined to less than 13 percent of the entire workforce and less than 10 percent of workers outside of government and public education. In 1995, John Sweeney, the president of SEIU, who had guided the union's growth since 1980, had been elected president of the AFL-CIO after running as an insurgent. Originally, he challenged the longtime incumbent, Lane Kirkland, and after Kirkland retired, Sweeney found himself running against Kirkland's second in command, Tom Donahue, who had once been a vice president of SEIU and a mentor to Sweeney. Initially greeted with enthusiasm by younger unionists and their liberal allies, Sweeney raised the labor movement's profile in the news media, expanded the unions' political action program, and increased the AFL-CIO's commitment to organizing, while urging individual unions to do the same.

But by 2001, the labor movement as a whole had stopped growing, the AFL-CIO was making fewer waves and headlines, and, like Kirkland before him, Sweeney became the target of criticism from other union leaders, including his successor as SEIU president, Andrew Stern. Having served as the president of a statewide union of social service employees in Pennsylvania and the national organizing director of the SEIU, Stern represented a rising generation of union activists who had come of age when basic industries and blue-collar jobs were in decline and traditional union tactics no longer succeeded. Under Stern's leadership, SEIU poured 30 percent of its resources into organizing. It built statewide industry-focused locals like 1199NW. It presented employers with the choice of facing confrontational tactics, such as the street demonstrations that were a regular feature of organizing campaigns among janitors, or creating cooperative relationships, such as the partnerships that Diane Sosne strived to build in the Seattle area. From 1996 through 2007, SEIU grew from 1 million to 1.9 million members.

Ten years into his presidency of the AFL-CIO, Sweeney solicited position papers from national unions about the future of the labor movement. These were posted on the AFL-CIO's Web site, prompting a rare public debate within the federation. The result was a discussion where almost everyone made important points, without any consensus emerging on how to prioritize these points or put them all together. Leading the debate, SEIU called for consolidating unions along industrial lines and pouring more resources into organizing, just as it had done in Washington State. Soon to be headed by Larry Cohen, who had helped to launch WashTech, CWA stressed member involvement and organizing new sectors of the workforce in industries where formal collective bargaining was not immediately attainable. The AFL-CIO Department for Professional Employees, now headed by Paul Almeida, and the IFPTE, now headed by Greg Junemann (who had been second in command in 2000 and had been actively involved in assisting the Boeing engineers' strike), each urged a greater emphasis on professional and technical employees and experiments with organizing based on workers' occupations, as well as their industries.

By the end of 2005, SEIU had left the AFL-CIO, together with the Teamsters, the Carpenters, the Laborers, the United Food and Commercial Workers, and UNITE-HERE, which included garment, textile, hotel, and restaurant workers, constituencies whose common denominator was that they tended to be low-wage immigrant workers. With the exception of the garment and textile workers in UNITE-HERE, few of these workers' jobs were threatened by imports or offshoring, and the strategists for the new labor federation—Change to Win—believed that with well-funded and carefully targeted campaigns, they could organize large numbers of these workers and lift their wages above the poverty level. But two years later, of all these unions, only SEIU was growing dramatically. Meanwhile, several unions that had remained in the AFL-CIO, including CWA, AFSCME, and the American Federation of Teachers (AFT), were also growing. In 2007, unions enjoyed a modest rebound, with a net increase of 311,000 members. The greatest growth was among health-care workers, where union membership increased by 142,000.

While SEIU, AFSCME, and AFT were continuing to organize professionals in government, education, and health care, few unions other than CWA and IFPTE had any success in organizing professionals and technicians in newer industries such as information technology, and their progress was excruciatingly slow. Early in a new century, neither the most effective unions nor the most progressive politicians nor the most astute academics have all the answers for the needs of the new workforce.

Nonetheless, the issues raised in the WTO protests, the Boeing engineers' strike, and the Microsoft temps' organizing efforts concerned workers who weren't reached by unions or even presidential campaigns. Indeed, the workplace conflicts in Seattle in 1999 and 2000 recall an earlier battle of Seattle—the general strike of 1919—which raised issues that were resolved by the New Deal, fifteen years later. Two days before the beginning of the Seattle general strike, the radical journalist Anna Louise Strong proclaimed in a famous editorial for the local *Union Record*: "We are undertaking the most tremendous move ever made by LABOR in this country, a move which will lead—*no one knows where!*"

Nine decades later, the demands by aircraft engineers, software testers, health-care workers, and metal workers for rewarding and fulfilling work resonate throughout the workforce. But like their more militant forebears, their dissatisfactions are leading . . . "no one knows where."

ACKNOWLEDGMENTS

How did a transplanted New Yorker living in Washington, D.C., write a book about workplace conflicts in Seattle? With a lot of help from friends and colleagues and a forgiving family.

During the summer of 1999, Liz McPike, the editor of *American Educator,* the professional issues journal of the American Federation of Teachers, commissioned me to write an article about new forms of unionism among professional and technical workers. In the course of researching the article, I interviewed Mike Blain and Marcus Courtney, who had just begun their efforts to organize the temporary employees at Microsoft. I also interviewed Larry Cohen, who was then the organizing director and now serves as president of the Communications Workers of America; he is one of a new generation of organizers who have assumed the leadership of their unions.

After the article appeared that fall, Eugenia Kemble, the executive director of the Albert Shanker Institute, asked me to write case studies about the Microsoft temps, the engineers and technicians at Boeing, and registered nurses in New Jersey for a report about professional and technical employees. During several trips to Seattle early in 2000, I met with Courtney, Blain, Barbara Judd, David Larsen, and other WashTech activists and Microsoft employees. I also met with leaders of the Boeing engineers' strike, including Charles Bofferding, Stan Sorscher, Doug Smith, and Craig Buckham of the Society of Professional Engineering Employees in Aerospace (SPEEA), as well as Paul Almeida, who was president of the International Federation of Professional and Technical Engineers (IFPTE) and has since become the president of the Department for Professional Employees at the AFL-CIO. In New Jersey, the president of the Health Professionals and Allied Employees, Ann Twomey, explained nurses' problems and professional aspirations.

The Shanker Institute's report included polling conducted by Geoff Garin and Guy Molyneux of Garin-Hart Research among engineers, information technology workers, and registered nurses—one of the most comprehensive studies ever conducted about professional and technical workers.

Since 2000, Kemble, Burnie Bond, and Randy Garton of the Shanker Institute continued to include me in research and discussions about professional and technical employees, encouraging me to pursue issues for which there aren't easy answers and on which we didn't always agree.

Early in 2004, I received the sort of e-mail that authors fantasize about—an invitation from Eric Nelson, a senior editor at John Wiley & Sons, to send him a proposal for a book. After going back and forth for several months about several ideas involving work in the United States, I mentioned that I had saved my notes from interviews with workers at Microsoft and Boeing in Seattle in the watershed year of 2000. "That's your book," Eric told me—workers in the showplace city of the New Economy at the turn of the new century. Thanks to Eric's insights, patience and editorial skills, that idea really did become a book. The editorial skills of Kimberly Monroe-Hill and Ellen Wright also were indispensable to this manuscript becoming a book.

By 2005, I was off and running, thanks largely to a grant from Bill Moyers and Lynn Wellhorsky at the Schumann Center for Media and Democracy. Moyers's passion for investigative journalism and social justice reflects his origins—he still remembers that his father first earned a decent wage when the factory where he worked was unionized.

For the last twelve years, I've benefited from being based at the Economic Policy Institute, a think tank that focuses on the condition of working Americans. Under the leadership of its founder, Jeff Faux, its president, Larry Mishel, and its vice president, Ross Eisenbrey, EPI has been the first to raise important issues, from the stagnant wages and increasing inequality to the off-shoring of professional and technical jobs. EPI also offers a friendly, intellectually stimulating environment and, for this noneconomist, one-stop shopping for scores of essential facts and analyses. Over the years, I have especially appreciated the insights and encouragement of other EPI staffers, including my initial contacts, Roger Hickey and Ruy Teixeira; a friend for more than twenty years, Nancy Coleman; and Eileen Appelbaum, Chris Barbee, Jared Bernstein, Heather Boushey (whose father was a machinist and union activist at Boeing), Karen Conner, John Cook, Nan Gibson, Elise Gould, Stephaan Harris, Ellen Levy, Joe Procopio, Rob Scott, and Noris Weiss Malvey.

During several more research trips to Seattle in 2005 and 2006, old and new friends, colleagues, and contacts were much more generous with their time and social networks than I had any right to expect. Susan Weiss and Kim Krummeck invited me to stay in their home and watch their dogs while they were away. An old friend from Brooklyn, who had moved to Seattle, Gretchen Donart introduced me to her wide range of acquaintances throughout the area. Carter Wright, who had been the researcher on another book that I had written and who was working for SEIU District 1199NW, was, as always, extraordinarily helpful and hardworking. Jonathan Rosenblum, who figures in several stories in this book and currently works for SEIU District 1199NW, provided remarkable assistance.

At SPEEA, Charles Bofferding and Stan Sorscher were always available to answer my questions and introduce me to people, including their adversaries. Geoff Stamper, who had been Boeing's chief negotiator, was also generous, forthright, engagingly honest, and transparently decent. At WashTech, Marcus Courtney was generous and patient beyond the limits of human nature. At SEIU District 1199NW, Diane Sosne, Emily Van Bronkhorst, Chris Barton, and Curt Williams were immeasurably accommodating and hospitable. At the United Steelworkers, Jim Woodward, Steve Powers, and Paul Whitehead were generous with their own time and arranged interviews with workers in Tacoma and Spokane. At the AFL-CIO, Rich Trumka, Denise Mitchell, and Rob McGarrah took time from their busy schedules. At the Washington State AFL-CIO and the Seattle Labor Council, Alan Link and Verlene Jones were helpful and informative. At the International Association of Machinists, Owen Hernstadt was a constant source of information. At the Economic Opportunities Institute, a progressive think tank in Seattle, John Burbank, Marilyn Watkins, and Laura Paskin provided me with insights, information, and office space.

In the fall of 2006, Dan Jacoby of the University of Washington's Labor Studies Center invited me to a conference about knowledge workers that offered me the opportunity to meet once again with many figures in the events of 2000 and to learn how the issues raised in these conflicts were being resolved. Jerry Baldasty and David Domke invited me to a seminar with students in the Communications Department, and an old friend, Paul Miller, hosted a party at his house where I met several leaders from Seattle's business, political, and legal communities.

In the "other" Washington (Washington, D.C.), Carolyn Jacobson introduced me to contacts in Seattle, including her colleagues from the Coalition of Labor Union Women. Mary Reardon introduced me to old friends in Seattle. Lisa Polisar located a book she had researched about hospital workers. And Dick Wilson lent me his collection of articles about the WTO protests.

Over the years, I've learned from several of the most insightful students of politics and the workplace, including Ruy Teixeira and Ralph Whitehead. Professor Richard Hurd of Cornell University's School of Industrial and Labor Relations has informed my understanding of professional and technical employees, as have Paul Almeida and David Cohen of the Department for Professional Employees and Greg Junemann of IFPTE.

Others with whom I've discussed economic, workplace, political, and demographic issues over the years include: Henry Bayer, Richard Bensinger, Heather Booth, Paul Booth, Jack Clark, Virginia Diamond, Page Gardner, Jim Grossfeld, Wade Henderson, Karen Lawson, Eleanor LeCain, Steve Lerner, Roberta Lynch, Tony Podesta, Jessica Smith, Marilyn Sneiderman, Phil Sparks, Ben Wattenberg, and Mildred Wurf. I've been fortunate to have worked for several of the most innovative and effective political and labor leaders of our times, including President Bill Clinton and AFSCME (American Federation of State, County and Municipal Employees) leaders Jerry Wurf, Gerald McEntee, and Bill Lucy. While researching and writing this book, I remembered that the social critic Michael Harrington, best known for calling attention to the plight of the poor, had predicted that the discontents of professional and technical workers would shape the future of U.S. politics.

My wife, Ruth Wattenberg, was as patient as anyone could be during the time it took to research and write this book. Having served as an organizer, editor, and policy expert for the American Federation of Teachers, she shared her experience and ideas about how workers and unions can promote quality. Early in my visits to Seattle, our son, Michael, remembered that he had heard that people in Seattle made airplanes, software, and coffee. When I told him I was talking to people who made airplanes and software, he, quite reasonably, asked when I would be talking to the people who made coffee. Our daughter, Lylah, was intrigued that I was house-sitting in Seattle for a couple who had two large dogs and assumed that I had purposely sought out a household with such interesting pets. Ruth, Michael, and Lylah have my love and gratitude for bearing with me as I researched and wrote this book.

NOTES

Introduction

1. Author's interview with Verlene Jones, Seattle, July 2005.
2. Jeff Faux, "Do the Seattle Protesters Have a Point?" *The International Economy*, July 2000.
3. Susan Gilmore, "WTO Poll: Police Did Well, Mayor Fumbled," *Seattle Times*, December 19, 1999.
4. Author's interview with Geoffrey Stamper, August 2005.
5. Author's interview with Jonathan Rosenblum, Seattle, June 2005.

1. Henry Kaiser's Orphans

1. Author's interview with Dave Carlson, Spokane, December 2005.
2. Biographical material about Henry Kaiser from Stephen B. Adams, *Mr. Kaiser Goes to Washington: The Rise of a Government Entrepreneur* (Chapel Hill: University of North Carolina Press, 1997), pp. 14–33; and "Henry J. Kaiser Is Dead at 85, Built $2 Billion Industrial Giant," *New York Times*, August 25, 1967.
3. Adams, Mr. Kaiser Goes to Washington, p. 100.
4. Doris Kearns Goodwin, *No Ordinary Time: Franklin and Eleanor Roosevelt: The Home Front in World War II* (New York: Simon & Schuster, 1994), pp. 416–418.
5. Adams, *Mr. Kaiser Goes to Washington,* pp. 152–153.
6. Author's interview with Alan Link, Seattle, August 2005.
7. Author's interview with Jim Woodward, Tacoma, August 2005.
8. Author's interview with Roseanne Miller, Tacoma, August 2005.
9. Author's interview with John Wheeler, Spokane, December 2005.

10. Author's interview with Alan Link, Seattle, June 2005.
11. This account of events in the strike draws upon Edward J. Wasilewski Jr., "A Look Back at the Kaiser Aluminum and United Steelworkers Dispute," Bureau of Labor Statistics, January 30, 2003.
12. Author's telephone interview with Paul Whitehead, March 2006.
13. Author's interview with Richard Prete, Spokane, December 2005.

2. FROM BLUE-COLLAR BLUES TO WHITE-COLLAR WOES

1. For an account of the Lordstown strike, see Stanley Aronowitz, *False Promises: The Shaping of American Working Class Consciousness* (Durham, NC: Duke University Press, 1992).
2. *Work in America: Report of a Special Task Force to the Secretary of Health, Education and Welfare* (Cambridge, MA: MIT Press, 1972), p. 13.
3. Ibid., p. 14.
4. President Richard M. Nixon, "Address to the Nation on Labor Day," September 6, 1971, www.presidency.ucsb.edu/ws/index.php?pid=3138&st=labor&st1, accessed March 3, 2008.
5. William Safire, *Before the Fall: An Inside View of the Pre-Watergate White House* (Garden City, NY: Doubleday, 1975), pp. 579–583.
6. "Current Statistics on White-Collar Employees," AFL-CIO Department for Professional Employees, 1999, and updates.
7. Ken Belson, "At Traditional Phone Companies, Jobs May Not Last a Lifetime," *New York Times,* December 5, 2005.
8. Ruy Teixeira and Joel Rogers. *America's Forgotten Majority: Why the White Working Class Still Matters* (Basic Books), p. x.
9. Joseph Nocera, "Living with Layoffs," *Fortune,* April 1, 1996.
10. Edmund L. Andrews, "Don't Go Away Mad, Just Go Away: Can AT&T Be the Nice Guy as It Cuts 40,000 Jobs?" *New York Times,* February 13, 1996.
11. Daniel H. Pink, *Free Agent Nation: How America's New Independent Workers Are Transforming the Way We Live* (New York: Warner Books, 2001).
12. Rand Wilson, "Part-Time America Won't Work: The Teamsters' Fight for Good Jobs at UPS," in *Not Your Father's Union Movement,* edited by Jo-Ann Mort. (London: Verso, 1998).

3. Graveyard Shift

1. All stories in this chapter involving Deanna Swenson are from the author's interview with her, Seattle, June 2005.
2. All stories in this chapter involving Curt Williams are from the author's interview with him, Seattle, June 2005.
3. All stories in this chapter involving Emily Van Bronkhorst are from the author's interview with her, Renton, December 2005.
4. Diane Sosne, "The Truth about Hospitals That Exist Only to Make Money," *Seattle Times,* July 11, 1997.
5. Author's interview with Verlene Jones, Seattle, July, 2005.
6. Suzanne Gordon, *Nursing against the Odds* (Ithaca, NY: Cornell University Press, 2006), p. 10.
7. Sosne, "The Truth about Hospitals That Exist Only to Make Money."
8. All stories in this chapter involving Donna Aring are from the author's interview with her, Seattle, June 2005.
9. Author's interview with Diane Sosne, Seattle, December 2005.
10. Author's interview with Gretchen Donart, Seattle, June 2005.

4. Caring Enough to Get Mad

1. Author's interview with Charles Bofferding, Seattle, March 2000.
2. See Richard Sennett, *The Culture of the New Capitalism* (New Haven, CT: Yale University Press), 2007.
3. See Lawerence Mishel and Richard Rothstein, "Response to Marc Tucker," Economic Policy Institute, June 1, 2007.
4. Stan Sorscher, "High-Tech Labor Shortage a Myth," *SPEEA Newsletter,* August 10, 2007, p. 1.
5. Ibid., p. 1.
6. Jube Shiver, Jr., "Alliance Fights Boost in Tech Workers Labor," *Los Angeles Times,* August 5, 2000.
7. David Brooks, "Bitter at the Top," *New York Times*, June 15, 2004.
8. Morley Winograd and Dudley Buffa, *Taking Control: Politics in the Information Age* (New York: Henry Holt, 1996), p. 2.
9. John B. Judis and Ruy Teixeira, *The Emerging Democratic Majority,* (New York: Scribner, 2002), p. 42.
10. John B. Judis and Ruy Teixeira, "Back to the Future: The Re-Emergence of the Democratic Majority," *The American Prospect,* June 2007.

5. CYBER PROLES

1. The accounts of David Larsen's experiences are from the author's interviews with him in Seattle in March 2000 and August 2005.
2. Walter Isaacson, "In Search of the Real Bill Gates," *Time*, October 20, 2005.
3. Richard Karlgaard, "Talent Wars," Forbes.com, October 31, 2005.
4. See Steve McConnell, *After the Gold Rush* (Redmond, WA: Microsoft Press, 1999).
5. Quotes and anecdotes involving Marcus Courtney are from the author's interviews with him by telephone in September 1999 and in Seattle in March 2000, June 2005, and December 2005.
6. Quotes are taken from the author's e-mails with James Fallows.
7. Darryle Estrine, "The Perma-Temp Contratemps," *Fast Company Magazine*, July 2000.
8. Author's interview with Anjani Millet, Redmond, WA, March 2000.

6. "AREN'T WE TECHNOLOGY WORKERS?"

1. Quotes and anecdotes about the class action lawsuit are from the author's interview with David Stobaugh, Seattle, October 2006.
2. The story of WashTech's founding is from the author's interview with Jonathan Rosenblum, June 2005.
3. Author's interview with Larry Cohen, Washington, D.C., September 1998.
4. The source for quotes and anecdotes about Mike Blain is the author's interviews with him by telephone in September 1998 and in Seattle in March 2000.
5. The source for quotes and anecdotes about Barbara Judd is the author's interviews with her in the Seattle area in March 2000 and August 2005.

7. "I KNOW WHAT IT'S LIKE TO BE TREATED REASONABLY"

1. Barbara Judd is the source for this and other e-mails that she received.
2. The source for the quotes and the anecdotes involving Squire Dahl is the author's interview with him in December 2005.

8. The Love-Hate Workplace

1. For varying findings on workers' job satisfaction, see the American Enterprise Institute's Web site, www.aei.org; Steven Greenhouse, "Three Polls Find Workers Sensing Deep Pessimism," *New York Times,* August 31, 2006; "U.S. Workers Hate Their Jobs More Than Ever," *FOXNews.com,* March 7, 2007; and Teresa M. McAleavy, "Workers More Dissatisfied, Survey Finds," *Seattle Times*, October 22, 2006.
2. Both quotes are from Kay Hymowitz, "Ecstatic Capitalism's Brave New Work Ethic," *City Journal* (Winter 2001).
3. Sylvia Ann Hewlett and Carolyn Buck Luce, "Extreme Jobs: The Dangerous Allure of the 70-Hour Workweek,"*Harvard Business Review,* December 2006.
4. Pamela Kruger, "Betrayed by Work," *Fast Company,* October 1999.
5. Ibid.

9. "A Company That Hires Engineers and Other People"

1. Boeing's history is recounted on its Web site, Boeing.com.
2. "Masters of the Air,"*Time,* April 7, 1980.
3. Author's interview with Charles Bofferding, Tukwila, April 2000.
4. For a history of SPEEA, see "Ingenuity, Activism Lead SPEEA through Challenges," *SPEEA Spotlite,* March 2004.
5. Author's interviews with Charles Bofferding, Tukwila, April 2000 and June 2005.
6. "Boeing: What Really Happened," *Business Week,* December 12, 2003.
7. Author's interview with Geoff Stamper, Seattle, August 2005.
8. Author's interviews with Charles Bofferding, Tukwila, April 2000 and June 2005.
9. Jeff Cole, "Selling Stonecipher to the Boeing Faithful—No. 2 Man Is Called Cold, but Says He's Misunderstood," *Seattle Times,* December 14, 1998.
10. Author's interviews with Stan Sorscher, Tukwila, April 2000 and June 2005.
11. John Greenwald, "Is Boeing Out of Its Spin?" *Time,* July 13, 1998.
12. Jeff Cole, "Wall St. Believers Give Up on Boeing—Analysts Who Held Hope Downgrade Stock Rating,"*Seattle Times,* December 3, 1998.
13. Jeff Cole, "Boeing's Cultural Revolution–Shaken Giant Surrenders Big Dreams for Bottom Line, " *Seattle Times,* December 13, 1998.

14. Laurence Zuckerman, "Boeing Weighs Tough Steps to Increase Profits," *New York Times,* February 25, 1999.

10. THE MAX PLANCK INSTITUTE FOR CYNICISM

1. Author's interview with Stan Sorscher, Tukwila, April 2000.
2. Chuck Taylor, "Flying High, or Eying the Bottom Line,"*Seattle Times*, July 9, 1999.
3. Ibid.
4. Nina Shapiro, "The Next Generation: The Bitter Strike at Boeing Underscores Sweeping Cultural Change at the Company," *Seattle Weekly*, March 8, 2000.
5. Author's interview with Stan Sorscher, Tukwila, April 2000.
6. Ibid.
7. Author's interview with Stan Sorscher, Tukwila, June 2005, and exchange of e-mails with Sorscher, December 7, 2005.
8. Author's interview with Doug Smith, Tukwila, April 2000.
9. Author's interview with Tom McCarty, Tukwila, June 2005.
10. Author's interviews with Charles Bofferding, Stan Sorscher, and other SPEEA leaders, Tukwila, April 2000 and June 2005; Steve Wilhelm, "Boeing Engineers' Union Retools for Stronger Stance," *BizJournals. com,* November 30, 1998.

11. "ON STRIKE *FOR* BOEING"

1. Author's interviews with Charles Bofferding, Tukwila, April 2000 and June 2005.
2. This account of the negotiations is from the author's interview with Geoff Stamper, Redmond, August 2005.
3. Jim Braham, "Prideless in Seattle,"*MachineDesign.com,* March 31, 2000.
4. Author's interview with Stan Sorscher, Tukwila, June 2005; and issues of the *SPEEA Newsletter* in December 1999.
5. Author's interviews with Stan Sorscher, Tukwila, April 2000 and June 2005.
6. For a report on how the slogan resonated nationally, see Steven Greenhouse, "Brains Develop Brawn on Picket Line,"*New York Times*, March 7, 2000.
7. Author's interview with Paul Almeida, Washington, D.C., December 2005.

8. Author's telephone interview with Richard Trumka, December 2005.
9. The account of the burn barrels is from the author's interview with Tom McCarty, Tukwila, June 2005, and his brochure, "How We Built the SPEEA Stove."
10. The account of the engineers' relationship with the FAA is from the author's interview with Paul Almeida, October 2005; and Chuck Taylor, "Boeing Strike Drags Down Profit Expectations, Stock,"*Seattle Times*, March 10, 2000.

12. ONE OF BOEING'S BEST YEARS EVER

1. The account of Stan Sorscher and Charles Bofferding's trip to the investment analysts' meeting is from the author's interview with Stan Sorscher, Tukwila, June 2005.
2. Author's interview with Paul Almeida, Washington, D.C., October 2005; and Stuart Eskanazi, "As Unions Applaud and Industry Watches, Boeing Makes Labor History," *Seattle Times,* February 13, 2000.
3. Author's interview with Paul Almeida, Washington, D.C., October 2005.
4. Ibid.

AFTERWORD

1. Dominic Gates, "Boeing Buys Peace with Its Engineers," *Seattle Times,* November 16, 2005.
2. William Dietrich, "Still Together after All These Years," *Pacific Northwest Magazine,* January 25, 2004.
3. Dominic Gates, "Boeing Buzzes about Source of Work," *Seattle Times,* March 9, 2003.
4. Ninan Shapiro, "The Outsourcing Source,"*Seattle Weekly*, May 5–11, 2004.
5. Bert Caldwell, "The Future Takes Flight at Trentwood," *The Spokesman-Review,* November 20, 2005.
6. Interview with Diane Sosne, Seattle, December 2005, and telephone interview, October 2007.
7. Bernadette Kenny, "The Coming Crisis in Employee Turnover," *Forbes.com*, April 25, 2007.
8. Tim Jones, "Obama's Mom: Not Just a Girl from Kansas," *Chicago Tribune,* March 27, 2007.

BIBLIOGRAPHY

GLOBALIZATION AND THE WTO PROTESTS

Borosage, Robert L. "The Battle in Seattle." *The Nation*. December 6, 1999.
Faux, Jeff. *The Global Class War: How America's Elite Lost the Future and What It Will Take to Win It Back* (Hoboken, NJ: Wiley & Sons, 2006).
Thottam, Jyotti. "Is Your Job Going Abroad?" *Time*. March 1, 2004.

HENRY KAISER, THE KAISER ALUMINUM COMPANY, AND THE UNITED STEELWORKERS OF AMERICA

Adams, Stephen B. *Mr. Kaiser Goes to Washington: The Rise of a Government Entrepreneur* (Chapel Hill: University of North Carolina Press, 1997).
Goodwin, Doris Kearns, *No Ordinary Time: Franklin and Eleanor Roosevelt: The Home Front in World War II* (New York: Simon & Schuster, 1994).
Hoerr, John P. *And the Wolf Finally Came: The Decline of the American Steel Industry* (Pittsburgh: University of Pittsburgh Press, 1988).

HEALTH-CARE WORKERS, LOCAL 1199, AND THE SERVICE EMPLOYEES INTERNATIONAL UNION

Bernstein, Aaron. "Can This Man Save Labor?" *Business Week*. September 13, 2004.
Fink, Leon B., and Brian Greenberg. *Upheaval in the Quiet Zone: A History of Hospital Workers Local 1199* (Urbana-Champaign: University of Illinois Press, 1989).

Gordon, Suzanne. *Nursing against the Odds: How Health Care Cost Cutting, Media Stereotypes and Medical Hubris Undermine Nurses and Patient Care.* (Ithaca, NY: Cornell University Press, 2005).

Kuttner, Robert. *Everything for Sale* (New York: Random House, 1999).

Sexton, Patricia Cayo, with Lisa Polisar. *The New Nightingales: Hospital Workers and Unions* (New York: Enquiry Press, 1981).

Stern, Andy. *A Country That Works: Getting America Back on Track* (New York: Free Press, 2006).

THE CONDITION OF WORKING AMERICANS AND THE AMERICAN LABOR MOVEMENT

Kazin, Michael. *The Populist Persuasion: An American History* (New York: Basic Books, 1995).

Lichtenstein, Nelson. *State of the Union* (Princeton, NJ: Princeton University Press, 2002).

Mishel, Lawrence, Jared Bernstein, and Sylvia Allegretto. *The State of Working America, 2006/2007* (Ithaca, NY: Cornell University Press, 2007).

Mort, JoAnn. *Not Your Father's Labor Movement: The New AFL-CIO and the Prospective Revival of American Labor* (New York: Verso, 1998).

Safire, William. *Before the Fall: An Inside View of the Pre-Watergate White House* (Garden City, NY: Doubleday, 1975).

Sweeney, John J., with David Kusnet. *America Needs a Raise: Fighting for Economic Security and Social Justice* (New York: Houghton-Mifflin, 1996).

Turkel, Studs. *Working: People Talk about What They Do All Day and How They Feel about What They Do* (New York: Pantheon, 1974).

THE MODERN WORKFORCE AND WORKPLACE AND PROFESSIONAL AND TECHNICAL WORKERS

Adams, Scott. *The Dilbert Principle: A Cubicle's Eye View of Bosses, Meetings, Management Fads & Other Workplace Afflictions* (New York: HarperBusiness, 1996).

Aronowitz, Stanley. *False Promises: The Shaping of American Working Class Consciousness* (Durham, NC: Duke University Press, 1992).

Ciulla, Joanne B. *The Working Life: The Promise and Betrayal of Modern Work* (New York: Three Rivers Press, 2001).

Committee on the Future of Work, chaired by Thomas R. Donahue. *The Changing Situation of Workers and Their Unions* (Washington, D.C.: AFL-CIO, 1985).

Ehrenreich, Barbara. *Bait and Switch: The (Futile) Pursuit of the American Dream* (New York: Metropolitan Books), 2005.

Freeman, Richard B., and Joel Rogers. *What Workers Want* (Ithaca, NY: Cornell University Press, 1999).

Grossfeld, Jim. *White-Collar Perspectives on Workplace Issues: How Progressives Can Make the Case for Unions* (Washington, D.C.: Center for American Progress), 2006.

Judis, John B., and Ruy Teixeira. *The Emerging Democratic Majority* (New York: Scribner, 2002).

Kahlenberg, Richard D. *Tough Liberal: Albert Shanker and the Battle over Schools, Unions, Race and Democracy* (New York: Columbia University Press, 2007).

Karoly, Lynn A., and Constantijn W. A. Paris. *The 21st Century at Work* (Santa Monica, CA: Rand Corporation), 2004.

Kusnet, David, and Peter D. Hart Research Associates. *Finding Their Voices: Professionals and Workplace Representation* (Washington, D.C.: Albert Shanker Institute), 2000.

Osterman, Paul, and Thomas A. Kochan, Richard M. Locke, and Michael J. Piore. *Working in America: A Blueprint for a New Labor Market* (Cambridge, MA: MIT Press, 2001).

O'Toole, James, and Edward E. Lawler III. *The New American Workplace* (New York: Palgrave Macmillan), 2006.

Pink, Daniel H. *Free Agent Nation: How America's New Independent Workers Are Transforming the Way We Live* (New York: Warner Books, 2001).

Reich, Robert B. *The Future of Success* (New York: Alfred A. Knopf, 2001).

————. *The Work of Nations: Preparing Ourselves for 21st Century Capitalism* (New York: Alfred A. Knopf, 1991).

Winograd, Morley, and Dudley Buffa. *Taking Control: Politics in the Information Age* (New York: Henry Holt, 1996).

Work in America: Report of a Special Task Force to the Secretary of Health, Education and Welfare. Foreword by Secretary Elliot A. Richardson (Cambridge, MA: MIT Press, 1973).

Microsoft, Part-Time and Temporary Workers, the Washington Alliance of Technology Workers, and the Communications Workers of America

Bahr, Morton. *From the Telegraph to the Internet* (Washington, D.C.: Welcome Rain Publishers), 1998.

Coupland, Douglas. *Microserfs* (New York: Regan Books, 1995).

McConnell, Steve. *After the Gold Rush: Creating a True Profession of Software Engineering* (Redmond, WA): Microsoft Press, 1999.

Tarlau, Jimmy, and David Nack. "The Communications Workers of America's Experience with Open Source Unionism." *Working USA*. December 2005.

Boeing, the Society of Professional Engineering Employees in Aerospace, and the International Federation of Professional and Technical Engineers

Gates, Dominic. "Boeing's Big Move." *The Industry Standard*. April 2, 2001.

Holmes, Stanley. "Boeing: What Really Happened."*Business Week*. December 15, 2003.

Newhouse, John. *Boeing versus Airbus: The Inside Story of the Greatest International Competition in Business* (New York: Alfred A. Knopf, 2007).

INDEX